GROWING
MINDS

Building Strong
Cognitive Foundations
in Early Childhood

Edited by
Carol Copple

National Association for the Education of Young Children
Washington, DC

National Association for the Education of Young Children
1313 L Street NW, Suite 500
Washington, DC 20005-4101
202-232-8777 • 800-424-2460
www.naeyc.org

NAEYC Books

Editorial Director
Bry Pollack

Senior Editor
Holly Bohart

Design and Production
Malini Dominey

Assistant Editor
Elizabeth Wegner

Editorial Assistant
Ryan Smith

Permissions
Lacy Thompson

Through its publications program, the National Association for the Education of Young Children (NAEYC) provides a forum for discussion of major issues and ideas in the early childhood field, with the hope of provoking thought and promoting professional growth. The views expressed or implied in this book are not necessarily those of the Association or its members.

Permissions

Excerpts from *Caring for infants & toddlers in groups: Developmentally appropriate practice*, 2d ed. (pp. 1–4, 7–10, and 14–17) by ZERO TO THREE (Washington, DC: ZERO TO THREE, 2008) are adapted with permission. Copyright © 2008 ZERO TO THREE: National Center for Infants, Toddlers, and Families.

Excerpts from *Enthusiastic and engaged learners: Approaches to learning in the early childhood classroom* (pp. 30–43 and 72–77) by M. Hyson (New York: Teachers College Press; Washington, DC: NAEYC, 2008) are adapted with permission. Copyright © 2008 Teachers College, Columbia University.

Excerpt from *Enthusiastic and engaged learners: Approaches to learning in the early childhood classroom* (pp. 133–38) by M. Hyson (New York: Teachers College Press; Washington, DC: NAEYC, 2008), based on information from "Child development tracker: Approaches to learning," *PBS Parents guide to child development* from pbsparents.org, is reprinted with permission of the Public Broadcasting Service and Teachers College Press.

Excerpts from *Making the most of plan-do-review: The teacher's idea book #5* (pp. 11 and 141) by N. Vogel (Ypsilanti, MI: High/Scope, 2001) are adapted with permission.

Excerpt from *Educating young children: Active learning practices for preschool and child care programs*, 2d ed. (p. 238) by M. Hohmann & D.P. Weikart (Ypsilanti, MI: High/Scope, 2002) is adapted with permission.

Excerpt from *Worms, shadows, and whirlpools: Science in the early childhood classroom* (p. 18) by K. Worth & S. Grollman (Portsmouth, NH: Heinemann; Newton, MA: EDC; Washington, DC: NAEYC, 2003) is reprinted with permission. Copyright © 2003 by Education Development Center Inc.

Credits

Cover illustrations: Copyright © James Yang
Cover design: Eddie Malstrom

Growing Minds: Building Strong Cognitive Foundations in Early Childhood

Library of Congress Control Number: 2011941837
ISBN: 978-1-928896-79-1
NAEYC Item #362

Carol Copple received her doctorate in human development from Cornell University and joined the faculty of Louisiana State University. As senior research psychologist at the Educational Testing Service, she directed a prekindergarten program for enhancing young children's thinking skills and wrote *Educating the Young Thinker: Classroom Strategies for Cognitive Growth* with Irving Sigel and Ruth Saunders. At the National Association for the Education of Young Children from 1993 to 2010, Dr. Copple headed the publications program, authored numerous books, and played a leading role in developing the association's position statements and education initiatives. She is now an early education consultant based in Nashville, Tennessee.

Contents

Carol Copple

About This Book

Since I first **began working with children I've** found their thinking fascinating. In my graduate program at Cornell in the 1970s, I gravitated to study of language and thought. It was the era when American scholars and educators were discovering the remarkable work of Jean Piaget, who showed us children's cognitive development as we had never seen it before.

We are always shaped, it seems, by the intellectual perspectives and concerns that are in the ascendance when we first seriously study a subject. At that time and place, there was more interest in children's evolving thought processes and their development as eager, proficient learners than in specific subject matter in the curriculum. And we were at the dawn of a revolution in views on poverty and educational disadvantage and in attacking them by giving poor children learning opportunities at an early age, most notably in Head Start. Efforts to understand and nurture children's cognitive development held a central place in research and educational programs throughout the decade.

In 1976 I was fortunate to receive a postdoctoral fellowship at the Educational Testing Service (ETS) with Irving Sigel, eminent pioneer in applying Piagetian and other cognitive theory and research to early childhood education. After a year I became director of the experimental preschool education program at ETS and for several years worked with Irv and the wonderful teaching staff to evolve teaching strategies that enabled children to become reflective, engaged thinkers. Though the "back to basics" movement was building steam, in our Educating the Young Thinker program we continued to focus intensely on fostering children's cognitive development and active, enthusiastic approaches to learning.

Through the pendulum swings since that time, I have remained what I guess could be called (albeit awkwardly) a "cognitivist." In the years I spent working at the National Association for the Education of Young Children (NAEYC) and watching the progress of education reform, I became increasingly aware of the importance of content knowledge and skills in early education. Enabling children to become excellent and eager learners is vital; it is also important to equip them with foundational skills and knowledge in language and literacy, mathematics, science, and other curriculum domains. This is one of the *both/and* principles that NAEYC and the field have sought to promote in its position statements and publications, particularly in the last two decades.

So it was with great enthusiasm that I undertook the development of this volume. NAEYC in its journals and books publishes a wealth of material that describes how young children develop cognitively and how teachers can promote this development. And the time is ripe for this book. I loved the idea of bringing together many of the gems in NAEYC publications and highlighting the importance of cognitive development—the "basic" underlying the other basics of learning. There is growing concern about educating American children so that as adults they will have the thinking skills needed in today's economy and the increasingly complex world we live in—21st century skills. Out of these enthusiasms and the exigencies of the present moment came *Growing Minds: Building Strong Cognitive Foundations in Early Childhood.*

The book is divided into two parts:

Part I (Cognitive Development from Birth through Age 8) uses chapter excerpts from *Developmentally Appropriate Practice in Early Childhood Programs Serving Children from Birth through Age 8* (NAEYC 2009) and other sources to summarize how young children develop cognitively and in their approaches to learning ("cognitive styles"); it also captures in very broad strokes how early childhood programs promote this development.

In Part II (Approaches for Promoting Cognitive Development in the Early Childhood Classroom) we take a closer look at pedagogy through ten NAEYC-published articles and chapters describing various classroom practices that foster children's cognitive growth.

Part I

Cognitive Development
from Birth through Age 8

Cognitive Development from Birth through Age 8

The opening selection of Part I is excerpted from "Development in the First Three Years of Life" from ZERO TO THREE's *Caring for Infants & Toddlers in Groups: Developmentally Appropriate Practice* (2d ed.). As you read it, you may have the initial reaction: "But this isn't about cognitive development, it's mostly about relationships." There is indeed much about relationships and social and emotional development in this selection. Yet it is entirely appropriate for *Growing Minds*, as babies and toddlers do their exploring and making sense of the world around them within the context of forming relationships. While for all ages cognitive development is embedded in the social world, this is especially true at the beginning of life.

Volumes of information are available on the various aspects of cognition of children ages 3–8. So the overview in Part I is necessarily selective, providing only a bird's eye view of cognitive development in the preschool, kindergarten, and primary years. The chapter excerpts for these periods are from NAEYC's 2009 *Developmentally Appropriate Practice in Early Childhood Programs Serving Children from Birth through Age 8* (3d ed.). The preschool chapter was written by Heather Biggar Tomlinson (formerly of the NAEYC professional development staff, currently living and working in Indonesia) and Marilou Hyson (researcher and former associate executive director at NAEYC, now a U.S. and international early childhood consultant). Heather Biggar Tomlinson wrote the kindergarten and primary chapters as well. Readers may want to refer to the full *Developmentally Appropriate Practice* volume to see how knowledge about children's cognition and other aspects of learning and development translate into effective, developmentally appropriate teaching practices. In the excerpts here, topics include brain development, concept acquisition, reasoning, representational thinking, self-regulation, and memory.

The topic of *approaches to learning*—the dispositions or learning styles characterizing the many ways that children engage with learning—does not typically fall under the heading of cognitive development. Yet children's varying approaches to learning relate in significant ways to how they function cognitively. Approaches to learning are powerful predictors of children's success in school and their learning of complex skills such as reading and math (Bowman et al. 2001). For example, approaches to learning, such as flexibility and persistence, clearly influence children's problem solving.

There are simply no sharp boundaries between the domains of development that we call cognitive, emotional, and social; and approaches to learning lie in the overlap among these. Moreover, teaching practices that foster cognitive processes also nurture children's positive approaches to learning, as discussed in the excerpts included from Marilou Hyson's wonderful volume *Enthusiastic and Engaged Learners: Approaches to Learning in the Early Childhood Classroom*, a copublication of Teachers College Press and NAEYC.

Reference

Bowman, B.T., S. Donovan, & M.S. Burns, eds. 2001. *Eager to learn: Educating our preschoolers.* Committee on Early Childhood Pedagogy, National Research Council. Washington, DC: National Academies Press.

Cognitive Development in the First Three Years of Life

Scientists **all over the world are studying** how very young babies listen to language; understand number concepts; learn from their changing perspectives as they roll over, sit, and stand; and always . . . always how they count on trusted adults to help them gain new awareness of themselves, others, and the world.

We are learning why relationships are so important to development. We are learning about individual differences such as temperament and developmental challenges, the influence of a family's and community's cultural beliefs, and the impact of early experiences on the brain. Because so many babies are in nonparental care, we are also studying both the positive effects and the challenges of providing group care for infants and toddlers.

Group care may provide unique opportunities to support relationships and learning. Infants and toddlers develop expectations about people and about themselves on the basis of how parents and others treat them. It is exceedingly important that in these first relationships, babies experience sensitive, affectionate care. When infants learn that adults meet their needs predictably and consistently, trust and emotional security develop. At the same time, infants and toddlers develop self-confidence as the adults around them help them master challenges in the world.

• Young infants (birth to 9 months) seek *security*.

• Mobile infants (8 to 18 months) eagerly engage in *exploration*.

• Toddlers (16 to 36 months) continue to form their *identity*.

Security, exploration, and identity formation are all important developmental factors in relationships and learning throughout the first three years of life. However, each dominates a different period. Security is the prime motivation for the young infant. Responsive adults help young infants to feel comfortable and to be focused as they develop a sense of trust in the adult's ability to understand them, keep them safe and secure, and make predictability possible.

Mobile infants rely on this foundation of security as they feel secure to move and explore. The quality of their experience as explorers becomes incorporated into their sense of who they are. They may begin to think of themselves as "someone who can make things happen and can learn about how my world works." As they venture out, they will check back with the adult to make sure they are safe. They also count on the adult to provide rich opportunities for them to investigate the world.

Although toddlers are naturally still very involved in exploration, this period of development is dominated by the work of forming an identity. As a toddler comes to understand his own experience and becomes aware of the experiences of others being separate from his, he is solidifying his sense of self.

Throughout the first three years of life, each child's development needs to be understood within the context of her relationships. Sensitive parents and teachers respond to all of the ways that infants and toddlers communicate their feelings, interests, and distress. They also change their actual responses as infants and toddlers grow. Providing security for a 6-month-old who is still establishing her sense of trust in the adult is a different challenge, for example, than providing security for a 12-month-old who is consumed with the urge to explore but needs to feel secure in order to venture into new territory. Nonetheless, the need to read the child's signals and to respond to what the child needs remains the same.

This chapter on development uses the central motivation of each period as an organizing principle as we describe the child's emerging capabilities.

Young infants (birth to 9 months)

Young infants need security most of all. They thrive on the warmth and caring that come from close relationships. Having someone special who responds quickly to their cues helps babies build a base of security that will support their exploration, learning, and identity formation.

ZERO TO THREE: National Center for Infants, Toddlers, and Families is a nonprofit organization that informs, trains, and supports professionals, policymakers, and parents in their efforts to improve the lives of infants and toddlers.

Babies are individuals with individual caregiving needs. Even newborns differ from one another in their biological rhythms and the way they use their senses (sight, hearing, touch, smell, and taste) to learn about the world around them. By the time they enter child care, most babies will have established distinct sensory preferences and activity patterns.

Babies enter the world ready for relationships. Very young infants show a particular interest in the people around them. They like to look and listen; they follow the father's voice as well as the mother's. Babies recognize and show interest in the sounds of their family's language, already heard for months in the womb. They look intently at the light and dark contours of the human face, and they can discriminate between an accurate drawing of a human face and one in which the main features are out of place. They can match the emotional tone of language with the expression on a person's face. Babies have many ways to participate in relationships.

By the time they are 3 months old (a time when many infants are first placed in group care settings), they are masters at attracting and holding the attention of familiar, responsive people. They can smile, laugh, cuddle, coo, reach out, and hold tight. They engage with their parents and infant care teachers in back-and-forth exchanges of gazes, grimaces, and grins. Adults learn how to understand these messages over time.

Babies delight in hearing language. They smile and gurgle when talked to and develop different types of cries to express different needs. Long before they speak in words, infants coo, babble, and then make sounds that imitate the tones and rhythms of adult talk—particularly those of their families and home culture. Before they understand even simple word combinations, they read gestures, facial expressions, and tone of voice and participate in the turn taking of conversation. An infant just a few months old will engage as a conversational partner: She coos, her infant care teacher coos back, and the infant coos in reply. If one partner turns away or becomes distracted, the other partner calls her back with a gesture or sound. Some particularly social babies even "converse" with each other!

Toward the end of the early infancy period,

© Tyler Hamlet

babies enjoy learning simple back-and-forth games that are traditional in their culture or the cultures of their infant care teachers. Peekaboo, pat-a-cake, "I roll the ball to baby," and hand-clapping games such as "*Debajo de un botón*" are just a few of the games that many infants learn.

Babies learn through movement. As they move their arms, legs, and other body parts and encounter the world through touching and being touched, babies become more aware of how their bodies move and feel. They soon discover that they can change what they see, hear, or feel through their own actions—how delightful to kick, see the mobile move, and be able to do it again!

Babies learn best when they are alert and calm. They can become deeply engrossed in practicing a newly discovered skill, such as putting their hands together to grasp an object or batting at a mobile circling over their crib. Through the repetition of actions, they develop their gross and fine motor skills and physical strength. They explore objects, people, and things by kicking, reaching, grasping, pulling, and letting go. Babies enjoy looking at

family pictures and at board books with pictures of other babies.

In a group setting, young infants like to watch other babies and older children, and they light up when a friend smiles and coos at them. Many young babies enjoy being "part of the action," at least for short periods. At the same time, they can be overwhelmed by too much social stimulation, and their excitement can turn quickly to tears. They depend upon adults to respond to their signs of interest, overstimulation, fatigue, or boredom and to help them keep their excitement or distress within bounds.

Babies use their senses and emerging physical skills to learn about the people and objects around them. They touch different textures and put things in their mouths. Babies learn to anticipate how familiar adults will respond to them, a skill that will evolve much later into an ability to "read" people and anticipate how to behave in new situations. Ideally, young infants are learning that their needs are understood and will be met. They are learning that new skills and new experiences most often bring pleasure, that determined efforts can lead to success, and that those they love will share their joy at each new accomplishment. These early experiences build a child's confidence, affecting her approach to learning far into the future.

Mobile infants (8 to 18 months)

As infants become mobile, exploration takes center stage. Like little scientists, they investigate everything they can get their hands—or mouths—on. "What will happen," they seem to ask repeatedly, "if I push this button or pull on this blanket or poke my friend Mikey?" A trusted infant care teacher becomes a secure base from which mobile infants can explore, checking back for reassurance and encouragement. Mobile infants develop feelings of confidence and competence as their infant care teachers share their pleasure in new discoveries and accomplishments. It is important for infant care teachers to remember that at this stage infants practice exploration but still need the security that trusted adults provide.

Mobile infants thrive on exploration and interaction. Mobility opens new worlds for infants. They can now move to what or whom they want by scooting, using their hands and bouncing forward, commando-crawling with stomach on the ground, one-legged stand-crawling, crawling on all fours, walking with assistance, and finally, toddling. They develop their large muscles as they creep, crawl, cruise, walk holding on to furniture or push toys, climb up onto couches and ramps, and descend stairs. Freedom to move about safely in an interesting, inviting environment is vital for these busy infants.

Mobile infants are fascinated by the daily activities of the other children and adults around them. Most likely they are found "in the fray," where they can observe what is going on and participate in their own way. They imitate actions they have seen, holding a comb to a doll's head, pretending to drink from a cup, and mimicking facial expressions of sadness or anger. The mental images mobile infants create of how things work and of sequences of peer and adult behaviors will become part of their rich repertoire of toddler play themes.

Mobile infants find their peers very interesting. Sometimes they smile and babble at each other socially. Other times they treat each other more like objects, experimenting to see what happens when they poke, prod, or crawl over them. They may choose a favorite friend to follow or imitate.

With mobile infants' new physical, cognitive, social, and emotional abilities come new discoveries and fears. They can look for a person who is momentarily out of sight, enjoy a game of peekaboo, and learn to wave bye-bye as they gain an understanding that people and objects exist even when they are out of sight. Although babies respond with differing degrees of intensity on the basis of both their individual temperaments and their experiences, almost all infants show some wariness of strangers during this period. A clown face, a firefighter in uniform, or a mask can be terrifying, especially if a trusted adult is not right there to provide comfort and reassurance.

Although new fears and anxieties are distressing to mobile infants and the adults who love them, these powerful feelings reflect new depths of understanding. Over these months, mobile infants are gradually developing an understanding that other people have their own experiences, feelings, and desires.

As they play, these young explorers can be totally absorbed. Opening and shutting, filling and dumping, and picking up and dropping are endlessly fascinating activities that challenge infants' mobility and dexterity as well as their ideas about objects and what they can do. They discover, test, and confirm that objects can be out of sight (inside a box or in a cabinet) and then found; that objects can be all together, separated into pieces, and then put together again; and that adults can be resources for reaching what has been dropped.

As they play and use their new physical skills, mobile infants learn the rudimentary rules of cause and effect. They learn to push buttons—on toys or a TV remote—and make interesting things happen. These infants use and manipulate tools (e.g., using a cup to scoop water). They also begin to group and compare objects and may enjoy a simple stacking or nesting toy. They demonstrate a basic understanding of quantities of *more* and *less*. They work intently at simple problems, like fitting a lid on a pan or picking up a slippery ice cube or a strand of spaghetti.

Using language helps mobile infants stay connected with their infant care teachers over small distances. As these infants build their vocabularies, they listen to the sing-song rhythms, elevated pitch, and exaggerated emphasis on important words and sounds that most adults naturally use when talking with them. Reciprocal conversations take place with adults, as infants use babbles, squeaks, and grunts. They begin to string together the familiar sounds of the languages in their environment into "expressive jargon" or "gibberish" that sounds a lot like sentences even though it does not contain meaningful words. The infants soon learn to respond to their name and to recognize the names of objects and people. They also learn to use simple gestures such as pointing, reaching up, pushing away, bouncing, and shaking their heads to signal their desires. Some will say their first words before their first birthdays; others will respond to words but be slower to use them.

Infant care teachers can encourage this interest in language by cuddling with one or two infants and reading simple board books to them several times each day. Pointing at pictures, naming people or objects, and making the sounds of animals in the pictures are good introductions to literacy and the importance of books.

Mobile infants love to play and interact with the caring adults in their lives and can use their new language and motor skills to participate in baby games that are traditional in their culture(s). These games may include versions of peekaboo, hand-clapping rhymes, bouncing games, and games that involve pointing or gesturing. As they learn these routines, babies will come to anticipate the fun parts and will laugh and gesture at the appropriate times.

The mobile infant is both practicing independence and using new ways to stay connected to those he loves and trusts to protect him as he moves about on his own. Eye contact, vocalizing, and gesturing take on added importance as tools for maintaining that connection, although physical contact continues to be essential. A strong, loving relationship with a trusted adult gives the mobile infant the secure base from which he can explore his world.

Toddlers (16 to 36 months)

Toddlers are primarily concerned with developing an understanding of who they are. Beginning at around 18 months, identity becomes the dominant theme for them. Developing this sense of self has a lot to do with their desire and drive for independence and control. Whether toddlers are still teetering with a wide-based gait, confidently getting around on two legs, or standing only with assistance, they are busy "standing up for themselves." They use their rapidly developing communication skills to indicate their desires and refuse what they do not want at the moment. As their social awareness expands, they pick up cultural messages about who they are and how they should be. Their most frequent statements are likely to include "No," "Mine," "Why," and "Me do it."

Of course, the sense of security that began to develop in the earliest months and the desire to explore (with increasing purposefulness) continue. Toddler care teachers can help toddlers find ap-

Kirsty, a 22-month-old who was just beginning to put words together, lived in a rural area. One winter day a fox trotted past the living room window. Kirsty's father pointed excitedly as it ran out of sight, then showed Kirsty the tracks in the snow. "See fox," said Kirsty the next morning. "Yes," replied her father, "we saw a fox." "Feet," said Kirsty. Her father elaborated. "Its feet made tracks in the snow," and Kirsty repeated "snow." Over the next several days, Kirsty told the fox story dozens of times, helped by her mother and father and then by her clued-in toddler care teacher. Kirsty's few contributions—"See fox," "feet," and "snow"—were soon supplemented with "run," "fast," "tracks," "tail," and "red" as the story grew more elaborate.

Kirsty is as excited as her parents and toddler care teacher by her new ability to use words to share a memory. Her father's delight encourages Kirsty to tell the story over and over again. Over time, her father scaffolds Kirsty's learning by adding just a bit more. Because Kirsty's parents and toddler care teacher talk frequently about the skills that Kirsty is working on and the new interests she is showing, Kirsty's mother and then her toddler care teacher are able to pick up with Kirsty where she and her father left off.

propriate ways to assert themselves by supporting their individuality, giving them choices whenever possible, and introducing social guidelines. Toddlers work very hard to understand social rules and get things right. The toddler care teacher fosters cooperation and facilitates the toddler's development of a strong sense of self. A well designed environment offers toddlers many chances to be in control as they participate in group play, fantasy play, and independent activities.

Young toddlers are busy exploring the world from their new, upright vantage point. At the same time they are, quite literally, gaining a new sense of themselves as either a "big boy" or a "big girl." They do the things they see the important people in their lives do, or at least they try. Reassured by the presence of a loved family member or toddler care teacher, they busily explore and construct an understanding of the world.

Toddlers are especially intrigued with the daily activities they see adults engage in and watch intently as grown-ups go about daily tasks of cooking, cleaning, building, and fixing. These experiences provide fuel for "stories" that toddlers tell over and over in their play, both with and without words. Instead of just pushing a truck, for example, they may drive it to a spot, fill it with sand, and then drive it to a new location to dump the sand. They might also use miniature figures to replay a frightening event, such as being barked at by a big dog or getting a "boo-boo."

Toddlers are fascinated by words. They constantly ask "Wha's dat?" and repeat words and phrases they hear. They enjoy following simple instructions, and, as they learn to talk, even give instructions to themselves. For example, a toddler may tell herself "No, no, no" or "Hot" as she tries to contain her exuberance. Toddlers can also use words to express strong feelings and to evoke what is not present. A child may repeat a phrase such as "Daddy come back" in a ritualistic way to comfort herself when feeling the sadness of separation, to reassure herself that the separation is not permanent.

Toddlers love to hear stories about themselves and the people and things they love. They also love books—especially sturdy ones they can easily manipulate, with clear pictures and lots of things to do—textures to feel, holes to peek through or poke fingers into, sounds to make, and actions to imitate. Illustrations of familiar objects and activities (or photo albums of favorite people) and simple, poetic text in their home language invite toddlers to join in the telling of the story. They do this in many ways: by repeating words and phrases, imitating the sounds of animals and machines, naming or pointing out pictures and details upon request, asking questions, and turning the pages. Many classic stories for toddlers involve searching for a mother, running away and coming back, being lost and found again, or doing something bad and being forgiven. These themes resonate with the toddler's ongoing struggles to balance his desires for independence and closeness, for being "big" and being a "baby."

As toddlers' verbal skills expand, so does their ability to use objects, to put together a series of actions in play, and to remember events for later reenactment. Adults are especially valued play partners because they can keep the story going as they respond to the child's lead by adding missing words or by suggesting next steps or new elements. An adult can support a toddler's need to repeat the same story over and over again, encourage her to do more of the storytelling each time, and help her to extend or elaborate on her story. Peers are also highly valued play partners as they heighten the emotional tone of play, take different roles, or share ideas for solving problems.

Through their experimentation with objects, language, and social interactions, toddlers enter a new phase of cognitive growth. They love to divide objects into categories by shape, size, color, or type. What toddlers are learning through play, observation, and exploration is truly amazing. They might call anything with four legs and a tail a "doggie" or remember which blocks go with the shape puzzle. They might line up rubber animals accord-

All of the children in Lei-Ann's family child care home are busy "writing letters." It started when Rosa was sick one day, and Nadia wanted to send her a get well card. Nadia, at 5, knew that a proper letter required a stamp and had to be put in a mailbox, so Lei-Ann gave her an envelope and a stamp and helped her write Rosa's address. Then the whole group took a walk to the mailbox. Noticing that her toddlers were fascinated with the idea that a letter could disappear into a box and end up at someone's house, Lei-Ann made up some address labels and return address stickers so the children could send each other mail—both within the group by putting them in a special box and, for really special messages, through the U.S. Postal Service.

Toddlers benefit from opportunities to imitate reading and writing in their pretend play. They can participate in these grown-up activities by scribbling "notes," making pictures and books, dictating words and seeing how they appear in print, and "reading" their messages.

ing to their height, find all of the cows, or even pair a big animal with a little one and call them "mommy and baby." They are developing increasingly sophisticated mental representations of the real world and mastering them through using them in play.

Toddlers' social awareness is far more complex than that of infants. They actively seek out their friends and especially enjoy imitating each other's behavior and engaging in group activities such as a simple game of follow the leader. Toddlers will work together to carry a large object, dig a hole in the sandbox, or make a bed for a doll. As their language and social skills become more sophisticated, they may begin to take on simple pretend play roles like doctor and patient or parent and child. They choose friends who share their interests and will play with them. Over time, in pairs or small groups, toddler friends develop their own rituals, favorite games, and deepening affections and attachments.

As they increasingly tune in to the social world, toddlers become particularly interested in their bodies and those of others. They begin to learn what it means to be a boy or a girl—both physically, when they notice differences in their body parts, and socially, especially as they notice the differences in gender roles within their culture. Some of this awareness develops as learning to use the toilet becomes an important issue during the third year of life, especially as children see peers giving up diapers. Toilet learning should begin when the child shows signs of interest and readiness. Adults need to follow the child's lead as she shows a desire for privacy when having a bowel movement in a diaper, expresses discomfort in a filled diaper, and shows interest in toileting.

Toddlers' exploration of the social world often involves conflict. The most basic conflict centers on "what is mine" and "what is yours." Toddlers react impulsively, but their feelings of empathy blossom as they negotiate these conflicts and see that other people have feelings too. They are beginning to understand that other people's thoughts and feel-ings may differ from their own (e.g., "I want to pull this lamp down, but Mama doesn't want me to"). Sometimes they try to do things they are told not to, just to see the other person's reactions. Toddlers can easily fall into despair at not getting what they want or when they sense the displeasure of a beloved adult; just as easily, they can react with true generosity and warmth. Through such experiences, toddlers build a sense of themselves as social beings: competent, cooperative, and emotionally connected.

Adapted with permission from *Caring for infants & toddlers in groups: Developmentally appropriate practice, 2d ed.* (Washington, DC: ZERO TO THREE, 2008), 1–4, 7–10, and 14–17. Copyright © 2008 ZERO TO THREE: National Center for Infants, Toddlers, and Families. All rights reserved.

Heather Biggar Tomlinson and Marilou Hyson

2

Cognitive Development in the Preschool Years

Some important **cognitive changes occur** during preschool, particularly in terms of mental representation. Whereas infants and toddlers have only a limited ability to form representations of their world (images, concepts) and hold them in memory, children in preschool possess more of that extraordinary ability. When asked about past or future events, preschoolers (unlike toddlers) are able to think about what happened weeks ago or anticipate what has not yet happened. They can create fanciful scenes (e.g., in which one child is a pilot and the other runs the control tower), coordinating roles and story lines, and by 4 and 5 years old, they do so with an awareness that they are acting out an imaginary idea (Sobel 2006). They become more efficient thinkers as they start to organize their thoughts into categories, and they show more sophisticated use of symbols through their use of pretend objects in play and drawings for learning and communicating.

In spite of their many advances, preschoolers can be illogical, egocentric, and one-dimensional in their thinking. Piaget referred to these years as a "*pre*operational" stage of development, emphasizing that children ages 2 to 7 are less capable in their thinking compared with older children. More recent research indicates that preschoolers have greater cognitive abilities than has been sometimes assumed, at least when children are in familiar situations and tasks are clearly explained to them.

Preschool children can appear to know or understand more—or less—than they actually do. At times they seem mature and relatively advanced in their thinking, and then later seem limited and inflexible. As preschoolers move from and between simpler to more complex thinking skills, it is helpful to remember that they are not merely functioning less effectively than older children or adults; their narrow focus on a limited amount of information at any given time is actually useful while they are learning so many things so rapidly (Bjorklund 2007). That is, because they are just on the cusp of grasping a variety of concepts, words, and skills at a new level, they learn best when they can attend to just one thing at a time (e.g., putting all the yellow crayons and chalk in one bin and purple crayons and chalk in another—cementing awareness of color) rather than attending to multiple things (e.g., yellow versus purple, crayons versus chalk, and broken versus whole, which is too many concepts to achieve success).

Below are brief descriptions of some influences on cognitive development, as well as characteristics of children's thought, that a preschool teacher might expect to see.

Influences of social interaction and play

As teachers are well aware, all learning for young children is interdependent: Cognitive development in the preschool years has important implications for children's social and language development, and social and language development play an essential role in stimulating cognitive growth. Children construct their understanding of a concept in the course of interaction with others (Berk & Winsler 1995; Vygotsky 1978).

In developing ideas about what "school" means, for example, children use what they hear people say about school, glimpses of buildings identified by others as schools, and stories about school that they have had read to them. Their initial ideas may be challenged, confirmed, elaborated on, or altered by subsequent interactions with peers, older children, or adults. And as Vygotsky demonstrated, much of children's understanding first occurs in communication with other people, then appears in "private speech" (thinking aloud), and eventually is internalized as thought. As children's memory, language, and other aspects of cognition improve and change, their relationships with others are affected.

Make-believe or pretend play, with guidance and support from adults, blossoms in the preschool years and allows children to make a number of cognitive gains as they try out new ideas and skills. Advances in children's play skills not only serve as indicators of preschoolers' advancing cognitive skills but also are crucial in fostering further cognitive development.

Heather Biggar Tomlinson is an early childhood education specialist consulting for UNICEF in Jakarta, Indonesia. **Marilou Hyson** is a U.S. and international early childhood consultant, former editor in chief of *Early Childhood Research Quarterly*, and former NAEYC associate executive director.

Other types of play, such as drawing or doing puzzles, are important too. But there is something special about social pretend play for preschoolers. When they engage in mature sociodramatic play (pretend play that involves communication with other children), children's interactions last longer than they do in other situations, children show high levels of involvement, large numbers of children are drawn in, and children show more cooperation (Creasey et al. 1998)—all of which have important benefits for children's cognitive (and other types of) development.

Toddlers, too, engage in pretend play, but by the time children reach preschool age, they usually show more sophisticated play, especially when they have had parents' and teachers' support and such play opportunities (Bodrova & Leong 2007).

They show their growing sophistication in a number of ways. They are more flexible and begin to substitute various objects for items needed in the play; leaves might become lettuce, and rocks, onions in the pretend soup being made. They move away from self-centered play to involve others; for example, instead of just pretending to drink from a cup, as a toddler might do, preschoolers might have a pretend party that involves welcoming a friend into their pretend home, passing out pretend cups, pouring and stirring pretend tea, and offering pretend cookies. Such a series of many steps and combinations of actions and interactions tends to be too complex for toddlers (Kavanaugh 2006; McCune 1993; Striano et al. 2001).

That is, by age 4 or 5, children often collaborate with a peer or peers to create a scene with various roles and story lines—say, a birthday party that includes a birthday boy, parents and friends, and a couple of different situations, perhaps opening gifts, a jealous sibling who gets in trouble, and time for candles and cake.

Piaget (1951) believed that pretend play strengthens newly acquired abilities to mentally picture different situations and allows children to take control of experiences in which they have little or no control in real life, such as going to the doctor's office or getting lost at the store. Vygotsky (1978) saw dramatic play, with its system of roles and rules (i.e., who does what and what is allowed in the play scenario) as uniquely supportive of self-regulation. Children's eagerness to stay in the play situation motivates them to attend to and operate within its structure, conforming to what is required by the other players and by the play scenario.

Indeed, research bears out the beliefs of these two prominent theorists and further extends our understanding of the benefits of play. A study of children from around the world, from Indonesia to Italy to Ireland (and the United States), showed that when preschool experiences at age 4 included lots of child-initiated, free-choice activities supported by a variety of equipment and materials—the kinds of environments that support play—these children had better cognitive (and language) performance at age 7 than their peers (Montie et al. 2006).

Other research shows that pretend play strengthens cognitive capacities, including sustained attention, memory, logical reasoning, language and literacy skills, imagination, creativity, understanding of emotions, and the ability to reflect on one's own thinking, inhibit impulses, control one's behavior, and take another person's perspective (Bergen & Mauer 2000; Berk 2006; Elias & Berk 2002; Kavanaugh & Engel 1998; Lindsey & Colwell 2003; Ruff & Capozzoli 2003).

Executive functioning

During the preschool years, the brain's cerebral cortex and the functions that ultimately regulate children's attention and memory are not fully developed, which accounts for some of the limitations in their capacity to reason and solve problems. They also haven't had as much experience as older children in being taught what to pay attention to or how to remember things, opportunity to practice self-regulation skills through sociodramatic play, and other environmentally supportive experiences. During the preschool years, as children have more instruction and opportunity to practice information-processing skills related to attention and memory, their skills improve.

Attention

Attention is crucial to our thinking because it decides what information will influence the task at hand. The ability to focus attention and concentrate enhances academic learning, including language acquisition and problem solving, as well as social skills and cooperation (Bono & Stifter 2003; Landry

et al. 2000; Murphy et al. 2007). As teachers know, preschoolers may have trouble focusing on details, spend only a short time on most tasks, and tend to be more distractible than older children, especially when required to listen passively or work on a prescribed task (Goldberg et al. 2001; Lin et al. 1999). But attention does become more sustained and under the child's control over the course of the preschool years.

For example, young preschoolers usually are not able to apply an attention strategy, whereas older preschoolers can use simple strategies. In one study, when doing a task in which the best strategy was to open only those doors with certain pictures on them (some doors pictured a type of house and other doors pictured a type of animal), 3- and 4-year-olds simply opened all the doors. But by age 5, children began to apply a selective strategy of opening only those doors with the relevant pictures on them—at least most of the time (Wood-Ramsey & Miller 1988).

Memory

As attention improves, so does memory and, more specifically, children's use of memory strategies. Memory strategies are deliberate mental activities that allow us to hold information first in working memory and then to transfer it to long-term memory. Preschoolers begin to use memory strategies, but these take so much effort and concentration that they are not very useful at first. As with other skills, memory strategies improve as preschoolers have opportunity and guidance to practice them (Berk 2009).

Younger children do not make effective use of memory strategies such as rehearsing a list or grouping items into meaningful categories (Bjorklund et al. 1994). Even when adults try to teach strategies for improving memory, younger children do not automatically or accurately apply the strategies in situations requiring memory.

But they do make memory-related gains in preschool. "Scripts" are schemas for routine events, such as going to the grocery store or eating lunch. As part of learning about their culture, children form script categories when items play the same role in a script (e.g., *peanut butter*, *bologna*, and *cheese* could be in the script category *lunch foods*). Three-year-olds are no more likely to group words

© Ellen B. Senisi

by script than by general category; that is, they are equally likely to pair any foods together (e.g., *broccoli* and *donut*) as they are to pair lunch foods together (*bologna* and *cheese*). Four-year-olds, on the other hand, are more likely to categorize words by a familiar script category (*lunch foods*) than by the broader general category (*foods*) (Nguyen & Murphy 2003). When words are highly associated, as they are in scripts, children do better on memory tasks (Krackow & Gordon 1998). (It is not until age 7 or so that children begin to use more abstract hierarchical taxonomies of categorization.)

In other words, preschoolers are more likely to understand and remember relationships, concepts, and strategies that they acquire through firsthand, meaningful experience. When 4- and 5-year-olds were either told to play with some toys or told to

simply remember them, they later remembered better the toys they had played with, because they spontaneously organized them mentally into meaningful groups based on their play activities, say, putting a shoe on a doll's foot or narrating their play ("*Fly away in this helicopter, doggie*") (Newman 1990).

When they do begin grouping items for memory, children naturally organize items by their everyday associations, such as *hat:head* and *carrot:rabbit*. Preschoolers who cannot recall multiple steps in a set of repeated directions can, however, relate specific, even sequential, events from highly salient experiences (e.g., a trip on an airplane, a visit to a theme park) from as long as a year before.

Other cognitive capacities

During the years from age 3 through age 5, children gradually develop their mental representation, logic and reasoning skills, conceptual and classification abilities, and other cognitive capacities.

Mental representation

Mental representations are internal depictions of information that our minds can manipulate—images or mental pictures of people or objects; concepts, which are categories by which the mind groups similar objects; and words, which are labels for these images and concepts now understood. Mental representation allows us to become more efficient thinkers and organize our experiences into meaningful, manageable, and memorable units (Berk 2009).

Children in the preschool years make exceptional advances in their ability to use mental representation. Around age 3, children begin to understand that an object can serve both as an object in its own right and as a symbol of something else; for example, a bowl can be a bowl, or it can be a hat, or a bed for a baby mouse (DeLoache 2006). This development reveals an extraordinary increase in children's ability to mentally or symbolically represent concrete objects, action, and events.

As their understanding of the connections between symbols and the real world becomes stronger, they realize that each symbol in their world corresponds to a specific state of affairs in everyday life and that a symbol does not have to have a strong resemblance to what it represents. For example, a stick picture of Ms. Hei and Puggles represents the teacher walking her dog, even though the drawn creatures and the real creatures look very little alike. This opens up many new avenues to knowledge and communication and prompts new abilities in various areas. Pretend play and drawing efforts are both excellent examples of how preschoolers advance in their ability to use mental representation, and symbolic thought in particular (Berk 2009).

Toddlers, given a crayon and paper, will scribble happily in imitation of others. When, at around age 3, children realize that pictures serve as symbols, they begin to draw as an artistic expression (Golomb 2004)—perhaps not in any greatly recognizable form in the beginning. But to themselves at least, the drawing depicts a recognizable shape, and that is what matters. For example, a child might draw a bunch of random squiggles and then ask the teacher to label the picture "Worms wrestling."

Children reach a major milestone around age 3 or 4 when they use lines as symbols for the boundaries of an object, usually a person. Four-year-olds might also draw more detailed features, such as eyes, a nose, and a smile. By age 5, preschoolers might be drawing more realistic and complex pictures with more conventional aspects—but even theirs have perceptual distortions because children are just beginning to represent depth (Braine et al. 1993; Toomela 2002). Just as their understanding of a bowl as a hat reveals dual representation, so their use of drawing shows that marks on a page hold meaning.

This increasing ability to use mental representation allows children to think ahead a bit before taking action, and their activities take on a more purposeful, goal-directed character (Friedman et al. 1987). Preschoolers can begin to separate their thoughts from their actions. They will not focus on the process of their thinking per se, but they begin to realize that what they think can be different from what they actually do.

For example, whereas toddlers continually repeat the same "mistake" and figure things out by doing something over and over, preschoolers can anticipate the consequences of their physical actions. For example, a child is more likely to anticipate a negative response from her teacher if she pulls her classmate's hair. She will not be able to control her impulse every time. But with the teacher's support in thinking of alternative ways to get what she wants (e.g., using her words, waiting her turn, sharing a toy) and with practice using empathy and self-regulation skills (e.g., through pretend play), she will do better each time.

Logic and characteristics of thought

Piaget believed children in the preschool years were illogical in many ways because they have a largely egocentric perspective (difficulty taking others' perspective), an inability to grasp the notion of conservation (that certain physical characteristics of objects remain the same even when their outward appearance changes), and a belief that inanimate objects have human thoughts, feelings, and wishes (Piaget 1930).

Although preschoolers do show these qualities and are certainly more limited than older children in their ability to reason, they are more advanced than Piaget assumed and than many adults might perceive. Children ages 3 to 5 do better on cognitive tasks than they did for Piaget—when the tasks occur with familiar elements and focus on one thing at a time (Berk 2009).

Reasoning

The ability to reason stems in part from our ability to take another's perspective. Preschoolers' thinking still tends to be egocentric; that is, they tend to take into account only their own point of view and have difficulty understanding how the world looks to other people. Instead, they assume that other people see and experience things the same way they do. For example, a child might share his graham cracker and peanut butter with his teacher when the teacher is sad, in the belief that she will be comforted by the same thing that comforts him. Three-year-olds who are shown that a candy box now holds pencils assume that others would likewise know it holds pencils—just like they do (Gopnik & Astington 1988).

But by age 4, children do have an awareness, albeit limited, of others' vantage points. For example, they will change the tone or level of their conversation when speaking with a toddler (Newcombe & Huttenlocher 1992; Gelman & Shatz 1978).

Even though research shows that preschoolers' capacities are at times underestimated, they do have limitations in their reasoning skills that affect learning. They have a limited understanding of ideas such as *time*, *space*, or *age*, for instance, and don't use these abstract concepts to help themselves reason unless the ideas are made real and relevant to their current lives.

That preschoolers are very concrete thinkers who focus on the tangible, observable aspects of objects is also apparent in their use of language. For example, a child may use the word *fuzzy* in relation to a peach skin or a blanket but have difficulty applying it to something abstract, as in "fuzzy thinking." And they typically reason from the particular to the particular ("*My dog is friendly, so this dog is*

friendly"), a natural result of their budding classification skills.

But in general, they show some ability to reason logically when tasks are simple, consistent with what they already know, and made relevant to their everyday lives (Berk 2009; Ruffman 1999).

Concept acquisition and classification

One of the main developmental goals of young children is to make sense of their world and organize it into meaningful and manageable categories or schemas. Preschoolers are answering for themselves two basic questions: What kinds of things are there in the world, and how do they relate to one another? (Siegler et al. 2006).

Children form basic categories first and gradually both expand to broader categories and narrow to more specific elements of the basic category. For example, they first recognize that a group of things with four legs that people sit on are called chairs; then they perceive the broader set (furniture) and more specific subsets (rocking chairs and La-Z-Boys—which is a more impressive classification than it sounds to adults, since La-Z-Boys are neither lazy nor boys).

Typically, preschoolers describe objects by their appearance and actions ("*the big, mean dog*"). They also organize information into categories based on attributes that define an object or an idea (e.g., four legs and you sit on it, four wheels and you ride in it), even if the members of this category look quite different (Mandler 2004). They may initially miss subtle differences in appearance that differentiate objects based on function (e.g., coin slot on a ceramic pig) but even toddlers perceive subtle defining features if adults explain them (Banigan & Mervis 1988). Preschoolers can also categorize by trait. For example, if told that two birds are sociable and one bird is shy, they know the two sociable birds (rather than the two that look alike) will prefer the same types of activities (Heyman & Gelman 2000).

In fact, preschoolers tend to conceptualize best when they understand why things are the way they are, or what matters in a comparison. For example, when told that wugs (imaginary animals) have claws, spikes, and horns because they like to fight, whereas gillies have wings because they do not like to fight and they fly away from wugs, 4- and 5-year-olds remember the physical features better than if they were not told why the creatures have their respective features (Krascum & Andrews 1998).

In part because the why matters in preschoolers' ability to conceptualize and remember, they are hungry for more and more explanations—explaining their seemingly endless stream of questions: "Why do cows moo?" "What do clouds feel like?" "Do the worms like to take walks?" The answers help preschool children learn how to think about the world and put things in categories (Siegler et al. 2006).

As children broaden their knowledge of things in the world and how those things go together, they more effortlessly categorize according to any number of attributes: length, color, weight, function, texture, and so forth. But young preschoolers have trouble focusing on more than one thing at a time and sticking with one feature (e.g., the color red) in sorting objects into a class (Brooks et al. 2003). Sec-

ondary attributes (e.g., size) tend to distract them from using one dimension consistently throughout the task. By age 4 or 5, however, children can sort and classify by more than one attribute of an object (e.g., color and size).

Because children are just beginning to understand part/whole and hierarchical relationships, they may have difficulty grasping that an object can be in more than one class ("*It's not a fruit—it's an apple!*") or recognizing that with six girls and four boys there are more children than girls, for example.

These types of classification skills have obvious links to curriculum areas. For example, from ages 3 to 5, children show increasing interest in mathematical and scientific concepts such as *number* and *quantity*; they start counting, measuring, comparing, and doing more complex matching activities. They start noticing and copying simple repeating patterns (e.g., long-short-long-short), and

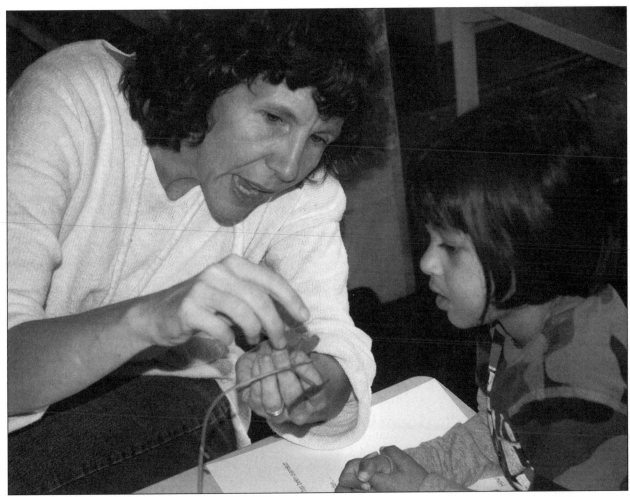

© Peg Callaghan

as they start organizing groups according to color or size, they start comparing them to see which has more objects.

Magical thinking

Young children's reasoning is influenced by their tendency toward magical thinking and animism—that is, giving lifelike qualities to inanimate objects. They may mistakenly think, for instance, that certain vehicles such as trains or airplanes can be living creatures because they move—not surprising as the objects are sometimes depicted with life-like features, such as headlights that look like eyes and appear to move on their own (Gelman & Opfer 2002). Or children might think a vacuum cleaner is a monster, or a thunderstorm means that God is angry.

Although individual differences in temperament play a big role in how fearful a child is, this tendency toward animism characterizes preschool cognition as a whole and accounts for many typical fears among this age group. They often believe also in the enchanted powers of fairies and goblins and such and believe that magic accounts for things they can't explain (Rosengren & Hickling 2000).

Even young preschoolers are savvy enough, however, to think that an action such as walking through a wall (which violates basic physical laws) would require magic, whereas taking a bath with one's shoes on (which merely breaks social convention) does not (Browne & Woolley 2004). Starting around age 4 or 5, children's magical beliefs begin to ebb as they realize magicians use tricks rather than magic or that Santa Claus is actually Uncle Kevin (Subbotsky 2004).

How quickly they give up their magical beliefs depends in part on culture, information from adults and older children, and religion. Regardless of how early it begins, the process of replacing magical thinking with more logical reasoning is gradual. Preschoolers will still be scared by scary stories and nightmares and monsters in the closet—and still believe in Santa for at least a few more years.

Promoting cognitive development in preschool

The cognitive processes described above will take several years to be well developed, in part because the preschool child's brain has yet to mature in some important ways, and in part because they have had little experience using the new skills and strategies learned, so each task requires enormous mental effort. The skills become more automatic and effortless only with practice—and plenty of support.

That support comes in the form of cues, questions, modeling, and other assistance from adults and other children. For example, as a child struggles with a puzzle piece, instead of directly showing him how to place the piece, the teacher might say, "What color is it? Where do you see that color on the puzzle?" or "Try turning it around another way." These types of questions and suggestions help children stretch to achieve that next level of understanding or performance. Say, with the teacher's prompt, the child finds where the puzzle piece fits. The teacher will continue this way, gradually reducing the amount of help as the child's skills improve, until eventually the child can succeed on his own. This kind of support, where the teacher (or a more competent peer) helps only just enough and until the child succeeds, is called scaffolding.

Of the many things that skilled teachers do to foster children's learning and intellectual development, one of the most important is ensuring guidance and ample time for sustained play. They realize its powerful benefits for cognitive development, including attention and memory gains and increased self-regulation (Bodrova & Leong 2005). To develop these skills, preschoolers particularly need to engage in sociodramatic play that is intentional, imaginative, and extended. Children negotiate with each other to take on different roles in the pretend scene, first discussing and then acting out a scenario, and using various props in different ways.

"Although 4-year-old children are capable of this kind of complex play, many preschool and even kindergarten age children still play at the toddler level, repeating the same sequence of actions within a very limited repertoire of play themes and roles," write Bodrova and Leong (2005, 4). Teachers need to help by giving children ideas for various scenes and roles; providing time, space, and play props and dress-up clothes; helping them implement some "rules" at first; and then backing away and letting children play with their peers alone so they internalize the skills needed to sustain play and develop cognitive (and other) skills.

Teachers take other active roles in promoting children's thinking and their acquisition of concepts and skills. These roles range from asking a well timed question that provokes further reflection or investigation to showing children how to use a new tool or procedure. Early childhood educators have evolved approaches that are very successful in promoting children's engagement in challenging, meaningful problems and enterprises—for instance, by encouraging children to plan and review their work and to represent what they know verbally, pictorially, and through other modes and media (Copple et al. 1984; Edwards et al. 1998; Forman 1994).

Preschoolers spontaneously pay attention to distinctive events and things, such as loud noises and brightly colored objects. Helping them to attend consciously to a specific aspect of something requires gentle scaffolding rather than generic demands to "Pay attention!" or "Listen!" which are not informative in honing children's attention. Preschoolers do not have the insight to know what specifically to pay attention to. A specific request or targeted question ("*Which two are alike?*") provides just enough structuring of the task to bring it within children's reach.

Attention advances most for children this age when they have opportunities to pursue their interests and try out new ideas and skills, especially through dramatic play (Bodrova & Leong 2007).

Research on cognitive development in preschool age children (e.g., Case & Okamoto 1996; Seifert 1993) leads to an important conclusion: Young children have age-related limits in their cognitive capacities, but they also have enormous capacities to learn and often underestimated capacities to think, reason, remember, and problem solve.

To demonstrate how teachers can promote cognitive skills in specific content and curriculum areas, an example using mathematics follows.

An example: Teaching mathematics

To be effective, preschool mathematics curriculum and instruction need to be engaging to children, consistent with their developmental level, and focused on the important concepts and processes on which subsequent math learning will build. Teachers also help children connect various mathematics topics to one another. This helps strengthen their grasp of concepts in each area as well as their beliefs about mathematics as a coherent *system*. Most good mathematics activities also develop language and vocabulary. For example, teachers can ask children wearing something red to get their coats *first*, those wearing blue to go *second*, and so on (Sarama & Clements 2006). Linking mathematics to other learning domains, such as literacy, strengthens both domains.

To promote math skills, teachers can:

• create learning environments to ensure that children "bump into interesting mathematics at every turn" (Greenes 1999, 46);

• investigate with children, observing what they do and say;

• answer children's questions and pose interesting questions and ideas for them to think about; and

• introduce the language of mathematics into everyday situations, and serve as examples by modeling math communication and investigation.

Children need to learn math concepts and relationships to become mathematical thinkers. Equally important, they need to learn basic but powerful things about problem solving and reasoning. For instance, children need to recognize that there are many different ways to solve a problem.

As children encounter mathematical challenges in the classroom or at home, teachers encourage them not only to tackle the problem but also to share their thinking with others. To promote children's mathematical thinking and learning, one of the most important things teachers can do is simply talk with them about problems, patterns, and mathematical connections using mathematical language (e.g., *more than*, *less than, tallest, five*) and listening to what they say. Such dialogue helps children think about what they are doing and makes their own thoughts clearer. In addition, it improves children's math vocabulary, introducing them to words and phrases useful in mathematical reasoning and problem solving.

In short, such interactions with children help to "mathematize" the experiences and informal knowledge. As Sarama and Clements (2006) note, "In all activities, especially teacher-directed activities, teachers need to help children connect their informal knowledge to their budding explicit knowledge of mathematics" (86).

Young children solve lots of problems that arise in their everyday lives, but they do so intuitively, often impulsively, and tend to rely on habit or trial and error. On entering school, children will encounter a greater range of problems, including many that require careful thinking and systematic investigation. The skills and cognitive structures needed to solve problems in this deliberate, logical way are not well developed in preschoolers. However, teachers can work to enhance children's problem-solving dispositions and abilities by creating a learning environment in which children feel free to take risks and search for solutions to problems.

Children become more conscious of their own reasoning and problem-solving strategies when teachers comment on what they are doing or ask about how and why they are doing it. For example, "Andre divided the playdough so that each person has the same amount. How did you do that, Andre?" and "If you mix the yellow and the blue, what will happen?"

In high-quality learning environments, children become increasingly persistent, flexible, and proficient problem solvers—and they learn to *enjoy* solving problems.

Adapted from C. Copple & S. Bredekamp, eds., *Developmentally appropriate practice in early childhood programs serving children from birth through age 8, 3d ed.* (Washington, DC: NAEYC, 2009), 129–40. Copyright © 2009 NAEYC.

References

Banigan, R.L., & C.B. Mervis. 1988. Role of adult input in young children's category evolution: An experimental study. *Journal of Child Language* 15: 35–47.

Bergen, D., & D. Mauer. 2000. Symbolic play, phonological awareness, and literacy skills at three age levels. In *Play and literacy in early childhood: Research from multiple perspectives*, eds. K.A. Roskos & J.F. Christie, 45–62. Mahwah, NJ: Lawrence Erlbaum.

Berk, L.E. 2006. Make-believe play: Wellspring for development of self-regulation. In *Play = learning: How play motivates and enhances children's cognitive and social-emotional growth*, eds. D. Singer, K. Hirsh-Pasek, & R. Golinkoff. New York: Oxford University Press.

Berk, L.E. 2009. *Child development.* 8th ed. Boston: Pearson/Allyn & Bacon.

Berk, L.E., & A. Winsler. 1995. *Scaffolding children's learning.* Washington, DC: NAEYC.

Bjorklund, D.F. 2007. *Why youth is not wasted on the young: Immaturity in human development.* Oxford: Blackwell.

Bjorklund, D.F., W. Schneider, W.S. Cassel & E. Ashley. 1994. Training and extension of a memory strategy: Evidence for utilization deficiencies in high- and low-IQ children. *Child Development* 65 (3): 951–65.

Bodrova, E., & D.J. Leong. 2005. Promoting student self-regulation in learning. *Education Digest* 71 (2): 54–57.

Bodrova, E., & D.J. Leong. 2007. *Tools of the mind: The Vygotskian approach to early childhood education.* 2d ed. Upper Saddle River, NJ: Pearson/Merrill Prentice Hall.

Bono, M.A., & C.A. Stifter. 2003. Maternal attention-directing strategies and infant focused attention during problem solving. *Infancy* 4: 235–56.

Braine, L.G., L. Schauble, S. Kugelmass & A. Winter. 1993. Representation of depth by children: Spatial strategies and lateral biases. *Developmental Psychology* 29 (3): 466–79.

Brooks, P.J., J.B. Hanauere, B. Padowski & H. Rosman. 2003. The role of selective attention in preschoolers' ruse use in a novel dimensional card sort. *Cognitive Development* 18: 195–215.

Browne, C.A., & J.D. Woolley. 2004. Preschooler's magical explanations for violations of physical, social, and mental laws. *Journal of Cognition and Development* 5: 239–60.

Case, R., & Y. Okamoto, eds. 1996. *The role of central conceptual structures in the development of children' thought.* Monographs of the Society for Research in Child Development, vol. 61, nos. 1–2, serial no. 246. Chicago: University of Chicago Press.

Copple, C., I.E. Sigel & R. Saunders. 1984. *Educating the young thinker: Classroom strategies for cognitive growth.* Hillsdale, NJ: Lawrence Erlbaum.

Creasey, G.L., P.A. Jarvis & L.E. Berk. 1998. Play and social competence. In *Multiple perspectives on play in early childhood education*, eds. O.N. Saracho & B. Spodek, 116–43. Albany, NY: State University of New York.

DeLoache, J.S. 2006. Mindful of SYMBOLS. *Scientific American Mind* 17 (1): 71–75.

Edwards, C.P., L. Gandini & G. Forman, eds. 1998. *The hundred languages of children: The Reggio Emilia approach—Advanced reflections.* 2d ed. Greenwich, CT: Ablex.

Elias, C., & L.E. Berk. 2002. Self-regulation in young children: Is there a role for sociodramatic play? *Early Childhood Research Quarterly* 17 (1): 216–38.

Forman, G. 1994. Different media, different languages. In *Reflections on the Reggio Emilia approach*, eds. L.G. Katz & B. Cesarone, 37–46. Urbana, IL: ERIC Clearinghouse on Elementary and Early Childhood Education.

Friedman, S.L., E.K. Scholnick & R.R. Cocking. 1987. Reflections on reflections: What planning is and how it develops. In *Blueprints for thinking: The role of planning in cognitive development,* eds. S.L. Friedman, E.K. Scholnick, & R.R. Cocking. New York: Cambridge University Press.

Gelman, S.A., & J.E. Opfer. 2002. Development of the animate-inanimate distinction. In *Blackwell handbook of childhood cognitive development*, ed. U. Goswami, 151–66. Malden, MA: Blackwell.

Gelman, R., & M. Shatz. 1978. Appropriate speech adjustments: The operation of conversational constraints on talk to two-year-olds. In *Interaction, conversation, and the development of language*, eds. M. Lewis & R.A. Rosenblum, 27–61. New York: John Wiley & Sons.

Goldberg, M.C., D. Maurer & T.L. Lewis. 2001. Developmental changes in attention: The effects of endogenous cueing and of distracters. *Developmental Science* 4: 209–19.

Golomb, C. 2004. *The child's creation of a pictorial world.* 2d ed. Mahwah, NJ: Lawrence Erlbaum.

Gopnik, A., & J.W. Astington. 1988. Children's understanding of representational change and its relation to the understanding of false belief and the appearance-reality distinction. *Child Development* 59 (1): 26–37.

Greenes, C. 1999. Ready to learn: Developing young children's mathematical powers. In *Mathematics in the early years*, ed. J. Copley, 39–47. Reston, VA: National Council of Teachers of Mathematics, and Washington, DC: NAEYC.

Heyman, G.D., & S.A. Gelman. 2000. Preschool children's use of trait labels to make inductive inferences. *Journal of Experimental Child Psychology* 77: 1–19.

Kavanaugh, R.D. 2006. Pretend play. In *Handbook of research on the education of young children*, 2d ed., eds. B. Spodek & O.N. Saracho, 269–78. Mahwah, NJ: Lawrence Erlbaum.

Kavanaugh, R.D., & S. Engel. 1998. The development of pretense and narrative in early childhood. In *Multiple perspectives on play in early childhood education*, eds. O.N. Saracho & B. Spodek, 80–99. Albany, NY: State University of New York.

Krackow, E., & P. Gordon. 1998. Are lions and tigers substitutes or associates? Evidence against slot filler accounts of children's early categorization. *Child Development* 69 (2): 347–54.

Krascum, R.M., & S. Andrews. 1998. The effects of theories on children's acquisition of family-resemblance categories. *Child Development* 69 (2): 333–46.

Landry, S.H., K.E. Smith, P.R. Swank & C.L. Miller-Loncar. 2000. Early maternal and child influences on children's later independent cognitive and social functioning. *Child Development* 71 (2): 358–75.

Lin, C.C., C.K. Hsiao & W.J. Chen. 1999. Development of sustained attention assessed using the continuous performance test among children 6–15 years. *Journal of Abstract Child Psychology* 27 (5): 403–412.

Lindsey, E.W., & M.J. Colwell. 2003. Preschoolers' emotional competence: Links to pretend and physical play. *Child Study Journal* 33: 39–52.

Mandler, J.M. 2004. *The foundations of mind: Origins of conceptual thought.* New York: Oxford University Press.

McCune, L. 1993. The development of play as the development of consciousness. In *New directions for child development*, no. 59, eds. M.H. Bornstein & A. O'Reilly, 67–79. San Francisco: Jossey-Bass.

Montie, J.E., Z. Xiang & L.J. Schweinhart. 2006. Preschool experience in 10 countries: Cognitive and language performance at age 7. *Early Childhood Research Quarterly* 21: 313–31.

Murphy, L.M.B., C. Laurie-Rose, T.M. Brinkman & K.A. McNamara. 2007. Sustained attention and social competence in typically developing preschool-aged children. *Early Child Development and Care* 177 (2): 133–49.

Newcombe, N., & J. Huttenlocher. 1992. Children's early ability to solve perspective taking problems. *Developmental Psychology* 28: 654–64.

Newman, L.S. 1990. Intentional and unintentional memory in young children: Remembering vs. playing. *Journal of Experimental Child Psychology* 50 (2): 243–58.

Nguyen, S.P., & G.L. Murphy. 2003. An apple is more than just a fruit: Cross-classification in children's concepts. *Child Development* 74 (6): 1783–806.

Piaget, J. 1930. *The child's conception of the world.* New York: Harcourt, Brace & World.

Piaget, J. 1951. *Play, dreams, and imitation in childhood.* New York: Norton.

Rosengren, K.S., & A.K. Hickling. 2000. The development of children's thinking about possible events and plausible mechanisms. In *Imagining the impossible*, eds. K.S. Rosengren, C.N. Johnson, & P.L. Harris, 75–98. Cambridge: Cambridge University Press.

Ruff, H.A., & M.C. Capozzoli. 2003. Development of attention and distractibility in the first 4 years of life. *Developmental Psychology* 39: 877–90.

Ruffman, T. 1999. Children's understanding of logical inconsistency. *Child Development* 70 (4): 872–86.

Sarama, J., & D.H. Clements. 2006. Mathematics in kindergarten. In *K today: Teaching and learning in the kindergarten year*, ed. D.F. Gullo, 85–94. Washington, DC: NAEYC.

Seifert, K. 1993. Cognitive development and early childhood education. In *Handbook of research on the education of young children,* ed. B. Spodek, 9–23. New York: Macmillan.

Siegler, R., J.S. DeLoache & N. Eisenberg. 2006. *How children develop.* 2d ed. New York: Worth Publishers.

Sobel, D.M. 2006. How fantasy benefits young children's understanding of pretense. *Developmental Science* 9: 63–75.

Striano, T., M. Tomasello & P. Rochat. 2001. Social and object support for early symbolic play. *Developmental Science* 4: 442–55.

Subbotsky, E.V. 2004. Magical thinking in judgments of causation: Can anomalous phenomena affect ontological causal beliefs in children and adults? *British Journal of Developmental Psychology* 22: 123–52.

Toomela, A. 2002. Drawing as a verbally mediated activity: A study of relationships between verbal, motor, visuospatial skills and drawing in children. *International Journal of Behavioral Development* 26: 234–47.

Vygotsky, L. 1978. *Mind in society: The development of higher psychological processes.* Cambridge, MA: Harvard University Press.

Wood-Ramsey, J., & P.H. Miller. 1988. The facilitation of selective attention in preschoolers. *Child Development* 59 (6): 1497–503.

Heather Biggar Tomlinson

Cognitive Development in the Kindergarten Year

Compared with younger children, kindergartners show more flexibility in their thinking, greater ability to conceptualize categories, advances in reasoning and problem solving, and gains in knowledge of the world, ability to pay attention, and use of memory. In short, kindergartners' thinking is reorganizing, gradually becoming more systematic, accurate, and complex. This transition—from preschool thought to the style of thinking more typical of middle childhood—is the major and well documented "5 to 7 shift" (Flavell et al. 2001; Newcombe 2005; Sameroff & McDonough 1994). It stems from a congruence of major changes in the brain and greater societal expectations and opportunities.

Brain development and a key shift in thinking abilities

New research in cognitive neuroscience shows that, given healthy environments, a child's neurological system develops dramatically during the early childhood years (Halfon et al. 2001). The first five to seven years of life are a sensitive period for brain development; the brain is especially responsive to stimulation, which prompts a massive wiring of neurons and sculpting of brain regions. The brain is more malleable than it will be later, making kindergarten an optimum time for learning and effective intervention with all children.

When children have appropriately stimulating surroundings, including interaction with responsive caretakers, rapid brain growth occurs during this time; from preschool to kindergarten, the brain grows steadily, increasing from 70 percent to 90 percent of its eventual adult weight (Thatcher et al. 1996). In addition to gains in size, the brain undergoes much reshaping and refining. There is a thickening of the coating of the nerve cells in the brain's cerebral cortex and "pruning" of neural networks that are not being used, allowing active portions of the brain to become more powerful. Such changes enable the child to better meet the particular demands of the environment. Profound changes also occur in the frontal lobes of the cerebral cortex, areas devoted to regulating thought and action.

At about age 5, children have nearly twice as many connections between neurons (synapses) as adults in some brain areas, including the frontal lobes. This overabundance of communication channels supports the brain's "plasticity," or high capacity for learning. It helps ensure that the child will be able to acquire basic human abilities even if some brain areas happen to be damaged. As the child interacts with others and the environment and learning occurs, the synaptic connections of the neurons become increasingly elaborate and committed to specific functions (Huttenlocher 2002; Nelson 2002).

The frontal lobes are important because they govern the inhibition of impulse, orderly memory, and the integration of information—capacities that facilitate reasoning and problem solving, as well as emotional self-regulation. All these skills improve considerably in the kindergarten child.

The interaction of these brain developments and stimulating, supportive environments leads to children's thought patterns becoming more systematic and organized. This is evident in the way children explore new situations, acquire concepts, respond to directions, play games, approach problems, and carry out everyday activities. By the end of kindergarten, children are more aware of patterns and regularities. They also begin to redefine confusing problems and combine concepts they previously used only alone. Kindergartners begin to recognize event sequences in many ways—as they appear in stories, in the physical world, in biological cycles within the physical world, in daily routines within the classroom, and in larger societal routines.

Kindergartners also demonstrate an emerging awareness of part/whole relationships. This development becomes more evident in the next few years as children's attention to stories and the complex connections between plot lines and characters' emotions as motivating factors grows. This awareness of part/whole relations is also evident in mathematics and science, in spontaneous comments such as "I see five fish—two blue ones and three yellow ones."

During kindergarten, children's thinking typically becomes less rigidly fixed and egocentric; it better accounts for multiple perspectives, is more

flexible, and is beginning to be able to transform ideas and representations (Dunn 1988; Halford & Andrews 2006; Harris 2006). In the physical domain, children can now grasp that the same object or set of objects can look very different depending on the observer's vantage point. In the social domain, children are better able to make inferences about what another person knows or feels. For example, if a child sees someone try to trick someone else, the child might infer that the child being tricked is unaware of what is happening.

In a variety of situations, children begin to see multiple sides of an issue. Unlike preschoolers, who assume that other people see things as they do, 5-year-olds begin to recognize that their own perspective on a situation may differ from someone else's—although this is an emerging ability that should not be expected on a regular basis. They may struggle to predict precisely what it is that someone else sees, but they are not surprised that another's view is different from their own. For example, a child may turn a book around so a friend can see it better. She begins to (but again, will not consistently) recognize that what her father would like as a gift is not what she would like. This awareness reflects an emerging ability to consider more information at one time.

An increase in flexible thinking is evident in other ways, as well. Children can mentally rearrange or transform information—they are less bound by the first thing they see or hear. For example, a kindergartner can figure out a couple of ways to combine blocks to create a structure of a particular shape. Or sometimes children can temporarily put aside their own feelings and be sensitive to the needs of another, especially if that person is a friend or loved one—and if there is no conflict with the child's own needs and desires.

This flexibility of thinking is apparent in geometric, spatial, and mathematical thinking. Children begin to apply visual spatial strategies and mental images to solve problems in the everyday world. Children understand that they can divide things, such as a cookie, so that everyone can have some—one thing becomes many. And they understand that a tangram with 10 separate pieces can be returned to its original appearance by putting the pieces together again—many things become one. This idea of applying visual spatial strategies

Heather Biggar Tomlinson is an early childhood education specialist consulting for UNICEF in Jakarta, Indonesia.

applies to stable objects, such as puzzles and their parts, and to things that move through space. With a bit of exploring, for example, children may be able to predict the expected pathway of a cone-shaped object rolling down an incline. They might discover that shadows are influenced by the orientation of the light source.

A child's skill in using these mental transformations will expand and improve throughout the course of middle childhood, but significant changes begin to appear in kindergarten. They continue to learn best with hands-on exploration of materials and with repetition.

In comparison with preschoolers, 5- and 6-year-olds are more likely to look for conceptual categories rather than just simple associations. For example, they understand that when they are looking for cereal in the grocery store, they probably will not find it in the dairy aisle. They also have a greater ability to think about their own thinking— that is, to engage in metacognition. To demonstrate,

as anyone who has shared a secret with a kindergartner knows, the child is able to recognize (with excitement!) that he knows something that someone else does not know ("*Let's surprise Ms. Plum by bringing cupcakes and lemonade for her birthday on Friday*"). They can reflect on how they know something ("*How do you know the plant will wilt if we don't water it all week?*"), make connections with other things they've learned ("*What does this remind you of that we examined last week?*"), and predict and plan for the future ("*What instructions should we give Mr. Sweenie to take good care of our pet rabbits during winter break?*").

A description of kindergartners' cognitive development and learning must include at least a brief account of their progress in two domains emphasized in the kindergarten curriculum—mathematics (discussed in this section) and literacy.

For each grade the National Council of Teachers of Mathematics has defined key learning goals (termed "curriculum focal points") based on children's abilities and mathematics educators' judgment about what children at that grade—in this case, kindergartners—need to learn to have a strong foundation for continued progress in math (NCTM 2006).

Research in math and literacy has contributed to our knowledge of what children of this age group are capable of learning and doing in these domains. To some extent, typical accomplishments in the kindergarten year reflect the expectations and instructions prevalent in many U.S. schools; they also reflect kindergartners' cognitive and perceptual abilities and their eagerness to learn to read and write and make sense of their world in spatial and numerical ways. Unfortunately, the potential for great gains in academic areas during the kindergarten year are not equally realized by all children. Children from low-income families and diverse cultural, linguistic, and racial backgrounds are at particular risk for not advancing in academic areas; as many as one-third of children entering kindergarten are already behind their peers (Carnegie Cor-

poration of New York 1998). The failure to achieve affects middle-class children as well (Zill & West 2001)—when education programs are not high quality, when families are not supported and involved, and when teachers are not well prepared and supported. The achievement gap that may evolve or widen in the kindergarten year distressingly leads to an ever-widening long-term gap in achievement (Carnegie Corporation of New York 1998).

As described in the following sections, children's advancing reasoning and problem solving, demonstrated in the various curricular areas, is supported by gains in knowledge of the world, attention, and memory.

Reasoning and representational thinking

Both brain development and experience contribute to give older children a larger memory span, and thus they are better able to hold in mind and consider, at times, two or more dimensions of an object

---

Promoting kindergartners' cognitive skills

Questions to encourage making connections between people, places, things, and events

Comparing—*finding similarities and differences; finding ways things "go together"; putting things in categories*

- How are these alike? Is there anything that doesn't belong in this group? What would be a good way of organizing things so we can tell what's here?
- What name could you give this group?
- This bottle holds almost eight scoops of rice. How many scoops do you think this jar will hold?

Quantifying—*finding out about how much and how many; breaking apart and recombining*

- How many of you have families with one child? two children? etc.…How many of you come from families with a grandma and five children? [Engage children in keeping track with tally marks or a bar graph.] So how many have more than one child?
- Can you show me another way to make…?
- [Compare quantities of unit blocks with different shapes or triangles, prisms, cylinders, etc.] Do we have the same number of each shape? Which one

has the most? Which has the least? What would be a good way to remember how many we have?
- When I cover some of the eight bears, look and see how many you can still see. How many do you think are hidden?

Sequences—*finding temporal and spatial order*

- Let's arrange our towers of cubes from shortest to tallest.
- Let's make a "timeline" that shows what happened first, last, and in-between.
- Let's lay out these pictures of food from hottest to coldest.

Spatial relationships—*finding positions*

- Suppose we want to put the chairs in two lines, like seats on a bus. How would we do that?
- Can you tell me how to get to the cafeteria from here?
- How many Big Blocks will it take to cover this rug?
- Do you think this shape would roll?

or event at once (Case 1998; Cowan et al. 1999). Kindergartners' advances in reasoning are initially fragile, and they may revert to earlier and more simplistic ways of thinking, including considering only one dimension at a time (AAAS 2008). Consequently, the kindergarten child's thinking sometimes seems limited and inflexible, and at other times quite advanced.

This move toward more complex thinking shows up in many ways. In everyday activities such as drawing pictures, for example, a 4- or 5-year-old often depicts people and objects separately, ignoring their spatial arrangement. Older kindergartners may be able to coordinate these two aspects so the drawing depicts both the features of objects and the objects' spatial relationship to one another. In creating stories, a similar progression takes place. Younger children focus on only a single character's actions and emotions; older children can combine two characters' actions and emotions in a single plot (Case & Okamoto 1996).

Because of variations in their experiences, interests, and goals, children display better developed thinking on some tasks than on others (Sternberg 2002). In this respect, culture is profoundly influential. For example, a child who comes from a cultural group in which children are expected to be quiet and learn through observing adults would have difficulty demonstrating her competence in a classroom where she is expected to speak up and address the adult in reciprocal conversation. But she might well have impressive competence in areas where she has ample experience, such as sorting and counting household items, caring for younger siblings, or collaborating with an adult in preparing a family meal. What is valued as "intelligent" behavior varies considerably from one cultural group to another (Sternberg & Grikorenko 2004).

Self-regulation and attention

Self-regulation skills, as previously mentioned, have both emotional and cognitive aspects. One of the

---

Activities to prompt thinking about thinking (metacognition)

Describing the present

- *Using connections*: Children plant a window box garden. The class talks about gardening, farming, and agriculture. They read books about gardening and visit a county experimentation farm. They plant their classroom gardens.

- *With words*: Each child starts a science journal and describes what is happening in the classroom garden. Dictations supplement drawings and children's writing.

- *In space*: Children make a chart showing the progress of plant growth, adding information three times a week.

- *By movement*: Children use their bodies to demonstrate how a plant grows.

Remembering the past

- *Using connections*: Ask: "Do you remember how you felt when we went into the jungle exhibit at the zoo? Did it remind you of anything you had done before?"

- *With words*: Ask children to describe something they saw at the zoo. Invite them to make a page for the memory album.

- *In space*: Have children build a model of the zoo with clay and other materials. Provide children with landscape and aerial photographs [but probably not maps] as memory supports.

- *By movement*: Ask: "Do you remember how the waves in the ocean tank moved? Let's pretend we are the waves."

Planning and predicting

- *Using connections*: Ask: "What do you think would happen if we put our plants in the closet?" "How many times will we need to fill the watering can to water each plant?"

- *With words*: Have children write/dictate directions for Mrs. Smith, who will take care of the plants while school is closed for vacation.

- *In space*: Engage children in making an illustrated chart that shows the steps in the sequence of how to take care of the plants.

- *By movement*: Ask: "What would a plant do if it didn't get water all week? Can you be the plant and show us?"

Reprinted from S.L. Golbeck. 2006. Developing key cognitive skills. In *K today: Teaching and learning in the kindergarten year*, ed. D.F. Gullo, 42–43. Washington, DC: NAEYC.

most important aspects of self-regulation in the cognitive domain relates to a child's ability to focus attention. The ability to not give in to distraction, to listen to what others are saying, and to focus on a given task for a productive length of time is crucial for success in school (for all ages, not just kindergarten). Self-regulation in kindergarten has been shown to correlate with achievement in math and reading, independent of a child's general level of intelligence (Blair & Razza 2007).

Kindergartners in well structured and supported classrooms can often work for 15 to 20 minutes at a time on a quiet, seated activity (Wood 2007). Their improved ability to focus and manage their attention contributes to transformations in their reasoning. Development of the frontal lobes of the cerebral cortex leads to greater cognitive inhibition—an improved ability, while engaged in a task, to prevent the mind from being distracted and straying to alternative thoughts (Bush et al. 2000). The capacity for cognitive inhibition, which already increases throughout the preschool years, improves dramatically beginning at about age 5 or 6 (Dempster 1993; Harnishfeger 1995; Sameroff & McDonough 1994). This increased ability enables children to focus more intently on the types of tasks they will encounter often in school. Still, kindergartners tend to have a limited attention span compared with older children or adults—unless they are pursuing self-chosen activities that are highly motivating to them. With the support of adults, kindergartners are also increasingly capable of planning; they can think out a short, orderly sequence of actions ahead of time and allocate their attention accordingly (Hudson et al. 1997).

Memory

The combination of brain growth and improved use of memory strategies eventually improve children's ability to recall information. However, kindergartners are not yet good at deliberate use of memory strategies unless teachers help them. When asked to recall items, such as a list of toys or groceries, children might rehearse on one occasion but not on another, and even when they do rehearse, their recall rarely improves. At this age, applying a memory strategy initially requires so much effort and attention that children have little attention left for the memory task itself (Schneider 2002). Nonetheless,

teachers can help children improve memory skills by prompting the use of strategies such as rehearsing information, organizing it into categories, or simply alerting children to the need to remember something.

Although they show limited memory for unrelated or non-meaningful information, kindergartners show good memory for information that is meaningful to them (Ely 2005). For example, at about ages 4½ to 5, children can give chronologically organized, detailed, and evaluative accounts of personal experiences, as this kindergartner illustrates: "We went to the lake. Then we fished and waited. I caught a big catfish! Dad cooked it. It was so good we ate it all up!" Increased memory capacity—when combined with teacher-guided opportunities to practice personal storytelling and other skills—is a manifestation of growing cognitive skills.

Promoting cognitive development in kindergarten

For all children to thrive academically and to reduce the achievement gap, schools and teachers should implement high-quality curricula and teaching strategies, embed teaching and learning in caring, nurturing relationships, and engage and empower families (Carnegie Corporation of New York 1998). One study of ethnically diverse, low-income families showed that increases in family involvement in school predicted improvements in children's literacy and mathematics skills (Dearing et al. 2008). Teachers should offer inviting, well organized classrooms and should establish warm and trusting relationships with children to create the conditions that foster children's thinking abilities. Emotional security frees children to devote energy to the cognitive tasks they encounter in the classroom. Organization of instruction allows for taking advantage of teachable moments in planned and systematic ways (Clements 2001).

Children continue to build on their early knowledge areas, and teachers who are sensitive to what children already know and think can help them refine and add to that base. Often these expanded ideas can be linked to specific curriculum content. For example, learning in science can be linked to children's own ideas about the physical world (Gelman & Brenneman 2004). If a child explains that we sleep "because it's nighttime," the teacher can build on that belief to explore the biological needs and rhythms of humans and other living organisms. Teachers also should help children connect concepts. Children can relate number concepts to geometry, for instance, by counting the sides of shapes or measuring the length of a rug, which strengthens their understanding of mathematics as a coherent *system* (Sarama & Clements 2006). The key for teachers is to understand the concepts themselves and also to understand how each child makes sense of the world and what interests him.

One way to support cognitive development is by asking children thought-provoking questions ("*How do you get to the cafeteria from here?*" or "*How could we remember how many we have?*") and making comments ("*I wonder how many big blocks it would take to cover the rug*" or "*Our plant didn't grow as much this week as before; I wonder if we did something differently*") that encourage children to think and reflect. Questions might focus on descriptions of events and changes in the physical and social world or on thought processes themselves, since kindergartners now have some capacity for metacognition. These questions encourage "thinking about thinking," directing children's attention to awareness of how they know something and how they might remember or solve a problem.

Teachers also promote cognitive development when they encourage children to record and document their knowledge by using various representational methods, such as words and gestures, writing, and drawing and by making diagrams, graphs, and models. Children are most highly motivated when sharing a message that is important to them. In such instances, children are likely to notice when their message is not getting across and perhaps grasp that it needs to be modified, though they are not yet skilled in knowing how to change the message to communicate more effectively. An important focus in the kindergarten year is enhancing children's understanding of the many ways that we use representations to communicate and share knowledge. A teacher might invite children to describe through words or actions something seen on a field trip to the zoo, create a page for a memory album, and build a model of the zoo (Golbeck 2006).

As with children of all ages, kindergartners learn from their interactions not only with adults, but also with peers. Children frequently test their ideas with peers and learn a lot from the reactions they receive. Sometimes the child's peers understand him and respond positively to his ideas; sometimes they do not. Teachers greatly promote kindergartners' cognitive development by recognizing the value of peer interactions for kindergartners' cognitive growth and by designing learning environments and planning experiences that encourage children to interact and collaborate.

Finally, children need to be able to make choices. Choices empower children to be active thinkers who challenge themselves. Teachers who offer children choices do not give up control, nor are they passive. Rather, they look for ways to be active participants in children's learning processes, while ensuring that the children are also active and engaged. Overall, the kindergarten year requires teachers to provide a nuanced balance for optimal cognitive development. On the one hand, there should be plenty of play, child choice, and verbal interaction; on the other, there should be adult-guided activities that are engaging to children and adaptable to their varying readiness. Kindergartners learn best under conditions in which adults guide and support their active efforts, with a gradual and measured introduction of more formal lessons.

It is also worth noting that most kindergarten age brain growth occurs in the course of everyday experiences as adults offer young children age-appropriate play materials and stimulating, enjoyable daily routines and social interaction: a shared meal, a picture book to discuss, a song to sing, or an outing at the park or another type of field trip. The resulting growth readies the brain for later, more advanced brain development, such as that necessary for reading comprehension, solving mathematical problems, or investigating scientific hypotheses (Huttenlocher 2002; Shonkoff & Phillips 2000). Hurrying a young child into mastering skills that depend on extensive training—such as advanced reading and comprehension, musical performance, or sports—runs the risk of overwhelming the brain's neural circuits and reducing its sensitivity to the experiences needed for healthy brain development (Bruer 1999).

Adapted from C. Copple & S. Bredekamp, eds., *Developmentally appropriate practice in early childhood programs serving children from birth through age 8, 3d ed.* (Washington, DC: NAEYC, 2009), 200–06. Copyright © 2009 NAEYC.

References

AAAS (American Association for the Advancement of Science). 2008. *Benchmarks.* Online: www.project2061.org/publications/bsl/online/index.php?home=true.

Blair, C., & R.P. Razza. 2007. Relating effortful control, executive function, and false belief understanding to emerging math and literacy ability in kindergarten. *Child Development* 78 (2): 647–63.

Bruer, J.T. 1999. *The myth of the first three years.* New York: Free Press.

Bush, G., P. Luu, & M.I. Posner. 2000. Cognitive and emotional influences in the anterior cingulate cortex. *Trends in Cognitive Sciences* 4: 215–22.

Carnegie Corporation of New York. 1998. *Years of promise: A comprehensive learning strategy for America's children.* Online: www.carnegie.org/sub/pubs/execsum.html.

Case, R. 1998. The development of central conceptual structures. In *Handbook of child psychology, Vol. 2: Cognition, perception, and language*, 5th ed., eds. D. Kuhn & R.S. Siegler, 745–800. New York: John Wiley & Sons.

Case, R., & Y. Okamoto, eds. 1996. *The role of central conceptual structures in the development of children's thought.* Monographs of the Society for Research in Child Development, vol. 61, nos. 1–2, serial no. 246. Chicago: University of Chicago Press.

Clements, D.H. 2001. Mathematics in the preschool. *Teaching Children Mathematics* 7 (4): 270–75.

Cowan, N., L.D. Nugent, E.M. Elliott, I. Ponomarev & J.S. Saults. 1999. The role of attention in the development of short-term memory: Age differences in the verbal span of apprehension. *Child Development* 70 (5): 1082–97.

Dearing, E., H. Kreider & H.B. Weiss. 2008. Increased family involvement in school predicts improved child-teacher relationships and feelings about school for low-income children. *Marriage & Family Review* 43 (3–4): 226–54.

Dempster, F.N. 1993. Resistance to interference: Developmental changes in a basic processing mechanism. In *Emerging themes in cognitive development: Foundations, Vol. 1*, eds. M.L. Howe & R. Pasnak, 3–27. New York: Springer-Verlag.

Dunn, J. 1988. *The beginnings of social understanding.* Cambridge, MA: Harvard University Press.

Ely, R. 2005. Language and literacy in the school years. In *The development of language*, 6th ed., ed. J.B. Gleason, 395–443. Boston: Allyn & Bacon.

Flavell, J.H., P. Miller & S. Miller. 2001. *Cognitive development.* 4th ed. Upper Saddle River, NJ: Prentice Hall.

Gelman, R., & K. Brenneman. 2004. Science learning pathways for young children. *Early Childhood Research Quarterly* 19: 150–58.

Golbeck, S.L. 2006. Developing key cognitive skills. In *K today: Teaching and learning in the kindergarten year*, ed. D.F. Gullo, 37–46. Washington, DC: NAEYC.

Halfon, N., E. Shulman & M. Hochstein. 2001. Brain development in early childhood. *Policy Briefs* 13: 1–4. Los Angeles: UCLA Center for Healthier Children, Family and Communities, California Policy Research Center.

Halford, G.S., & G. Andrews. 2006. Reasoning and problem solving. In *Handbook of child psychology, Vol. 2: Cognition, perception, and language*, 6th ed., eds. D. Kuhn & R. Siegler. Hoboken, NJ: John Wiley & Sons.

Harnishfeger, K.K. 1995. The development of cognitive inhibition: Theories, definitions, and research evidence. In *New perspectives on interference and inhibition in cognition*, eds. F.F. Dempster & C.J. Brainerd, 176–204. San Diego: Academic Press.

Harris, P.L. 2006. Social cognition. In *Handbook of child psychology, Vol. 2: Cognition, perception, and language*, 6th ed., eds. D. Kuhn & R. Siegler. Hoboken, NJ: John Wiley & Sons.

Hudson, J.A., B. Sosa & L.R. Shapiro. 1997. Scripts and plans: The development of preschool children's event knowledge and event planning. In *The developmental psychology of planning: Why, how, and when do we plan?*, eds. S.L. Friedman & E.K. Scholnick, 77–102. Mahwah, NJ: Lawrence Erlbaum.

Huttenlocher, P.R. 2002. *Neural plasticity: The effects of environment on the development of the cerebral cortex.* Cambridge, MA: Harvard University Press.

NCTM (National Council of Teachers of Mathematics). 2006. *Curriculum focal points for prekindergarten through grade 8 mathematics: A quest for coherence.* Reston, VA: Author.

Nelson, C.A. 2002. Neural development and lifelong plasticity. In *Handbook of applied developmental science, Vol. 1*, eds. R.M. Lerner, F. Jacobs, & D. Wertlieb, 31–60. Thousand Oaks, CA: Sage Publications.

Newcombe, N.S. 2005. *What do we mean when we say modularity?* Master lecture presented at the biennial meeting of the Society for Research in Child Development, April 7–10, Atlanta, GA.

Sameroff, A., & S.C. McDonough. 1994. Educational implications of developmental transitions. *Phi Delta Kappan* 76 (3): 188–93.

Sarama, J., & D.H. Clements. 2006. Mathematics in kindergarten. In *K today: Teaching and learning in the kindergarten year*, ed. D.F. Gullo, 85–94. Washington, DC: NAEYC.

Schneider, W. 2002. Memory development in childhood. In *Blackwell handbook of childhood cognitive development*, ed. U. Goswami, 236–56. Malden, MA: Blackwell.

Shonkoff, J.P., & D.A. Phillips, eds. 2000. *From neurons to neighborhoods: The science of early child development.* A report of the National Research Council. Washington, DC: National Academies Press.

Sternberg, R.J. 2002. Intelligence is not just inside the head: The theory of successful intelligence. In *Improving academic achievement*, ed. J. Aronson, 227–44. San Diego: Academic Press.

Sternberg, R.J., & E.L. Grikorenko. 2004. Why we need to explore development in its cultural context. *Merrill-Palmer Quarterly* 50: 369–86.

Thatcher, R.W., G.R. Lyon, J. Rumsey & J. Krasnegor. 1996. *Developmental neuroimaging.* San Diego: Academic Press.

Wood, C. 2007. *Yardsticks: Children in the classroom, ages 4–14.* 3d ed. Turner Falls, MA: Northeast Foundation for Children.

Zill, N., & J. West. 2001. *Entering kindergarten: Findings from the condition of education, 2000.* Washington, DC: U.S. Dept. of Education, National Center for Education Statistics.

Heather Biggar Tomlinson

4

Cognitive Development
in the Primary Grades

Children in the primary grades make great strides in cognitive development. A gradual but significant shift in cognitive abilities occurs in most children between about ages 5 and 7, such that children under 5 think and reason differently than those 7 and older (Case & Okamoto 1996; Piaget 1952; Piaget & Inhelder 1969; Sameroff & McDonough 1994; White 1965).

Between 5 and 7, children become more proficient and flexible in their use of mental representations and begin to acquire the ability to think about things more dimensionally and to solve a wider range of problems, a finding that holds in studies of children around the world (Rogoff et al. 1975). Children this age enjoy reading, spelling, printing activities, board games, and computer games. They are interested in nature, simple science experiments, collecting and sorting, learning about weights and the value of coins, creating a finished product from their work, and discerning the line between fantasy and reality, as with magic tricks or the tooth fairy.

During the primary years, the brain continues to develop. Changing cognitive capacities at this age are in part the result of processes such as lateralization, wherein the two hemispheres of the brain start to function more efficiently as learning occurs. Brain lateralization further improves with maturation of the corpus callosum (the tissue connecting the two halves of the brain), and this speeds mental processing of information (Harris 1986). Also during this period, the synapses of the brain (the connections that transmit information from one neuron to another) go through "pruning," a process of eliminating neurons that are not often activated, which scientists speculate improves efficiency (Chugani 1996; Dana Alliance on Brain Initiatives 1996).

After age 7, most children will have achieved some or all of this important brain restructuring. This brain development, it is important to note, is the result of an interaction between the biological changes occurring at this time of life and the experiences that children have in the environment. In effect, brain development shapes and is shaped by learning (Bransford et al. 2003).

The changes in brain structure and processes are important not only in and of themselves but also because they influence how children interact with the environment—and how people in the environment interact with children. There are changes in the expectations, demands, and structuring by adults of the social and cultural context within which children live (Vygotsky 1978). Adults from all different cultures expect more of children in this age group as compared with when they were younger; around ages 5 to 7, children experience more responsibilities and more adult-like chores and roles (Rogoff et al. 1975).

The changes that occur in children's cognition during these years equip them to perform the mental operations required for reading, mathematics, and other content learning in the early grades. These changes affect not only their academic and intellectual functioning but also social cognition, moral reasoning, and language abilities. However, individual and cultural differences contribute to wide variation in children's abilities.

Concept acquisition and reasoning

By first grade, most children exhibit more flexible, multidimensional thinking. Changes in children's cognition occur gradually and unevenly, and children will occasionally and temporarily revert to earlier ways of thinking. Primary grade children continue to need lots of hands-on, experiential learning (AAAS 2008). When presented with a new concept, primary grade children need physical actions or direct experiences to help them grasp the idea, much as adults need vivid examples and illustrations to grasp unfamiliar concepts (Pica 2004).

Although children in second or third grade can solve some abstract problems (such as determining place value), they are not yet able to grasp highly complex, abstract concepts or learn by text or direct instruction alone. While they can symbolically or mentally manipulate concrete concepts, it will be some time before they can mentally manipulate abstract ideas; for example, use certain mathematical algorithms, grasp dates in history, or fully comprehend the irreversibility of death. Accordingly, while children can use symbols such as words and

numerals to represent objects and relations, they still need concrete reference points.

Unlike younger children, whose reasoning is often from the particular to the particular, primary grade children gradually gain the ability to engage in syllogistic logic. By age 8 or 9, for example, most children know that if stick A is longer than stick B, and B is longer than stick C, then A is also longer than C, at least when they encounter such problems in reality rather than as hypothetical situations. Similarly, primary grade children are better able to engage in spatial reasoning. For instance, 5- and 6-year-olds are confused about left/right directionality when facing a person. By age 7 or 8, most children can mentally reverse the directions and understand left and right from a perspective other than their own (Berk 2008).

Children's capacity for classification—the ability to group objects by common attributes—extends during these years to the ability to use more than one attribute to classify and understand class inclusion; that is, the capacity for an object to be a member of more than one group simultaneously. To a greater extent than kindergartners, primary grade children understand part/whole relationships. They understand that with a group of four cats and five dogs, for example, there are more animals than dogs.

During the primary grades, children typically master seriation and sequencing. Seriation is the ability to place objects in order by length, weight, or size. Sequencing requires the ability to hold two pieces of information simultaneously—noting that an object is both larger than one object and smaller than another. These abilities are examples of children's increasing capacity to decenter from a single focus and consider multiple perspectives. In other words, thinking becomes more multidimensional.

Although primary grade children have largely move beyond the egocentrism of their preschool thinking, a form of egocentrism particular to reasoning emerges during this period: Children can become fixated on the validity of their own hypotheses and will change the facts to fit a hypothesis rather than modify the hypothesis because the facts do not support it. For example, if a 7-year-old comes to believe that he is not a good athlete because he has not scored any goals on the soccer field, he may hold fast to this belief despite specific

Heather Biggar Tomlinson is an early childhood education specialist consulting for UNICEF in Jakarta, Indonesia.

evidence to the contrary. Children get better at separating evidence from theory as they get older (Kuhn & Dean 2004).

As primary grade children increasingly become able to understand the viewpoints of others and focus on several aspects of a problem at one time, they become able to reverse their thinking. They can mentally go through a series of steps and then reverse them or understand that one operation can undo another, for example, that subtraction can undo or reverse addition. These capabilities have important implications for the kinds of problems that children can solve.

Although considerable individual variation exists and abilities depend on exposure through teaching (Fuchs et al. 2008), children in the primary grades generally develop a true understanding of measurement and mathematical problems. By age 6 or 7, most children's understanding of one-to-one correspondence and number is complete. For instance, they realize that the number of cookies (eight, say) does not change when the cookies are rearranged, distributed, or divided into different subsets (5 + 3, 6 + 2, and so on). These concepts develop in some predictable order (e.g., number followed by mass, length, area, and weight, respectively).

Executive functioning

By the primary grades, children are expected to and are ready to start learning on demand, according to Vygotsky and his followers (Elkonin 1972; Zuckerman 2003). This means children must be able to focus their attention, remember things on purpose, and be able to compare the process and findings of their own learning with teacher expectations (Bodrova & Leong 2007). Many of the changing cognitive abilities and developments in the brain, particularly in the prefrontal cortex, that allow a child to learn on demand are the higher mental functions executive functioning or cognitive control. Executive functioning includes abilities such as planning, organization, being able to shift thought or attention, inhibiting distracting thoughts, and sustained and sequenced behavior; it also involves "working memory," or the ability to hold information actively in mind while performing tasks (Mahone & Silverman 2008).

These are all self-regulatory skills that allow someone to make use of appropriate strategies to complete a job, such as building a model car or creating a classroom habitat for worms. These higher mental functions are indeed skills to be cultivated, not just the result of becoming older, like getting in new teeth, which requires no effort or application. The abilities are just beginning to emerge in the early primary grades and, like other skills, they should be taught, are dependent on one's motivation, and improve with practice (Bodrova & Leong 2007; Mahone & Silverman 2008; Nelson et al. 2006).

Self-regulation of thought and attention

Many classroom activities and real-world tasks require children to selectively focus attention on relevant information—whether through listening, watching, or reading—while simultaneously filtering out irrelevant information that distracts from the activity at hand.

Starting around age 6, children do improve in their ability to focus attention on demand and to ignore distracting information—although teachers and parents should recognize that this is a skill that is not fully developed until adolescence (Casey et al. 2001; Ridderinkhof et al. 1997). Whereas 6- and 7-year-olds will continue to struggle with focusing attention on what matters most versus what is irrelevant, 8-year-olds and older children will have somewhat less trouble with this (Rueda et al. 2004).

This growing skill allows children to engage in sustained work, and they appreciate having time to finish their work now that they can concentrate for somewhat longer periods (Wood 2007).

Of course, the ability to pay attention relates to children's ability to learn various subjects. For example, in the area of literacy, being able to focus on information that matters and ignore what does not helps children correctly formulate complex sentences and recall in an organized way information they have heard from a story (Purvis & Tannock 1997). Problems paying attention can lead to learn-

ing difficulties, such as an inability to remember or even recognize words previously learned (Cutting et al. 2003).

Planning and organization

To solve problems requiring a series of steps—in other words, to plan—one has to postpone action in order to weigh alternatives, organize task materials, and remember each step in the right order (Berk 2009). Children who are able to form and carry out a plan are more likely than others to develop other advanced cognitive skills (Hyson et al. 2006). But planning is not necessarily easy. Activities that may seem commonplace and effortless for adults (such as baking a cake or completing a three-digit subtraction problem) actually involve many steps that must occur in a certain sequence. Planning for and completing these activities involve first thinking about all the necessary steps ahead of time and then allocating attention appropriately (Scholnick 1995).

Because of primary grade children's enhanced ability to classify and sort, they may do quite well at organizing materials (e.g., for baking a cake). However, they might have trouble knowing by themselves the order in which things should be done or how to break down the steps into individual actions. With subtraction, for example, children have to know that they must always subtract the bottom row from the top row (rather than, say, smaller digit from larger digit), work across columns from right to left, and "borrow" before subtracting from a column with too few.

Primary grade children show an interest in time, and their concepts of time are improving but still are not mature. Not until after age 8 are children reasonably accurate in placing events in time sequence. They can generally categorize past, current, and future events, but they are not yet able to use dates to sequence historical time—another example of their ability to reason about concrete, but not abstract, concepts (Barton & Levstik 1996; Thornton & Vukelich 1988). Therefore, it is not always possible for a primary grade child to plan ahead without considerable guidance from an adult.

Memory

Being able to retain and recall new information is essential for success in school, and children's maturing capacity to use working memory in the primary grades greatly assists with their learning. For example, with reading, children's freedom from using repetition and great effort to remember word meanings allows them to move toward comprehension (Beck & McKeown 2007; Cutting et al. 2003). Most information-processing theorists attribute primary grade children's improved ability to solve problems to their increased capacity to store information and retrieve it from memory. Their increased memory capacity, use of memory strategies, and awareness of mental processes (metacognition, metamemory) allow them to be more reflective and interested in reviewing their work.

Before age 6, children usually don't think about the process of thinking, instead focusing on the outcomes of their thinking. Between ages 7 and 10 and continuing into adolescence, children begin to understand their own capacity to construct knowledge, select and transform information, and distinguish between and select various memory strategies (Flavell 2000; Kuhn 2000; Schwanenflugel et al. 1998).

Children younger than age 9 rarely use memory organization strategies on their own (Bjorklund 1988), but teachers can actively promote primary grade children's expanding ability to think about their own memory functioning—that is, their metamemory. They might teach children to reorganize a list of words so that like words are clustered together (e.g., apples, pears, and bananas are all fruits; koalas, pandas, and grizzlies are all bears), making them more meaningful (Cutting et al. 2003). Or they might encourage using mental imagery, so that children remember unusual material by creating a picture in their mind (Craig & Baucum 2002). One simple but effective strategy is for teachers to simply remind children, "This is something you will need to remember."

During the primary grade years, children show improved capacity in both short- and long-term memory, although again these capacities are not yet mature. For example, the adult capacity for short-term memory is seven chunks or bits of information (words, numbers, phrases, etc.); preschoolers can hold only two or three chunks, while 7-year-olds can usually retain five. By the beginning of third grade, children usually are well on their way toward

automatic retrieval by memory (e.g., of number combinations as their major strategy to solve mathematics problems) (Fuchs et al. 2008).

Once information is in short-term memory, it must be transferred to long-term memory if it is to be retained. Information in short-term memory is in danger of being forgotten, of course, especially when new information interferes. This is why children need time and opportunities to consolidate new learning before the next concepts are introduced. When the curriculum moves along at too rapid a pace, it is not surprising that children cannot remember what has already been taught and that topics have to be re-taught (an all too common occurrence in American schools).

During the primary grade years, children become better able to employ memory strategies such as rehearsal (repeating information to remember it) and organization (grouping information into similar categories). Children begin to apply these memory strategies more systematically (e.g., distinguishing vowels from consonants or remembering the multiplication tables) as the demands of school increase. The primary grade child is better able than a younger child to retain decontextualized information, but adults help greatly by structuring the memory tasks, making them meaningful, and guiding children to systematically use memory strategies.

Children's improved memory during this age period is in large part a result of their increasing body of accumulated knowledge and concepts. In other words, children's experiences and memories provide categories or structures to which they can more readily connect new experiences. As adults are aware, when we know a lot about a topic, we find new information on this topic more meaningful and easier to retain and retrieve. Information-processing theorists believe that school-age children's improved memory capacity is due largely to the fact that primary grade children have accumulated more knowledge to which to connect new information or experiences than their younger counterparts. This theoretical perspective argues that children's limited concrete thinking is not just the result of age-related constraints on cognition, it is also a lack of prior knowledge in the content area (Metz 1995).

© Terri Gonzalez

Promoting cognitive development in the primary grades

Compared with preschoolers and kindergartners, school age children are more logical and flexible in their thinking, have more knowledge of the world, have improved memory, and can better sustain their attention. But compared with adults, 6-, 7-, and 8-year-olds are novices in virtually every cognitive area, and their thinking and reasoning reflect this shallow level of prior knowledge.

Children in the primary grades enjoy challenges that test their growing skills as long as they can achieve success with the challenges. Children can become perfectionistic (Wood 2007), but teachers can support children by helping them enjoy the process of the task and feel good about effort exerted, rather than focusing on praise for the product (Hyson 2008). Children may show a type of egocentrism in their logic where they change the facts to fit their hypothesis, but they are not being deliberately obstinate in holding on to their views. Rather, they are working through a developmental phase in their reasoning skills. Teachers can help them correct misconceptions by patiently questioning assump-

tions or creating ways to test hypotheses.

To find a good balance between challenging children and ensuring their success, teachers will find national benchmarks or key learning goals helpful. Consider mathematics as an example. For each grade, the National Council of Teachers of Mathematics (NCTM) has defined key learning goals (termed "curriculum focal points") based on children's abilities and mathematics educators' judgment about what children at that grade need to learn to have a strong foundation for continued progress in math (NCTM 2006). NCTM's curriculum focal points are especially useful for prioritizing and organizing mathematics curriculum and instruction.

The focal points document was developed in an attempt to bring consistency, coherence, and focus to the mathematics curriculum in the United States, which is often described as "a mile wide, and an inch deep." The report is not a curriculum; instead it describes the specific concepts and skills that should be addressed at each grade level. More so than other subject areas, mathematics is a sequential discipline in which earlier understandings provide an essential foundation on which later skills and concepts build.

No matter what the subject area, teachers should keep learning concrete, relevant to children's everyday lives, and connected to previously learned material. A new concept must have a tangible referent, something real and familiar. Children are more likely to learn about, say, measurement and distance if the task is fun and imaginative yet based in their reality; for example, determining how far a ladybug has moved across the table (Tyminski et al. 2008). Likewise, a unit on water will mean more to children when they can relate it to their own lives. They may experiment with its properties in various conditions (e.g., in the freezer, on the countertop, after two minutes in the microwave), measure its weight in different amounts (a cup, a bucket, a bathtub), or determine the amounts needed by the cactus on the desk versus the African violet on the window sill.

All of these tasks would be more meaningful than, say, discussing water's subatomic particles—which would have no meaning in children's daily lives. A child in the early grades is still several years away from being able to reason about a hypothetical situation or an abstract concept.

Teachers can promote cognitive development by using periods of focused instruction about a specific new skill or concept within integrated curriculum studies and long-term projects (lasting weeks or months) that enable children to gain deeper knowledge and understanding of a topic. Trying to cover every topic of study quickly leads to shallow learning. Rather, encouraging the primary grade child to pursue a topic—or an interest or hobby—in some depth supports concept development. Children can develop "expertise" in any area that is of intellectual interest to them—stars, rocks, state flags—and the habits of mind they develop from deep study in one area are broadly applicable to learning in other areas. By providing challenging, high-quality choices in the topics of study, teachers help children persist and stay engaged, enhancing their learning (Brophy 2004).

When guiding children in a task, teachers should remember to be specific. For example, teachers sometimes direct children to "pay attention," meaning to ignore distractions and focus on the task at hand. The problem with such directions is that they require children to read between the lines, so to speak, and infer what specifically the teacher wants them to pay attention to. If a child doesn't succeed at the task, perhaps the child was paying attention but was focusing on the wrong aspect of the task. A child who reads, "We wents to the store to buys a apple" and declares the sentence correct may be responding to the meaning of the sentence, because the class did go to the store to buy apples, rather than considering the grammatical errors in the sentence (Bodrova & Leong 2007). Teachers can help children focus their attention by being specific about where it is that children should focus their thoughts and efforts.

Adults should not expect children in the primary grades to be fully aware of their thought processes yet; they can help them advance in planning, attention, memory, and other cognitive processes by engaging children in cooperative or shared activities that allow them to perform at the next higher level of functioning, by using verbal reminders and prompts, and by using writing and drawing activities to improve self-reflection (Bodrova & Leong 2007; Zuckerman 2003).

Adapted from C. Copple & S. Bredekamp, eds., *Developmentally appropriate practice in early childhood programs serving children from birth through age 8, 3d ed.* (Washington, DC: NAEYC, 2009), 271–81. Copyright © 2009 NAEYC.

References

AAAS (American Association for the Advancement of Science). 2008. *Benchmarks.* Online: www.project2061.org/publications/bsl/online/index.php?home=true.

Barton, K.C., & L.S. Levstik. 1996. "Back when God was around and everything": Elementary children's understanding of historical time. *American Educational Research Journal* 33 (2): 419–54.

Beck, I., & M.G. McKeown. 2007. Increasing young low-income children's oral vocabulary repertoires through rich and focused instruction. *Elementary School Journal* 107 (3): 251–71.

Berk, L.E. 2008. *Infants and children: Prenatal through middle childhood.* 6th ed. Boston: Pearson/Allyn & Bacon.

Berk, L.E. 2009. *Child development.* 8th ed. Boston: Pearson/Allyn & Bacon.

Bjorklund, D.F. 1988. Acquiring a mnemonic: Age and category knowledge effects. *Journal of Experimental Child Psychology* 45: 71–87.

Bodrova, E., & D.J. Leong. 2007. *Tools of the mind: The Vygotskian approach to early childhood education.* 2d ed. Upper Saddle River, NJ: Pearson/Merrill Prentice Hall.

Bransford, J., A.L. Brown & R.R. Cocking, eds. 2003. *How people learn: Brain, mind, experience, and school.* A report of the National Research Council. Washington, DC: National Academies Press.

Brophy, J. 2004. *Motivating students to learn*. 2d ed. Mahwah, NJ: Lawrence Erlbaum.

Case, R., & Y. Okamoto, eds. 1996. *The role of central conceptual structures in the development of children's thought*. Monographs of the Society for Research in Child Development, vol. 61, nos. 1–2, serial no. 246. Chicago: University of Chicago Press.

Casey, B., S. Durston & J. Fossella. 2001. Evidence for a mechanistic model of cognitive control. *Clinical Neuroscience Research* 1: 267–82.

Chugani, H.T. 1996. Neuroimaging of developmental nonlinearity and developmental pathologies. In *Developmental neuroimaging: Mapping the development of brain and behavior*, eds. R.W. Thatcher, G.R. Lyon, J. Rumsey, & N. Krasnegor. San Diego: Academic Press.

Craig, G.J., & D. Baucum. 2002. *Human development*. 9th ed. Upper Saddle River, NJ: Prentice Hall.

Cutting, L.E., C.W. Koth, E.M. Mahone & M.B. Denckla. 2003. Evidence for unexpected weaknesses in learning in children with Attention-Deficit/Hyperactivity Disorder without reading disabilities. *Journal of Learning Disabilities* 36 (3): 259–69.

Dana Alliance on Brain Initiatives. 1996. *Delivering results: A progress report on brain research*. Washington, DC: Author.

Elkonin, D. 1972. Toward the problem of stages in the mental development of the child. *Soviet Psychology* 10: 225–51.

Flavell, J.H. 2000. Development of children's knowledge about the mental world. *International Journal of Behavioral Development* 24: 15–23.

Fuchs, L.S., D. Fuchs, S.R. Powell, P.M. Seethaler, P.T. Cirino & J.M. Fletcher. 2008. Intensive intervention for students with mathematics disabilities: Seven principles of effective practice. *Learning Disability Quarterly* 31 (2): 79–92.

Harris, A.C. 1986. *Child development*. St. Paul, MN: West.

Hyson, M. 2008. *Enthusiastic and engaged learners: Approaches to learning in the early childhood classroom*. New York: Teachers College Press; Washington, DC: NAEYC.

Hyson, M., C. Copple & J. Jones. 2006. Early childhood development and education. In *Handbook of child psychology, Vol. 4: Child psychology in practice*, 6th ed., eds., K.A. Renninger & I. Sigel, 3–47. New York: John Wiley & Sons.

Kuhn, D. 2000. Why development does (and does not) occur: Evidence from the domain of inductive reasoning. In *Mechanisms of cognitive development*, eds. R. Siegler & J. McClelland, 221–49. Mahwah, NJ: Lawrence Erlbaum.

Kuhn, D., & D. Dean, Jr. 2004. Connecting scientific reasoning and causal inference. *Journal of Cognition and Development* 5: 261–88.

Mahone, E.M., & W. Silverman. 2008. ADHD and executive functions: Lessons learned from research. *Exceptional Parent* 38 (8): 48–51.

Metz, K. 1995. Reassessment of developmental constraints on children's science instruction. *Review of Educational Research* 65 (2): 93–127.

NCTM (National Council of Teachers of Mathematics). 2006. *Curriculum focal points for prekindergarten through grade 8 mathematics: A quest for coherence*. Reston, VA: Author.

Nelson, C.A., K.M. Thomas & M. de Haan. 2006. Neural bases of cognitive development. In *Handbook of child psychology, Vol. 2: Cognition, perception, and language*, 6th ed., eds. D. Kuhn & R. Siegler, 3–57. Hoboken, NJ: John Wiley & Sons.

Piaget, J. 1952. *The origins of intelligence in children*. New York: International Universities Press.

Piaget, J., & B. Inhelder. 1969. *The psychology of the child*. New York: Basic.

Pica, R. 2004. *Experiences in movement: Birth to age eight*. 3d ed. Clifton Park, NY: Delmar Learning.

Purvis, K.L., & R. Tannock. 1997. Language ability in children with attention deficit hyperactivity disorder, reading disabilities, and normal controls. *Journal of Abnormal Child Psychology* 25: 133–44.

Ridderinkhof, K., M.W. van der Molen, G. Band & T. Bashore. 1997. Sources of interference from irrelevant information: A developmental study. *Journal of Experimental Child Psychology* 65: 315–41.

Rogoff, B., M. Sellers, S. Pirotta, N. Fox & S. White. 1975. Age of assignment of roles and responsibilities to children. *Human Development* 18: 353–69.

Rueda, M.R., J. Fan, B.D. McCandliss, J.D. Halparin, D.B. Gruber, L.P. Lercari & M.I. Posner. 2004. Development of attentional networks in childhood. *Neuropsychologia* 42 (8): 1029–40.

Sameroff, A., & S.C. McDonough. 1994. Educational implications of developmental transitions. *Phi Delta Kappan* 76 (3): 188–93.

Scholnick, E.K. 1995. Knowing and constructing plans. *SRCD Newsletter* (Fall): 1–2, 17.

Schwanenflugel, P.J., R.L. Henderson & W.V. Fabricius. 1998. Developing organization of mental verbs and theory of mind in middle childhood: Evidence from extensions. *Developmental Psychology* 34: 514–24.

Thornton, S., & R. Vukelich. 1988. Effects of children's understanding of time concepts on historical understanding. *Theory and Research in Social Education* 16: 69–82.

Tyminski, A.M., M. Weilbacher, N. Lenburg & C. Brown. 2008. Ladybug lengths: Beginning measurement. *Teaching Children Mathematics* 15 (1): 34–37.

Vygotsky, L. 1978. *Mind in society: The development of higher psychological processes*. Cambridge, MA: Harvard University Press.

White, S.H. 1965. Evidence for a hierarchical arrangement of learning processes. In *Advances in child development and behavior*, eds. L.P. Lipsitt & C.C. Spiker, 187–220. New York: Academic Press.

Wood, C. 2007. *Yardsticks: Children in the classroom, ages 4–14*. 3d ed. Turner Falls, MA: Northeast Foundation for Children.

Zuckerman, G. 2003. The learning activity in the first years of schooling: The developmental path toward reflection. In *Vygotsky's educational theory in cultural context*, eds. A. Kozulin, B. Gindis, V.S. Ageev, & S.K. Miller, 177–99. Cambridge: Cambridge University Press.

Marilou Hyson

5

Becoming Enthusiastic and Engaged

Today, the children in this Head Start class are doing something different. Velma, the group's new assistant teacher, has planned an activity in which each child will make his or her own playdough. To introduce the activity, she uses the morning group time to show the children each of the ingredients as well as a finished ball of playdough.

After this introduction, the children all go to one long table, where each child has been given a small pile of flour. Velma pours some salt onto each child's pile and leaves the container on the table. Despite the teachers' reminders not to touch the flour yet, some children poke it with their fingers, while a few children blow at it vigorously. Sam stands quietly with his hands at his sides, looking down at the materials.

Velma tells the children to make a little hole with their fingers, so that she can add a bit of water and oil to each child's pile of flour and salt. Next, the children are to use their hands to mix the dough. Each child seems to have her or his own way of doing this: Claudia gets some flour on her patent leather shoes and looks down, worried, while Luz jumps right in but then makes a face and wipes her hands dramatically on a towel, laughing with the other girls at her end of the table when her hands get too sticky to suit her. Ricardo is completely absorbed in the feel of the dough rubbing it between his fingers and trying out the different textures as he mixes it. As he does this, he spies the container of salt on the table and surreptitiously dumps a large quantity onto his dough.

Some of the children seem deeply engaged in trying to mix the ingredients, squeezing, flattening, and pulling bits of unmixed flour into their ball of dough. Other children lose interest or give up quickly, and still others are almost giddy with the excitement of these new materials. Some, like Sam, take a long time to become involved; yet once Sam begins, he coils his small ball of playdough into delicate, imaginative shapes. Gradually most of the children focus on the dough-mixing process as they begin to see results.

Children are born with an innate urge to

connect with the people and things in the world. Unless they have significant disabilities or are living in desperate circumstances, babies are constantly touching, tasting, reaching, babbling—enthusiastic and engaged! But many things influence how those approaches to learning may develop in future months and years. As the children participate in Velma's playdough-making activity, multiple factors invisibly surround each child and the class as a whole, affecting how each child develops enthusiasm and engagement in learning. This section is about those factors—those "circles of influence."

Which "Approaches to Learning"?

Does the child enter into new experiences and tasks with enthusiasm, or with hesitance? Does she or he stick with a task when it is challenging, or tend to seek out an easier activity? These are some of the variations in children's *approaches to learning*, one of the key dimensions of school readiness identified by the National Education Goals Panel (1995). Hugely influential in school and life success, children's approaches to learning (sometimes called *cognitive styles* or *learning styles*) are grounded not entirely in cognitive development, nor entirely in emotional development or personality. Which are these approaches to learning? Experts do not all produce exactly the same list, but the following dimensions appear in most lists in one form or another:

Curiosity/Initiative. Choosing to engage and participate in new and challenging activities.

Persistence. Sticking to and completing tasks and activities.

Attention. Focusing on a task or teacher-directed activity with deliberate concentration.

Self-direction (or Self-regulation). Setting goals, making choices, and managing time and effort with independence.

Flexibility. Approaching problems or situations in a number of ways and able to shift from one to another in seeking a solution

Sources:
Conn-Powers, M. 2006. All children ready for school: Approaches to learning. Early Childhood Briefing Paper Series. Indiana Institute on Disability and Community, Early Childhood Center. Online: www.iidc.indiana.edu/styles/iidc/defiles/ECC/SRUD-ApproachestoLearning.pdf.
Hyson, M. 2008. *Enthusiastic and engaged learners: Approaches to learning in the early childhood classroom.* New York: Teachers College Press; Washington, DC: NAEYC.

—Carol Copple

Using Bronfenbrenner's ecological perspective on development as a framework, I will describe these intersecting circles of influence on children's approaches to learning, beginning with each child's individual and developmental characteristics, and then moving outward to the family, community, school, and culture.

Before beginning this discussion, I should raise a few cautions. First, the examples I give are just that—examples. They are not intended to describe exhaustively every possible influence on children's positive approaches to learning. You may think of or may have experienced even more. Second, the results of research apply only to large groups of children. General patterns may not apply to *specific* children, schools, or families. Third, we cannot "connect the dots" between any potential influence and any particular approach to learning in a simple cause-effect way. And, finally, children also influence their own development—the path of development

Marilou Hyson is a U.S. and international early childhood consultant, former editor in chief of *Early Childhood Research Quarterly*, and former NAEYC associate executive director.

is two-way. For example, although Velma's way of communicating with the children influences their behavior, at the same time the children's reactions also influence the way she responds to them.

What influences children's approaches to learning? An ecological perspective

Urie Bronfenbrenner's ecological perspective on human development may help organize an overview of the many intersecting influences on children's approaches to learning (Bronfenbrenner 2000; Bronfenbrenner & Morris 2006). Bronfenbrenner's theory emphasizes that, although every child brings certain "givens" into the world, he or she is constantly participating in many settings and systems, not only being affected by but also affecting those settings and systems. The children who are busy making playdough are no exception. Certainly, the experiences and interactions children have in their immediate environment are the most important contributors to their development. For each young child, the most influential experiences take place within the family and within the family's cultural practices. However, the child's experiences most likely also include early care and education programs, health care settings, and other community settings.

As Bronfenbrenner's theory further emphasizes, members of those settings also connect with and influence one another. For example, teachers, families, and health care providers may communicate regularly about a child's chronic illness. Further removed from the child's daily life, but also important in influencing her or his development, are settings and contexts such as the parents' workplace (e.g., does Luz's mother's employer make it possible for her to spend time at her child's school?). The outermost "circle" includes broad influences such as cultural values, customs, and public policies, which affect in many, sometimes indirect, ways how children are treated and what is expected of them in every setting.

Individual differences in children's characteristics

"They're just born that way"—or are they? There's no doubt that Sam, Ricardo, and Luz have each had a unique Sam-ness, Ricardo-ness, and Luz-ness since they were born. Sam's parents and grandparents say that they've noticed his cautious way of encountering new experiences since he was a baby. But does that mean that everything about Sam's approaches to learning was determined at birth? Not at all. When we take a closer look, in this chapter and later in the book, we will see that many factors influence the directions in which these seemingly fixed characteristics develop.

Temperament, learning styles, and multiple intelligences

Like other children, Sam has a distinctive, individual pattern of behaving and interacting with this world. In his case, it expresses itself in a cautious, somewhat fearful approach to new experiences (as we saw when he held back from even touching his playdough ingredients), combined with lots of persistence, even to the point of stubbornness, after he gets acquainted with a new experience. Just as children are born with their own eye color, body type, and so on, they come into the world with distinctive

behavioral styles—individual patterns of behavior that are probably genetically influenced and that tend to persist over time (Rothbart & Bates 2006).

These characteristics include differences in children's levels of distractibility, approach/withdrawal from new situations, adaptability, intensity, persistence, and attention span. When Sam grows up, it's more likely than not that he will approach his first job in the same cautious way that he approached his first week in Head Start.

Besides temperament, much has been written about children's so-called "cognitive styles" or "learning styles" (Rider 1997). Some of this research suggests children have inborn preferences for processing information in either a visual, auditory, or physical way. Observing Ricardo's deep sensory absorption in mixing and manipulating the dough, one might see him as having a strong physical or "kinesthetic" learning style.

Similarly, Howard Gardner's (1993) theory of multiple intelligences describes seven primary types of intelligence. According to Gardner, individual children show early and persistent differences in their strengths in each area, resulting in a unique profile for each child. For example, the profile of social, active Luz might include strong emphasis on "interpersonal intelligence" and "bodily/kinesthetic intelligence," while Sam's strengths might be in the area of "spatial intelligence." Whether described as temperament, learning styles, or multiple intelligences, these kinds of differences may form the early roots of children's distinctive approaches to learning.

Girls, boys, and approaches to learning

Does the fact that a child is a girl or a boy have some influence on her or his approaches to learning? Looking at the children making playdough, on average the girls appeared more planful and persistent than the boys—more self-regulated, if you will. Many of the girls approached the dough-making task in a focused, systematic way. And the only children who blew on the flour, dumped salt out of the container, or intentionally plopped a ball of dough onto the rug were boys.

Generally speaking, research confirms these impressions. Prekindergarten and kindergarten girls are apt to be more attentive and persistent as they work on learning tasks, whereas boys are likely to be more distractible and disruptive (McWayne et al. 2004). Teachers are apt to view boys, especially boys living in poverty, as especially distractible and hard to teach (Childs & McKay 2001). And girls' greater attentiveness and persistence seems to explain some of their commonly observed superiority to boys in kindergarten literacy achievement (Ready et al. 2005).

Inborn, maybe, but not set in stone

So some tendencies and behaviors related to children's approaches to learning seem to be inborn. However, these tendencies are not set in stone, and that is good news for early childhood educators and families. Even something like temperament (Rothbart & Bates 2006), which is thought to be essentially "wired in," shows itself and develops differently depending on the extent to which people in a child's environment encourage its expression. Depending on the fit of their own temperament with that of a child, parents and teachers may try to change certain aspects of a child's temperament. For example, even if Sam tends to be reluctant to try new things, if Sam's parents and teachers encourage a bit more risk-taking, he may well shift his typical style to some extent, though he may never be a daring experimenter like his classmate Ricardo.

Many people have pointed out that children can develop strengths that go beyond their preferred learning style or innate abilities. While respecting children's early and persistent individual differences, educators can intentionally provide experiences to broaden children's repertoire of effective learning behaviors.

The same point can be made with respect to gender. Although the research shows some gender differences in children's approaches to learning, good early childhood programs can create opportunities for all children—boys and girls—to strengthen their persistence, flexibility, intrinsic motivation, and every other component of positive approaches to learning.

However, while acknowledging and respecting all of these individual differences, a major theme of this book is that children are not simply born with positive or negative approaches to learning. Labels like "Joachim is just not an attentive child," or "Kaeylin is basically unenthusiastic" will limit rather than expand children's capacities.

Approaches to learning grow up: The influence of development

Having seen that the first "circle of influence" includes all of the innate characteristics that children bring into the world, let's look now at examples of the important developmental changes in children's approaches to learning from birth through the early grades of school. The Head Start children in our example are 4 years old or have just turned 5. If we had visited them the year before, would we have seen them express their enthusiasm and engagement in the same ways? To some extent, yes: Sam as a 3-year-old was probably hesitant yet also creative, and Luz would have most likely been impulsive and exuberantly sociable. But in the past year, major changes in the children's physical, cognitive, social, emotional, and language development have created new opportunities (and sometimes new challenges) in using those key approaches to learning.

Theoretical perspectives

Why is this? Developmental theorists and researchers have described some of the pathways, trajectories, or sequences in which aspects of children's approaches to learning may develop—too many, in fact, to discuss in this chapter. Below are just a few illustrative examples. Some theories of child development offer insight into how approaches to learning may develop, even though none of these theories specifically uses the term "approaches to learning" in describing these behaviors. For example, the descriptions of typical developmental crises at each stage of Erikson's (1950) theory could be considered in terms of the different ways that children might approach learning tasks. In the preschool years, Erikson describes children as struggling with issues of initiative, approaching tasks with great bursts of bold energy and intrusiveness. These behaviors seem typical of at least some of the 4-year-olds in their first encounter with making playdough. Erikson's theory predicts that in a few years these children would approach such a task quite differently, when their central developmental crisis will revolve around issues of "industry versus inferiority." At that point, children might typically be concerned about the right way to make the playdough, thinking in terms of what bakers or sculptors might do and comparing their product with a culturally relevant standard.

Similarly, Vygotsky's theory describes sequences in the development of self-regulation, a central component of what we are calling the approaches-to-learning dimension of engagement. Developmentally, this group of 4-year-olds is becoming better able to act in a "deliberate, planned manner" (Bodrova & Leong 2007, 127), but for now, many children in the class are still in a more reactive mode, impulsively responding to their feelings and their immediate environment. When Ricardo sees the big container of salt, for example, he grabs it and dumps it without being able to stop himself from acting on his impulse. Although Ricardo's impulsiveness may be an extreme example, most of the children in this class are still having great difficulty regulating their own behavior when faced with such a new, entrancing, and potentially messy stimulus!

Research in neuroscience and cognitive development

New research in brain development offers additional insights into the development of approaches to learning. Neuroscientists would emphasize that maturation of the brain is one key factor, allowing older children to regulate their own behavior to a much greater extent than when they were younger. Furthermore, researchers see important developments in early childhood in those aspects of the brain's workings that are called "executive function," the ability to deal with problems (such as turning a pile of flour into a ball of playdough) in a deliberate yet flexible way (Rothbart et al. 2007; Zelazo et al. 2003). To do this, the brain needs to coordinate a number of mental processes; these include organizing, focusing attention, sustaining effort, monitoring, and self-regulating. These cognitive processes are similar to, and may be important underpinnings of children's approaches to learning.

The development of specific components

Beyond brain development, other researchers have tracked the very early development of some specific components of approaches to learning—again, without necessarily using that term. For example, Barrett and colleagues (1993) described stages in development of children's "mastery

motivation," from birth to age 3: First, babies try to control events or toys; then they try to meet some standards (what the researchers call "task-related mastery"); and finally, toddlers evaluate themselves based on comparing their own performance with some specific standards.

Researchers have also traced the development of achievement motivation in children (this work is well summarized in Wigfield et al. 2006). For instance, children as young as 2½ react to failure by showing negative emotion or avoiding looking at adults. Researchers also find developmental changes in how children interpret their failure. Very young children, under age 2, are not concerned about what others think of their performance; next, children begin to care what adults think; and as they get older, they become able to evaluate their own success or failure. Yet even in preschool there are individual differences, with some 4- and 5-year-olds reacting very negatively to failure on learning tasks.

Children with disabilities

As we think about the development of children's approaches to learning over the early childhood years, it is important to keep in mind that this pathway may be different for children who have developmental delays or disabilities. For a child with a disability, certain components of approaches to learning may take longer to develop, or the child may show enthusiasm or engagement with behaviors different from those of a typically developing child. For example, one of the children making playdough is Teresa, who has Down syndrome. Although she is the same chronological age as her classmates, Teresa's developmental age limits her current ability to sustain engagement in the playdough-making task (de Kruif & McWilliam 1999). Another child in the class, Raymond, has been diagnosed with autism; this disability creates challenges in his ability to use flexible problem-solving strategies. For example, Raymond does not change his technique for mixing the dough even when that strategy does not lead to success, and he does not turn to other children for ideas or help in solving the challenge of how to mix the dough.

However, one cannot generalize about children with disabilities. First, each child who has a disability is also an individual, with the individual

quirks and characteristics that all children have. Teresa's neighbor Brock also has Down syndrome, but he has a very different style of behavior than Teresa, although both have the same disability and are the same age. Second, different disabilities may have different implications for the development of positive approaches to learning. Zachary has mild cerebral palsy, but the disability has not affected Zachary's development of any aspects of positive approaches to learning. His only difficulty is that other children and adults sometimes do not understand his words when he tries to express his enthusiasm or desire for engagement in a task. Like Zachary, Brock, Raymond, and Teresa, *all* children have potential to develop positive approaches to learning, though perhaps on different timetables and in different ways.

Family influences

Children are not just individuals but are members of families and communities. Chapter 9 will recom-

mend ways in which early childhood programs may partner with families to support children's positive approaches to learning. This chapter simply describes some of the ways in which families make a difference.

A major influence on approaches to learning is the quality of a child's relationship with her or his family. Children with secure attachment relationships are likely to develop more persistent, enthusiastic, and curious ways of approaching problem-solving tasks, from the toddler years into preschool and kindergarten (Arend et al. 1979; Waters et al. 1979). These relationships might explain at least some of the individual differences in the Head Start children's reactions to the new experience of making their own playdough. More generally, children who have strong "relatedness" to their parents "may enter the classroom with . . . a willing attitude and the desire to concentrate on the classroom agenda" (Furrer & Skinner 2003, 159). Furrer and Skinner, along with Howes and Ritchie (2002), have also found that children who are closer to their parents may subsequently form closer relationships with their teachers—relationships that in turn influence their level of academic motivation and engagement.

Parents' own beliefs about learning, and the way they translate those beliefs into action, may also influence their children's approaches to learning. For example, research suggests that children whose parents encourage them to become involved in learning for its own sake (not just to receive rewards) have greater intrinsic motivation to learn (Gottfried et al. 1994).

The influence of school

At an early age, most children in the United States begin to spend time in out-of-home care and education programs. Whether it is a child care center, a family child care home, prekindergarten, a Head Start classroom, kindergarten, or the primary grades, "school" is an important circle of influence on young children's approaches to learning, both directly and indirectly (through the school's relationship with families). The potential sources of influence include children's relationships with their teachers, as well as the quality of the program, curriculum, and teaching practices.

Relationships with teachers

Among the many benefits of children's positive relationships with their teachers (Pianta 2000), a very important plus is the positive effect on children's motivation to learn. As Furrer and Skinner (2003) put it,

> Feelings of relatedness tapped by measures of school climate and quality of teacher-student relationships, as well as feelings of belonging, inclusion, acceptance, importance, and interpersonal support, have been linked to important academic outcomes, including self-efficacy, success expectations, achievement values, positive affect, effort, engagement, interest in school, task goal orientation, and school marks. (p. 149)

Although Furrer and Skinner's statement is based on research with somewhat older children, it is likely that these positive connections between teacher-child relationships and children's motivation to learn begin much earlier. In a study of children's engagement in classroom activities in North Carolina child care centers, researchers from the Frank Porter Graham (FPG) Child Development

Center (2001) found that in programs where the teachers were especially warm and sensitive, a higher percentage of children were observed to be actively engaged.

In addition to benefiting from close relationships with teachers, children also model their own approaches to learning on those they see in their teachers. Teachers who themselves have more of a "mastery orientation" (learning to become more competent, rather than just to pass a test or get a reward) influence the children in their classrooms to be more mastery-oriented and to have more intrinsic motivation to learn (Midgley 2002).

Other aspects of program quality

Besides the influence of a teacher's relationship with children, other aspects of quality in early childhood education are able to influence children's positive approaches to learning. These range from overall program quality to more specific aspects of curriculum and teaching practices.

For example, in the FPG study, the researchers found that the level of program quality correlated with the extent and level of the children's engagement (FPG Child Development Center 2001). Children in higher quality classrooms were more likely to be engaged in activities in a more sophisticated and focused way than children in programs rated as lower in quality. The effect of program quality on children's engagement was especially evident in classrooms that served toddlers rather than older preschoolers. As the researchers noted, it may be that in order for toddlers to become and remain engaged, they must have the sort of teacher support and scaffolding provided in higher quality classrooms.

Much research indicates that positive approaches to learning will be supported by an early childhood curriculum that fosters children's choice, independence, and planning, and that offers children activities with appropriate levels of challenge and complexity (Hyson et al. 2006; Stipek & Seal 2001). Similarly, Rimm-Kaufman and colleagues (2005) found that the way early childhood teachers organize the environment and interact with children makes a difference in children's involvement in learning. For example, children are more involved when teachers rely more on small groups and when they build or elaborate on children's own ideas.

Studies of older children, summarized in Midgley (2002), Wigfield and Eccles (2002), and Wigfield and colleagues (2006), have found that children's motivation to learn and their engagement in learning are supported by teaching practices that communicate clear expectations, encourage children's active involvement and collaboration, and give children helpful guidance without overcontrolling every aspect of children's actions.

Cultural influences

Bronfenbrenner and others have emphasized that culture's influence is pervasive, connecting with and permeating every other system that influences a child's development (Bronfenbrenner 2000; Rogoff 2003). This section suggests some of the many ways in which culture may influence young children's approaches to learning.

In most early childhood programs today, the class is culturally diverse. Little research has examined cultural influences on specific aspects of children's approaches to learning. Studies of how children develop their motivation to learn have primarily been conducted with White, middle-class children. But many researchers, though not focusing specifically on approaches to learning, have studied broader cultural influences on children's development (Rogoff 2003; Schweder et al. 2006). Their insights may indirectly help us understand how linguistic and cultural diversity may affect children's enthusiasm and engagement.

Whatever their culture, all children probably share certain essentials that we are calling positive approaches to learning. Enthusiasm is evident in all children; children in every culture can be interested, joyful, and motivated to learn. Engagement is also part of all children's behavioral repertoire; children in every culture can be attentive, persistent, flexible, and self-regulated. But within these essentials, culture still remains a powerful influence on how children's approaches to learning develop and are expressed in their behavior. Let's look at a few examples.

First, children growing up in different cultures may vary in how persistent, attentive, or self-regulated they seem to be. For example, Blinco (1992) found that on the average, Japanese first-graders were significantly more persistent in completing tasks than their U.S. counterparts. The most likely explanation is that broad cultural values influence how much families may encourage their children's persistence. For many U.S. families, persistence may not be an important value, at least for younger children.

Most descriptions of approaches to learning focus on children's *individual* feelings and behaviors—the child's own attention, persistence, engagement, motivation, and so on. Yet the United States is in the minority in its dominant cultural emphasis on individualism and independence. Seventy percent of the world's cultures have a more collaborative, interdependent orientation than is found in the dominant U.S. culture. In these cultures, group efforts are valued and encouraged far more than the efforts made by individuals (Gutierrez & Rogoff 2003; Rogoff 2003).

Many of the culturally diverse children enrolled in U.S. early childhood programs may have been encouraged to adopt those collaborative values by their families and community. Although this point has often been made about children from non-U.S. cultures, Ladson-Billings (1995; 1997) and others have noted the same orientation toward cooperative approaches to learning among many African American students, as well as among American Indian and Alaska Native children (Pewewardy & Hammer 2003).

Culture also influences children's responses to various kinds of learning tasks and experiences. We know that children tend to be more motivated to engage in tasks that are optimally challenging—neither too far above nor too far below their capacities. But this match depends greatly on what the child's cultural environment considers challenging, and what experiences the child has had within that culture. What is an interesting challenge within one culture may be routine within another. In the playdough-making activity, some of the children were frustrated at first when they tried to combine the ingredients, apparently having had few experiences with this process. In contrast, many of the Hispanic children in the class help their mothers and grandmothers make tortillas every day. Mixing, slapping, and stretching the dough were second nature for these children; using these skills in a new activity created much enjoyment and engagement.

Culture also influences how children display their approaches to learning. Some cultures value and encourage vivid expressions of emotion; in other cultures, children may be less expressive in showing their interest and joy, though their underlying feelings may be the same (Hyson 2004). Similarly, when children focus their attention on a learning task, culture may influence whether they show this attention in intense gazes or in sidelong glances, and whether children explore the learning material physically or simply watch others demonstrate the activity (Rogoff 2003).

A final example: Children's culture may also influence how they respond to the other circles of influence as they develop positive approaches to learning. In an earlier section, we saw that positive approaches to learning are enhanced when children have warm relationships with their teachers. This is true for all children but seems especially important for ethnic minority students who tend to flourish when teachers combine warm, personal relationships with high expectations (Brophy 2004; Delpit 2006).

This discussion of cultural influences should end by emphasizing that children's culture is a great potential asset to their approaches to learning. Culturally responsive teaching increases the chances that all children, whatever their culture, language, and ethnicity, will develop enthusiasm and engagement—perhaps stimulated by different things and expressed in different ways, but always benefiting their development and learning.

Looking back and looking forward

This section has described the many interlocking circles of influence that can produce positive approaches to learning for young children. As we have seen, children come into the world with some basic behavior patterns or temperament/learning style characteristics. Some children may also come into the world with disabilities or developmental delays. Yet these individual characteristics are only part of the picture. Complex influences, ranging from family to school to culture to public policies, work together to affect each child's enthusiasm for and engagement in learning.

As we trace these processes, we should also remember that early childhood professionals can positively affect children's approaches to learning by becoming involved in each of these circles of influence. For example, early childhood educators can align their classroom practices with families' cultural values; they can select curriculum that intentionally fosters interest, engagement, persistence, and other positive approaches to learning; they can work to understand and influence public policies that might promote attention to approaches to learning. Together, these and other actions may have substantial effects on children's enthusiasm and engagement, and ultimately on their development and learning.

*   *   *

In the following excerpt from *Enthusiastic and Engaged Learners*, Marilou Hyson considers the place of approaches to learning in five education models. She chose these particular models because all are widely known and available to programs; comprise the entire curriculum rather than a single subject; and give explicit attention to various components of children's approaches to learning.

Hyson also looks at one content-specific curriculum, the Young Scientist Series, from the perspective of approaches to learning. (Its developers, Ingrid Chalufour and Karen Worth, describe the content and pedagogy of the Young Scientist Series more fully in Part II of this volume.)

Curriculum to promote positive approaches to learning

Early childhood curriculum models or approaches may differ on many dimensions, including the curriculum's explicitness or structure, its comprehensiveness, and its mix of teacher- and child-guided activities. These differences do not necessarily make one curriculum better than another. However, in a joint position statement, two national early childhood organizations urge programs to "Implement curriculum that is thoughtfully planned, challenging, engaging, developmentally appropriate, culturally and linguistically responsive, comprehensive, and likely to promote positive outcomes for all young children" (NAEYC & NAECS/ SDE 2003). In the position statement, the organizations outline specific indicators of a curriculum that is likely to promote good outcomes for children:

• Children are active and engaged

• Goals are clear and shared by all

- Curriculum is evidence-based
- Valued content is learned through investigation and focused, intentional teaching
- Curriculum builds on prior learning and experiences
- Curriculum is comprehensive
- Professional standards validate the curriculum's subject-matter content
- The curriculum is likely to benefit children

These criteria describe an effective curriculum in terms such as *challenging, engaging, valued content,* and *responsive*—terms that are similar to those we have used to describe the components of positive approaches to learning. This suggests that if an early childhood curriculum fully meets the NAEYC and NAECS/ SDE criteria for good curriculum (2003), it is likely (though not guaranteed) to support the development of positive approaches to learning.

With these criteria as a general guide, let us examine selected curriculum models to see the extent to which they are likely to promote positive approaches to learning. The examples were chosen for several reasons: They are relatively well known and available to programs, and in different ways each includes a relatively explicit emphasis on various components of children's approaches to learning. This discussion is not intended to endorse any of the models, or to slight others. Rather, the object is to illustrate some ways in which familiar curricula have incorporated a focus on enthusiasm and engagement. The descriptions are necessarily brief and are focused only on those aspects that are relevant to this book. The references cited in each section provide more extensive information on the specific curricula from their developers or implementers. For other perspectives on various early childhood curriculum models, see Goffin and Wilson (2001), Kessler and Swadener (1992), and Seefeldt (1999).

The examples begin with five curricula that would be considered comprehensive (i.e., curricula that were designed to address many areas of children's development and learning) and conclude with one content-specific example—a science curriculum.

Montessori curriculum

Contemporary Montessori education has grown out of Maria Montessori's pioneering work in the early 20th century (Torrence & Chattin-McNichols 2000). Mixed-age groups of children work independently and in small groups, often with manipulative, self-correcting materials specially designed to help children construct an understanding of concepts. Teachers observe children's development and respond by providing materials, a consistent structure, and encouragement of learning. They demonstrate the purpose and use of materials but then allow children to investigate independently.

Montessori education is premised on the belief that children are intrinsically motivated to learn and to feel deep joy in learning. One of the central tenets of Montessori education is the importance of children developing what Maria Montessori called "self-direction," or what might be termed "self-regulation" from an approaches-to-learning perspective (Montessori 1995; Torrence & Chattin-McNichols 2000). According to Montessori, inner discipline develops from opportunities to discover something of deep interest and to act on that interest in purposeful ways. These opportunities are intentionally built into the materials and daily routine of a Montessori classroom.

Engagement, or what Montessori called "concentration," is another key goal in the Montessori curriculum. The story is told that Maria Montessori once demonstrated to dubious visitors the power of children's concentration by watching a child who was utterly absorbed in manipulating a set of cylinders that she held in her lap. Montessori then quietly lifted up the child, chair and all, and moved her to another part of the room without the child's ever shifting attention from her self-chosen task (Montessori 1964). This utter absorption in learning may be unusual, but an emphasis on intrinsic motivation, love of learning, persistence, and focused attention is at the heart of Montessori education.

High/Scope curriculum

Initially influenced by Piaget's theory of development, and more generally by constructivism, the High/Scope curriculum was designed to develop children's understanding of essential concepts of space, time, number, and classification, as well as other important developmental outcomes (Hohman & Weikart 1995). According to the developers, the curriculum is built around teacher- and child-initiated learning activities in five main curriculum content areas: approaches to learning; language, literacy, and communication; social and emotional development; physical development, health, and well-being; and arts and sciences. An important feature of this curriculum is its focus on underlying concepts or big ideas, rather than on mechanical skills. The curriculum is organized around key developmental indicators (formerly known as "key experiences"); active learning promotes understanding of these and other concepts.

Several features appear to intentionally support some of the components of approaches to learning. For example, the High/Scope curriculum has a strong emphasis on children's planning. The daily schedule is built around a so-called "plan/do/review" sequence. First, in a group meeting, children are guided in planning how they will use their free-choice time in various learning areas *(plan)*. Children then have substantial blocks of time to involve themselves in these activities *(do)*. Following this work time, the children gather again in small or large groups to recall, represent, and reflect on their activities, using language or other media *(review)*. The curriculum's emphasis on child-initiated activities is intended to support sustained interest and engagement, which are other aspects of positive approaches to learning. At the same time, teacher-initiated activities and interactions not only support conceptual and skill development but also enhance children's attention and persistence in their activities.

Tools of the Mind

The newest of the comprehensive curricula discussed in this section, Tools of the Mind (Bodrova & Leong 2007), was developed to put into practice the developmental and educational ideas of the Russian psychologist Lev Vygotsky (1978). Again, many of the emphases

in this curriculum are consistent with and foster children's positive approaches to learning. In the preschool years, the primary goal of the curriculum is *self-regulation,* which is also seen as a key developmental accomplishment of the age group. "At the end of kindergarten, young children should be able to regulate their physical and emotional behaviors, and some of their cognitive behaviors" (Bodrova & Leong 2007, 127). A variety of activities and "mediators" are designed to support children's increasing self-regulation. Because of its central role in helping children develop cognitive and social competence, make-believe play is the central activity in the Tools of the Mind preschool curriculum. Before each extended pretend play period, children engage in a "play planning" process, using drawings and scaffolded writing to represent their ideas about what and with whom they will play, which again contributes to self-regulation. During the play period itself,

© Susan Woog Wagner

teachers promote children's in-depth involvement, helping them persist in and elaborate on their make-believe play ideas.

The development of self-regulation, which includes physical, emotional, and behavioral regulation, sets the stage for the later development of motivation to learn, which this theory describes as happening in the primary grades. The primary-grades curriculum emphasizes clear, explicit standards for children's performance, accompanied by helpful "mediators" and teachers' scaffolding. Intellectual curiosity or "enquiry motivation" is another important outcome during the primary grades. Although not identical to the notion of intrinsic motivation, this concept is similar and equally important (Bodrova & Leong 2007). The environment, learning tasks, and teacher behaviors that are emphasized in the Tools of the Mind curriculum are intended to foster this intellectual curiosity.

The Creative Curriculum

Developed by Teaching Strategies (Dodge et al. 2002), the Creative Curriculum aims to support a comprehensive set of child outcomes. Several components under our approaches-to-learning umbrella—persistence, curiosity, and flexibility, for example—are included in the outcomes that this curriculum emphasizes and assesses. The results of these assessments are used in ongoing curriculum planning based on children's strengths and challenges.

The curriculum emphasizes child choice within a classroom organized around interest centers such as blocks, art, dramatic play, and literacy. The use of the term "interest centers" suggests a focus on building on children's motivation to explore and learn. Another key emphasis in the curriculum is creating a classroom community (Dodge & Bickart 2002), which is a potential support for children's enthusiasm and engagement in learning. A major goal of the Creative Curriculum is teaching children how to learn, through teachers' involvement with children individually and in small groups.

The Project Approach

"Projecks can be edukashional. Projecks can be fun."
    —Travis (Diffily & Sassman 2002, 1)

A project is an in-depth study of a particular topic.

Used at all levels of education, project-based learning or "applied learning" (Diffily & Sassman 2002) has been advocated by Katz and colleagues as a valuable approach in early childhood education programs from the preschool years through the primary grades (Chard 1998; Helm & Katz 2001; Katz & Chard 2000).

In project-based learning, children work together as they investigate problems or questions that are meaningful to their lives. They define the questions they wish to explore, track down information in developmentally appropriate ways, and share their learning with others through presentations or other kinds of documentation. Those who have developed and implemented this approach to curriculum describe children gaining a deeper knowledge of content, as well as better research and problem-solving abilities.

Additionally, the Project Approach is seen by its developers as having a number of benefits that map onto the components of approaches to learning. For example, project work is said to increase children's self-direction and motivation to learn. Positive learning dispositions (Katz 1993; 1995) may be strengthened when children engage in extended, meaningful project work. Interest and joy in learning are likely to be stimulated because of the topics chosen by the class to investigate. And because projects take place over time, children are called on to focus their attention and to persist in sometimes challenging learning tasks.

Young Scientist Series

Each of the preceding five curricula addresses multiple areas of children's development and learning. Increasingly, however, programs, school districts, or states are turning to subject- or content-specific curricula in areas such as literacy, mathematics, and science. Sometimes these curricula supplement a comprehensive curriculum, and sometimes a set of content-specific curricula is used in place of a comprehensive curriculum.

One example of a content-specific curriculum that incorporates many of the approaches-to-learning emphases is the Young Scientist curriculum (Chalufour & Worth 2003; 2004; 2005). With support from the National Science Foundation, the series, designed for children ages 3–5, includes curriculum guides in three areas: discovering nature, building structures, and exploring water. Whatever the topic, the teaching plans outlined in this curriculum always have three phases, starting with "Engage"—an initial whole-group time for the teacher to spark children's interest in the materials that will be available. Then considerable time, up to an hour a day, is provided for children to "Explore" the materials. Teachers use this time to support children's problem-solving efforts, sustained attention, and persistence in challenging tasks (such as using a turkey baster to pull water in and squirt it out). The interests children develop during these open explorations may then lead to focused explorations of phenomena such as water drops. In the last phase, teachers can "Extend" the explorations into other, related areas of the curriculum. In approaches-to-learning terms, the curriculum strengthens dispositions as well as helping children construct understandings of scientific phenomena. "Scientific dispositions" that are emphasized in this curriculum, and that are part of the National Science Teachers Association's standards, include curiosity, eagerness to explore, an open mind (which in approaches-to-learning terms might be considered flexibility), and delight in being a builder, an explorer, or a discoverer.

Taking a closer look

Whether you are already using one of these curricula or are considering adopting one of them, you will need to go beyond these brief descriptions to analyze both the overall value of the curriculum and its specific attention to children's enthusiasm and engagement. Do keep in mind, however, that these are not the only curricula that might be considered for their approaches-to-learning focus.

Adapted with permission from M. Hyson, *Enthusiastic and engaged learners: Approaches to learning in the early childhood classroom* (New York: Teachers College Press; Washington, DC: NAEYC, 2008), 30–43 and 72–77. Copyright © 2008 Teachers College, Columbia University.

References

Arend, R., F.L. Gove, & L.A. Sroufe. 1979. Continuity of individual adaptation from infancy to kindergarten: A predictive study of ego-resiliency and curiosity in preschoolers. *Child Development* 50 (4): 950–59.

Barrett, K. C., G.A. Morgan & C. Maslin-Cole. 1993. Three studies on the development of mastery motivation in infancy and toddlerhood. In *Mastery motivation in early childhood: Development, measurement, and social processes*, ed. D.J. Messer, 83–108. New York: Routledge.

Blinco, P.M.A. 1992. A cross-cultural study of task persistence of young children in Japan and the United States. *Journal of Cross-Cultural Psychology* 23 (3): 407–15.

Bodrova, E., & D.J. Leong. 2007. *Tools of the Mind: The Vygotskian approach to early childhood education*. 2d ed. New York: Prentice Hall.

Bronfenbrenner, U. 2000. The ecology of developmental processes. In *Handbook of child psychology: Vol. 1. Theoretical models of human development*, 5th ed., eds. W. Damon & R. M. Lerner, 993–1028. New York: Wiley.

Bronfenbrenner, U., & P.A. Morris. 2006. The bioecological model of human development. In *Handbook of child psychology: Vol. 1. Theoretical models of human development*, 6th ed., W. Damon & R.M. Lerner, 793–28. New York: Wiley.

Brophy, J.E. 2004. *Motivating students to learn*. 2d ed. Mahwah, NJ: Erlbaum.

Chalufour, I., & K. Worth. 2003. *Discovering nature with young children* (Young Scientist Series). St. Paul, MN: Redleaf Press.

Chalufour, I., & K. Worth. 2004. *Building structures with young children* (Young Scientist Series). St. Paul, MN: Redleaf Press; Washington, DC: NAEYC.

Chalufour, I., & K. Worth. 2005. *Exploring water with young children* (Young Scientist Series). St. Paul, MN: Redleaf Press.

Chard, S. 1998. *The Project Approach: Making curriculum come alive* (Book 1). New York: Scholastic.

Childs, G., & M. McKay. 2001. Boys starting school disadvantaged: Implications from teachers' ratings of behaviour and achievement in the first two years. *British Journal of Educational Psychology* 71 (2): 303–14.

de Kruif, R.E.L., & R.A. McWilliam. 1999. Multivariate relationships among developmental age, global engagement, and observed child engagement. *Early Childhood Research Quarterly* 14 (4): 515–36.

Delpit, L. 2006. *Other people's children: Cultural conflict in the classroom* 2d ed. New York: New Press.

Diflily, D., & C. Sassman. 2002. *Project-based learning with young children*. Portsmouth, NH: Heinemann.

Dodge, D.T., & T.S. Bickart. 2002. How curriculum frameworks respond to developmental stages: Birth through age 8. In *Issues in early childhood education: Curriculum, teacher education, and dissemination of information. Proceedings of the Lilian Katz Symposium*, ed. D. Rothenberg, 33–41. University of Illinois at Urbana-Champaign: Early Childhood and Parenting Collaborative.

Dodge, D. T., L.J. Colker & C. Heroman. 2002. *The creative curriculum for preschool*. 4th ed. Washington, DC: Teaching Strategies.

Erikson, E. H. 1950. *Childhood and society*. New York: Norton.

Frank Porter Graham Child Development Center. 2001. *The quality and engagement study. Final report* (R. A. McWilliam, Principal Investigator). Chapel Hill, NC: Author.

Furrer, C., & E.A. Skinner. 2003. Sense of relatedness as a factor in children's academic engagement and performance. *Journal of Educational Psychology* 95 (1): 148–62.

Gardner, H. 1993. *Multiple intelligences: The theory in practice.* New York: Basic Books.

Goffin, S.G., & C.S. Wilson. 2001. *Curriculum models and early childhood education: Appraising the relationship* 2d ed. Upper Saddle River, NJ: Prentice Hall.

Gottfried, A.E., J.S. Fleming & A.W. Gottfried. 1994. Role of parental motivational practices in children's academic intrinsic motivation and achievement. *Journal of Educational Psychology* 86 (1): l04–13.

Gutiérrez, K., & B. Rogoff. 2003. Cultural ways of learning: Individual traits or repertoires of practice. *Educational Researcher* 32 (5): 19–25.

Helm, J., & L. Katz. 2001. *Young investigators: The Project Approach in the early years.* New York: Teachers College Press.

Hohman, M., & D.P. Weikart. 1995. *Educating young children: Active learning practices for preschool and child care programs.* Ypsilanti, MI: High/Scope Press.

Howes, C., & S. Ritchie. 2002. *A matter of trust: Connecting teachers and learners in the early childhood classroom.* New York: Teachers College Press.

Hyson, M. 2004. *The emotional development of young children: Building an emotion-centered curriculum.* 2d ed. New York: Teachers College Press.

Hyson, M., C. Copple & J. Jones. 2006. Early childhood development and education. In *Handbook of child psychology: Vol. 4. Child psychology in practice*, eds. K.A. Renninger & I. Sigel, 3–47. New York: Wiley.

Katz, L.G. 1993. *Dispositions: Definitions and implications for early childhood practices.* Urbana, IL: ERIC Clearinghouse on Elementary and Early Childhood Education.

Katz, L.G. 1995. Dispositions in early childhood education. In *Talks with teachers of young children: A collection*, ed. L.G. Katz, 47–69. Norwood, NJ: Ablex.

Katz, L., & S. Chard. 2000. *Engaging children's minds: The project approach.* 2d ed. Stamford, CT: Ablex.

Kessler, S.A., & B.B. Swadener, eds. 1992. *Reconceptualizing the early childhood curriculum: Beginning the dialogue.* New York: Teachers College Press.

Ladson-Billings, G. 1995. Toward a theory of culturally relevant pedagogy. *American Education Research Journal* 32 (3): 465–91.

Ladson-Billings, G. 1997. *The dreamkeepers: Successful teachers of African American children.* San Francisco: Jossey-Bass.

McWayne, C.M., J.W. Fantuzzo & P.A. McDermott. 2004. Preschool competency in context: An investigation of the unique contribution of child competencies to early academic success. *Developmental Psychology* 40 (4): 633–45.

Midgley, C. ed. 2002. *Goals, goal structures, and patterns of adaptive learning.* Mahwah, NJ: Erlbaum.

Montessori, M. 1964. *The Montessori method.* New York: Schocken Books.

Montessori, M. 1995. *The absorbent mind.* New York: Henry Holt & Co.

National Association for the Education of Young Children & National Association of Early Childhood Specialists in State Departments of Education. 2003. *Early childhood curriculum, assessment, and program evaluation: Building an effective, accountable system in programs for children birth through age 8.* Joint position statement. Online: www.naeyc.org/positionstatements/cape.

National Education Goals Panel. 1997. *Getting a good start in school.* Washington, DC: U.S. Government Printing Office.

Pewewardy, C., & P.C. Hammer. 2003. Culturally responsive teaching for American Indian students. *ERIC Digest ED482325.* Urbana, IL: ERIC Clearinghouse on Rural Education and Small Schools. Retrieved March 15, 2008, from http://www.eric.ed.gov:80/ERICDocs/data/ericdocs2sql/content_storage_O10000019b/80/lb/8b/07.pdf.

Pianta, R.C. 2000. *Enhancing relationships between children and teachers.* Washington, DC: American Psychological Association.

Ready, D.D., L.F. LoGerfo, D.T. Burkam & V.E. Lee. 2005. Explaining girls' advantage in kindergarten literacy learning: Do classroom behaviors make a difference? *Elementary School Journal,* 106 (1): 21–38.

Rider, R.J. 1997. On the nature of cognitive style. *Educational Psychology* 17 (1,2): 29–49.

Rimm-Kaufman, S. E., K.M. La Paro, J.T. Downer & R.C. Pianta. 2005. The contribution of classroom setting and quality of instruction to children's behavior in kindergarten classrooms. *Elementary School Journal* 105 (4): 377–94.

Rogoff, B. 2003. *The cultural nature of human development.* New York: Oxford University Press.

Rothbart, M. K., & J.E. Bates. 2006. Temperament. In *Handbook of child psychology: Vol. 3. Social, emotional, and personality development*, ed. N. Eisenberg, 99–166. New York: Wiley.

Rothbart, M.K., B.E. Sheese & M. Posner. 2007. Executive function and effortful control: Linking temperament, brain networks, and genes. *Child Development Perspectives* 1 (1): 2–7.

Schweder, R.A., J.J. Goodnow, G. Hatano, R.A. LeVine, H. Markus & P.J. Miller. 2006. The cultural psychology of development: One mind, many mentalities. In *Handbook of child psychology: Vol. 1. Theoretical models of human development*, eds. W. Damon & R.M. Lerner, 716–92. New York: Wiley.

Seefeldt, C., ed. 1999. *The early childhood curriculum: Current findings in theory and practice.* 3d ed. New York: Teachers College Press.

Stipek, D., & K. Seal. 2001. *Motivated minds: Raising children to love learning.* New York: Holt.

Torrence, M., & J. Chattin-McNichols. 2000. Montessori education today. In *Approaches to early childhood education*, 3d ed., eds. J.L. Roopnarine & J.E. Johnson, 191–219. Upper Saddle River, NJ: Prentice Hall.

Vygotsky, L. S. 1978. *Mind and society: The development of higher mental process.* Cambridge, MA: Harvard University Press. (Original work published 1930, 1933, 1935)

Waters, E., J. Wippman & L.A. Sroufe. 1979. Attachment, positive affect, and competence in the peer group: Two studies in construct validation. *Child Development* 50 (3): 821–29.

Wigfield, A., & J.S. Eccles, eds. 2002. *Development of achievement motivation.* San Diego, CA: Academic Press.

Wigfield, A., J.S. Eccles, U. Schiefele, R.W. Roeser & P. Davis-Kean. 2006. Development of achievement motivation. In *Handbook of child psychology: Vol. 3. Social, emotional, and personality development*, 6th ed., eds. W. Damon, R.M. Lerner, & N. Eisenberg (Vol. Ed.), 933–1002. New York: Wiley.

Zelazo, P.D., U. Müller, D. Frye & S. Marcovitch. 2003. The development of executive function in early childhood. *Monographs of the Society for Research in Child Development,* 68 (3, Serial No. 274).

Examples of Developmental Changes in Children's Approaches to Learning

RESEARCH SHOWS that if children start school with a strong set of attitudes and skills that help them "learn how to learn," they will be better able to take advantage of educational opportunities. While some learning skills come naturally to children, others can be developed through a supportive environment.

SNAPSHOTS

	1–2 years	2–3 years
	One-year-olds are in the act of discovering the world. They enthusiastically use their senses to purposefully explore everything they can. They find pleasure in causing things to happen and in completing basic tasks. They also enjoy sharing interesting learning experiences with adults, and may use gestures and simple sounds or speech to ask adults questions. Since language skills are still developing, one-year-olds rely more heavily on nonverbal, physical strategies to reach simple goals.	Two-year-olds enjoy using their senses to explore the world, and can solve simple problems with the "trial and error" method. They will practice an activity many times to master it, and can complete short-term, concrete tasks. Their budding language skills and desire to learn prompt many "why," "what," and "how" questions. This year typically marks the beginning of pretend play, where two-year-olds experiment with familiar objects and situations to process their experiences.

INITIATIVE, ENGAGEMENT, AND PERSISTENCE

	1–2 years	2–3 years
Decision-Making	Indicates preferences nonverbally or with simple language (e.g., points to an apple and pushes banana away).	Makes choices (e.g., food, clothes, toys, activities) based on preferences, sometimes in opposition to adult choices (e.g., child says, "No jacket. Want hat!").
Attention	Focuses attention on interesting sights or sounds, often in shared experiences with adults (e.g., sits on father's lap looking at a picture book).	Increases ability to sustain attention, especially when it directly influences an activity (e.g., repeatedly stacks blocks and knocks them down).
Persistence and Task Completion	Shows pleasure in completing simple tasks (e.g., drops clothespins into a bucket and smiles and claps when all are inside).	Completes self-chosen, short-term, concrete tasks. Practices an activity many times to gain mastery (e.g., repeatedly moves magnetic letters on and off the refrigerator).

3–4 years	4–5 years	5–6 years
Three-year-olds increasingly know what they want and express their preferences. While playing, they are better able to ignore distractions and focus on the task at hand. They will even persist in completing something that is a bit difficult. Learning still happens primarily through exploring, using all the senses. Their growing language skills allow for more complex questions and discussion, and they can think more creatively and methodically when solving problems.	When it comes to learning, four-year-olds are developing greater self-control and ingenuity. Their pretend play is more complex and imaginative, and can be sustained for longer periods. They can also make plans and complete tasks. Four-year-olds want to try new experiences. They also want to be more self-reliant, and seek to expand the areas of their lives where they can be independent decision-makers.	Five-year-olds are creative and enthusiastic problem solvers. They offer progressively more imaginative ideas for how to do a task, make something, or solve longer-term or more abstract challenges. As they participate in a variety of new experiences, five-year-olds ask more analytical questions and weigh their choices. They are also more social as they learn new things and prefer activities that involve other children.
Becomes increasingly deliberate when choosing preferred activities and companions (e.g., child says, "I want to play at Jeremy's house today.").	Further expands areas of decision-making (e.g., child may say, "This morning I'm going to work on my Lego building.").	Deliberates and weighs choices (e.g., may spend a long time thinking about whether to go to the store with mom or to stay home and help dad).
Is able to focus attention for longer periods of time, even with distractions or interruptions, as long as the activity is age-appropriate and of interest (e.g., can repeatedly solve and dump out a wooden puzzle, even with the TV on in the background).	Has an increased ability to focus attention, and can ignore more distractions and interruptions (e.g., at preschool, can focus on a drawing even when other children are nearby; might say, "I'll play with you later. I want to finish this.").	Can maintain focus on a project for a sustained period of time (e.g., spends a rainy day building a complicated fort out of chairs and blankets, complete with props and signs). Is able to return to an activity after being interrupted.
Persists with a wider variety of tasks, activities, and experiences. Keeps working to complete a task even if it is moderately difficult (e.g., persist with a somewhat challenging wooden puzzle).	Is increasingly able to complete tasks, even those that are longer-term and less-concrete (e.g., keeping track of the days until his or her birthday on a calendar). Has greater ability to set goals and follow a plan (e.g., child says, "I'm going to pick up all these branches," and then works until it is done).	Persists in longer-term or complex projects, with supervision. Can return to projects begun the previous day. Uses self-talk and other strategies to help finish difficult tasks and assignments from adults (e.g., a school project to make an alphabet book).

	1–2 years	2–3 years
Self-Help and Independence in Learning	Increasingly tries to help with self-care activities (e.g., feeding, undressing, grooming). When reading with adults, may want to hold the book or try to turn the pages. Collects information about the world using the senses.	Has a growing interest in and ability to perform routine tasks independently (e.g., puts napkins on the table before dinner).
CURIOSITY AND EAGERNESS TO LEARN		
Participation in Varied Experiences	Actively participates in a variety of sensory experiences (e.g., tastes, touches, pats, shakes).	Is able to participate in a broader array of experiences (e.g., exploring outdoor playground equipment, climbing on rocks, investigating contents of kitchen cabinets, paging through books), thanks to increased physical and cognitive skills.
Questioning	May seek information from adults by pointing to an interesting object, and then giving a questioning look, making a vocal sound, and/or saying a single world. In the second half of the year, children will be able to combine works to ask simple questions (e.g., says, "What that?" or "Who coming?").	May ask many "why," "what," and "how" questions about a variety of sights, sounds, and experiences (e.g., asks, "Why mommy crying?").
Eagerness to Learn	Shows physical and vocal pleasure when exploring objects and other things. Finds pleasure in causing things to happen (e.g., picks up bells and rings them, then smiles broadly when each one sounds different).	Continues to show enthusiasm and pleasure in daily explorations. Enjoys solving simple problems (e.g., successfully puts on own hat after several tries, then happily jumps up and down).
REASONING AND PROBLEM SOLVING		
Flexibility and Resilience	Tries a variety of physical strategies to reach simple goals (e.g., when a cart gets stuck while being pushed through a door, he or she turns the cart a different way and tries again).	Becomes more systematic in using language and physical approaches to solve problems, but may become stuck on one solution (e.g., tries numerous strategies for nesting a set of cups of graduated sizes, but may keep pushing harder to get a large cup to fit into a smaller one).

3–4 years	4–5 years	5–6 years
Expands abilities to independently complete a range of self-help skills (e.g., feeding, undressing, grooming). May refuse adult assistance (e.g., tries over and over to pull on a sweater and pushes mom's hands away when she tries to help).	Increasingly makes independent choices and shows self-reliance (e.g., chooses clothes, feeds, and dresses self).	Chooses and follows through on self-selected learning tasks. Shows interest and skill in more complex self-help skills (e.g., decides to learn to skate, zips jacket, prepares a snack).
Continues to seek and engage in sensory and other experiences (e.g., listens to stories, plays with friends, takes trips to the fire station).	Asks to participate in new experiences that he or she has observed or has hear of others participating in (e.g., says, "Jack goes fishing. Can I?").	Tries an even wider range of new experiences, both independently and with peers and adults (e.g., goes on a camping trip with grandparents, tries to learn to play piano like older brother). May deliberately take risks when learning new skills.
Continues to ask numerous questions, which are becoming more verbally complex (e.g., asks, "How we get to Nana's house?").	Asks questions about future events, as well as about the here and now (e.g., asks, "When will we go to Sarah's house again?").	Asks higher-level questions (e.g., asks, "What would happen if we had no food? Or "Why was Raymond mad at me?").
Seeks out new challenges (e.g., tries to dress a doll or put together a new construction toy).	Starts to show more enthusiasm for learning letters, shapes, and numbers (e.g., while looking at a book with dad, points to a word that contains the letter "S" and says, "S! That's in my name! What is that word?").	Expands verbal and non-verbal enthusiasm for learning new things, including academic (e.g., reading, writing) and physical skills (e.g., riding a bike).
Continues to become more flexible in problem-solving and thinking through alternatives (e.g., when trying to put on shoes, talks to self about what to do first. If the shoe won't easily go on one foot, he or she tries the other foot.).	More flexible and able to draw on varied resources in solving problems (e.g., tries to build a large structure with blocks, but the building keeps falling down. After several failed attempts, he or she tries making a larger base. May also look at how other children have made their buildings.).	Is increasingly able to think of possible solutions to problems. Can use varied and flexible approaches to solve longer-term or more abstract challenges (e.g., when planning to have friends over on a rainy day, thinks about how to deal with a limited space to play).

	1–2 years	2–3 years
Help-Seeking	Uses gestures and (toward the end of the year) simple language to get help when "stuck" (e.g., extends arms toward grandfather and says, "Up Up!" when trying to get into large chair).	Continues to expand use of language to get help, but may refuse assistance even when needed (e.g., may say, "I need help!" when trying to get a little car into the garage, but then says, "Do it myself!" when help arrives).
Thinking Skills	Discovers aspects of the physical world using early language skills and purposeful exploration with the senses (e.g., turns a plastic bucket over and over, raising and lowering the handle thoughtfully).	Grows in abilities to recognize and solve problems through active exploration, including trial and error (e.g., tries to get a large pillow into a small container by turning it this way and that; eventually folds up pillow so it fits).
INVENTION AND IMAGINATION		
Pretending	Pretends one object is really another with simple physical substitutions (e.g., picks up a wooden block and holds it to his or her ear like a phone).	Engages in simple pretend play with familiar objects and situations (e.g., puts doll to bed and lays blanket over her).
Creative Approaches to Situations	Uses objects in new and unexpected ways (e.g., puts saucepan on head, laughs uproariously).	Expands use of objects, art materials, and toys in new and unexpected ways (e.g., takes bath towels out of a closet and drapes them over chairs, crumples up paper in interesting shapes when pasting onto cardboard).

3–4 years	4–5 years	5–6 years
Increasingly able to ask for help on challenging tasks (e.g., says, "Can you put Teddy's pants on?").	Seeks help from both adults and peers, and has a greater understanding of the kind of help that may be needed (e.g., says, "Can you hold this end of the string for me, so I can tie this?").	Analyzes complex problems more accurately to identify the type of help needed (e.g., says, "I think I know how to play this game, but I think you'll have to help me get started. Then I can do the rest.").
Thinks more systematically. Benefits from conversations with adults and peers, as well as physical investigation.	Grows in ability to understand abstract concepts, especially when his or her thinking is supported by physical interaction with materials (e.g., systematically pours sand into measuring cups, then looks at and comments on amounts).	Continues to benefit from hands-on experiences to support more abstract thinking skills (e.g., makes a book about last summer's vacation trip, complete with sections for each place visited, drawings to illustrate, and labels written with adult help).
Grows in ability to sustain pretend play with other children (e.g., plays in pretend kitchen with friend, serving "cookies"). Takes on familiar roles (e.g., mom or dad) in pretend play.	Engages in more sustained and complex pretend play (e.g., creates a long scenario with several other children, taking a pretend trip with many stops). Expands the roles acted out in pretend play. Is less dependent on realistic props.	Collaborates with other children in extended and complex pretend play, taking on more varied roles and situations (e.g., acts out roles of lions, hunters, rescuers, and other animals in a dramatic and sustained scenario).
Plays creatively with both language and objects. Expresses inventive ideas in an expanding set of situations (e.g., creates interesting scenes with small plastic animals; strings nonsense words together, "Mommy, nommy, sommy, tommy").	Offers creative, unusual ideas about how to do a task, how to make something, or how to get from one place to another (e.g., says, "I've got a great ideal Let's walk backwards to the kitchen!").	Offers increasingly creative, unusual ideas about how to do a task, how to make something, or how to get from one place to another (e.g., asks, "Let's use these old boxes to make a spaceship! Where's some paint?").

Part II

Approaches for Promoting Cognitive Development in the Early Childhood Classroom

Symbolic Thought in the Early Years

Near the end of the second year of life, mental representation can be seen in the child's reproducing of an event seen earlier, that is, deferred imitation (Piaget 1962). Also emerging at this time are the more advanced levels of what Piaget called object permanence—recognizing that an object exists even when it is out of sight. For example, a child sees an object disappear into the adult's closed hand and then sees the adult put his hand under a cloth, a hat, and finally a cup, leaving the button under the cup. Having attained an advanced level of object permanence, the child knows to look for the button under the cup. Object permanence can also be seen in children's daily activities. For instance, children late in the second year of life find it necessary to make only occasional visual checks for the mother, far fewer than they did at a younger age (Bronson 1973). In all these ways children manifest the transition to representational thinking at around 18 to 24 months. This advance in thinking is also apparent in children's symbolic or pretend play.

Moving from their first imitations of simple actions, such as pretending to drink from an empty cup, preschool children become capable of greater symbolic thought in their dramatic play, for example, using an object to represent another, taking on roles, and spinning scenarios far removed from the here and now. To do these things not only requires a degree of symbolic capacity but also increases children's facility in symbolic thinking. In **"Chopsticks and Counting Chips: Do Play and Foundational Skills Need to Compete for the Teacher's Attention in an Early Childhood Classroom?"** Vygotskians Elena Bodrova and Deborah Leong describe the development of mature dramatic play and how their educational approach supports it. As to whether play and foundational (academic) skills are at odds in the classroom, their emphatic answer is no. In their approach, Tools of the Mind, play (particularly dramatic play) has been found to enhance academic learning as well as cognitive and social-emotional development. Yet, the play must be the right kind—rich in role play, with children planning and interacting as they set the scene and sustain the play over time. Children do not achieve this level of play without supportive scaffolding, Bodrova and Leong argue. And today many children no longer receive this support from their social environments outside of school. The educational approach described here supplies this support with an active set of strategies that nurture high-level play, and thus cognitive development and academic learning.

Pretend play is one powerful medium for developing symbolic thought and representational abilities; another fertile context is in-depth exploration of a problem or project of strong interest to the children. As they work collaboratively in such an enterprise and adults encourage their use of various representational media to convey their ideas, children's thinking processes, knowledge, and representational competence grow. The seminal work of the schools of Reggio Emilia has shown the incredible potential of investigations and projects, and many North American educators inspired by Reggio Emilia have explored these ideas in American and Canadian contexts. In their article **"Moving into Uncertainty: Sculpture with 3- to 5-Year-Olds"** educators Carol Anne Wien, Bobbi-Lynn Keating, Annette Coates Comeau, and Barbara Bigelow describe the investigations of children in Halifax, Nova Scotia. The children grapple with the question of what sculpture is and with problems ranging from the artistic ("How can I make my sculpture look like a chameleon?") to the physical ("How can I make my creation stand up?"). The authors note: "The teachers learned as much as the children, and this joining of minds enlivens teaching and makes every move fresh and stimulating" (82). Indeed, both teachers and children encountering a sense of excitement and satisfaction in the classroom is a recurring thread in these descriptions of engaging, cognitively-rich learning activities.

In most accounts of how children learn and develop, language development receives strong emphasis, and rightly so. Getting far less attention, though of great importance, is the development of spatial understanding. The significance of the spatial domain—and the relatively slight attention it receives among educators—led me to include here an excellent review article on the subject. Authored by Susan Golbeck, professor and researcher at Rutgers University, **"Building Foundations for Spatial Literacy in Early Childhood"** explains why it is important for young children to acquire spatial understanding and robust skills in imagining, representing, and analyzing the spatial world. Use of two- and three-dimensional representations as tools for perceiving and communicating about our spatial worlds—in other words, spatial literacy—is embedded in the various disciplines in the curriculum and in a great many of the careers and daily activities that adults engage in. Drawing from cognitive and educational research, Golbeck describes how young children begin to anchor themselves in space and advance in their spatial sense. And drawing from the research base, she provides useful guidance for teachers on promoting young children's spatial understanding and skills.

References

Bronson, W.C. 1974. Mother-toddler interaction: A perspective on studying the development of competence. *Merrill-Palmer Quarterly* 20 (4): 275–301.

Piaget, J. 1962. *Play, dreams and imitation in childhood.* New York: Norton. (Original work published 1945)

Elena Bodrova and Deborah J. Leong

6

Chopsticks and Counting Chips: Do Play and Foundational Skills Need to Compete for the Teacher's Attention in an Early Childhood Classroom?

For the Chinese New Year, May's parents give her some sweets to share with her classmates. "Let's play Chinese restaurant," suggests the teacher after the children finish their snack. Children run to the housekeeping area and start emptying the cupboards. "But we don't have any Chinese food," remarks Taylor, examining plastic hamburgers. "No chopsticks," says Nita, holding up spoons and forks. "Can you pretend you have them?" asks the teacher. "How about using pencils as chopsticks and counting chips as food?" "No, I want to play family," answers Nita, settling into the familiar routine of stirring a pot as Taylor begins to place plastic hamburgers on the plates.

What is happening here? Why don't the children engage in a new play scenario? Should we worry about these children's apparent lack of pretend play skills, and if so, how can teachers intervene?

These might not be the most burning questions on the minds of preschool and especially kindergarten teachers. In an age of rising expectations and tougher academic standards, educators are more likely to pay attention to issues that seem to be more closely related to school readiness. "I used to have a lot more play," sighs a kindergarten teacher, "and now my principal does not understand why I want to keep the playhouse in my room. She thinks children should play at home and come to school to learn."

Why play belongs in the early childhood classroom

Would you agree with this principal's position? At first it does make sense—many preschool and kindergarten programs run for a half-day only, and spending time on play seems like a luxury. Maybe home is the place where play belongs. In our own memories we see ourselves spending a lot of time playing with our friends, and most of this play did take place outside the classroom. At that time it never occurred to teachers that they should provide any kind of support for children's play—it was taken for granted that most children knew how to play, and those who did not would learn from other children.

These nostalgic memories are probably the reason some teachers and school administrators are reluctant to consider play as important a part of the classroom as other activities. However, when asked to describe how children play today, most educators agree that play has in fact changed from what it used to be 30 or even 20 years ago. Nowadays young children spend less time at home playing with their peers and more time playing alone, graduating from educational toys to video and computer games.

When they do engage in sociodramatic play, children rarely try a new theme, preferring instead to act out the familiar scenarios of family, school, and doctor. Even books and TV shows filled with information about realistic as well as fantasy settings and characters often fail to inspire children to turn their housekeeping area into a space station or animal hospital. Teachers (as well as families) comment that today's children tend to rely on realistic toys and props, and they have a hard time using their imaginations to invent a substitute for a prop they do not have. Children often resort to repeating aggressive actions over and over again instead of developing involved play scenarios.

> "What a wonderful castle!" exclaims the teacher as she admires a structure Esai and Spencer have just completed in the block area, "Do you want to play knights and dragons?" continues the teacher, reminding the boys about the book they read in class. "I see you have enough knights in your castle, and it is strong enough to protect them from the biggest dragon." The boys seem puzzled. "We do not have any dragons," says Esai after a long pause. Spencer looks around to see if there are some dragons. He glances at the science area where numerous boxes of plastic dinosaurs and crocodiles are stacked under the reptiles poster. He looks back at the teacher. "No, we do not have any dragons," Spencer says.

The home and classroom experiences of many children may not be sufficient to produce the rich,

Elena Bodrova is Principal Researcher at Mid-Continent Research for Education and Learning. **Deborah Leong** is Professor Emerita of Psychology and Director of the Tools of the Mind Project.

imaginative play that has long been considered an inherent characteristic of early childhood. Many factors contribute to this state of affairs:

- changes in the social context (children spend more time in the company of same-age peers who may not be as effective play mentors as older siblings or friends)
- increasing academic demands of preschool and kindergarten programs
- the tendency of toy manufacturers to produce ever more realistic playthings

To combat these negative factors, early childhood teachers would need to support play development at least at the same level as they support the development of fine motor skills or phonemic awareness. But it is hard to expect all early childhood teachers to follow this advice because, outside of the early childhood community, play is not universally recognized as a medium for learning.

"I am finding myself between a rock and a hard place," admits a former preschool teacher who now writes books for the parents of young children. "Because I work for a publishing company, I need to meet the demands of our customers. However, being an early childhood educator, I know that if I write only what is in demand, it would not be right for the children. All parents want now are worksheets, and they want them in their babies' hands as early as possible."

In practice, the need to promote foundational skills, such as phonological awareness or listening comprehension, in young children and the need to support their play appear to be competing for teachers' time and attention. But in theory it should not be this way. Research on play accumulated over the past several decades makes a convincing case for the benefits of supporting a high quality of pretend play. A number of studies show the links between play and many foundational skills and complex cognitive activities such as memory (Newman 1990), self-regulation (Krafft & Berk 1998), distancing and decontextualization (Howes & Matheson 1992; O'Reilly & Bornstein 1993; Sigel 2000), oral language abilities (Davidson 1998), symbolic generalization (Smilansky & Shefatya 1990), successful school adjustment (Fantuzzo & McWayne 2002), and better social skills (Corsaro 1988).

In many of the recent studies focusing on the relationship between play and literacy, play interventions resulted in an increase in children's use of literacy materials and their engagement in literacy acts, as well as gains in specific literacy skills such as phonological awareness (for a review of the research, see Roskos & Christie 2001). Not only does play help children develop skills and concepts necessary to master literacy and math, it also builds the foundation of more general competencies that are necessary for the children to learn successfully in school and beyond.

Considering what we know about the effects of play on young children's learning and development, the disappearance of play from early childhood classrooms looks even more alarming. As the opportunities for children to engage in high-quality play outside school become less and less common, early childhood teachers might soon be children's only play mentors.

The task of supporting play while making sure children meet school expectations may seem impossible, especially given the constraints of a typical early childhood program. However, we believe it can be done.

During our years of work with preschool, Head Start, and kindergarten teachers, we found that knowing the characteristics of high-level play and being able to support these characteristics not only results in richer, more imaginative play but also has a positive effect on the development of foundational skills, including cognitive and emotional self-regulation and the ability to use symbols. These foundational skills in turn make it possible for the children to achieve higher levels of mastery of specific academic content, such as literacy (e.g., Bodrova & Leong 2001; Bodrova et al. 2003).

The Vygotskian approach to play

Our analysis of play is based on the works of Lev Vygotsky and his students (Bodrova & Leong 1996; 2004). While Vygotsky's views of play are familiar to the Western educational community (e.g., Berk 1994; Berk & Winsler 1995), the work of his students, Daniel Elkonin in particular, is relatively unfamiliar in the West.

Elkonin [1904–85] is known in the United States primarily through the use of Elkonin Blocks in Reading Recovery and other remedial reading programs. In Russia, Elkonin's research (1978) on phonemic awareness is only part of his legacy; his study of play is another substantial contribution to the field.

Having studied learning in primary grade students and younger children, Elkonin was a strong opponent of lowering the school-entry age in Russia. He argued that not only would it not help increase student achievement, it would also result in pushed-down curriculum and the elimination of play from the lives of preschoolers and kindergartners. As an alternative he developed a highly successful curriculum for the primary grades that allows elementary school teachers to teach all requisite skills and concepts without adding more academic content to the existing preschool and kindergarten curricula.

Elkonin identified four principle ways in which play influences child development. All four expected outcomes of play activity are important for preparing the foundations for subsequent learning that takes place in primary grades (Elkonin 1977; 1978).

1. **Play affects the child's motivation.** In play, children develop a more complex hierarchical system of immediate and long-term goals. In fact, play becomes the first context where young children demonstrate their ability to delay gratification—something preschoolers are known to struggle with in most other situations.

2. **Play facilitates cognitive decentering.** The ability to take other people's perspectives is critical for coordinating multiple roles and negotiating play scenarios. Assigning different pretend functions to the same object involves cognitive decentering. This newly acquired competency will later enable children to coordinate their cognitive perspectives with those of their learning partners and teachers. Eventually this ability to coordinate multiple perspectives will be turned inward, leading to the development of reflective thinking and metacognition.

3. **Play advances the development of mental representations.** This development occurs as the result of a child separating the meaning of objects from their physical form. First, children use replicas to substitute for real objects; then they use new objects that are different in appearance but can perform the same function as the object prototype. Finally, most of the substitution takes place in the child's speech with no objects present. Thus the ability to operate with sym-

bolic substitutes for real objects contributes to the development of abstract thinking and imagination. (It is important to note that Vygotskians believe that imagination is an expected outcome of play, not a prerequisite for it.)

4. **Play fosters the development of deliberate behaviors—physical and mental voluntary actions.** The development of deliberateness in play becomes possible because the child needs to follow the rules of the play and because play partners constantly monitor each other to make sure that everyone is following the rules. At first, this deliberateness is demonstrated in physical actions (e.g., a child moves on all fours when playing a cat or stays still when playing a guard), social behaviors, and changing speech registers in language use. Later, this deliberateness extends to mental processes such as memory and attention.

According to Vygotskians, only when these four outcomes are in place can a young child profit fully from academic activities. If these foundations are missing, the child may experience various difficulties adapting to school, be it in the area of social interactions with teachers and peers or in the area of content learning.

The kind of play that helps children develop all four foundations is defined by the combination of the imaginary situation children create (a scenario), roles for the people and perhaps objects, and rules about what the players can and cannot do in the scenario (Vygotsky [1966] 1977; [1930-35] 1978). Outside the Vygotskian framework, this kind of play is often labeled *sociodramatic play, role play*, or *pretend play* to distinguish it from other playlike activities such as stacking blocks on top of each other or playing games.

By the time children turn 4, they are capable of engaging in this kind of complex play with multiple roles and symbolic use of props. However, in reality many preschool- and even kindergarten-age children still play at the level typical of toddlers, spending most of their play repeating the same sequence of actions as long as they stay in the same role. We use the term *immature play* to distinguish this play from the *mature play* that should be expected of older preschoolers and kindergartners. Although mature play does in fact contribute to children's learning and development in many areas, immature play does not provide these benefits.

It seems to us that in many instances when parents or school administrators propose replacing play in an early childhood classroom with more academic activities, they are prompted by the fact that the play they see in these classrooms is actually happening at an immature level. It is hard to argue for the value of play that is repetitive and unimaginative.

Following Vygotsky's principle of *learning leading development* (Vygotsky [1930-35] 1978), we designed a system of interventions to scaffold play in children who for some reason did not receive adequate support for their play at home or at school (e.g., Bodrova & Leong 2001; Bodrova et al. 2002). Each strategy targets one or more characteristics of mature play. This article shares some of our insights into how early childhood teachers can promote mature play.

Helping children create an imaginary situation

When children create an imaginary situation, they assign new meanings to the objects and people involved. As a result they practice operations on meanings that are mentally more sophisticated than operations on real objects. It is apparent, however, that the cognitive benefits of engaging in imaginary actions depend on the kinds of props and toys children use: realistic and specific props do not require a great deal of imagination.

A good way for teachers to support the development of imaginary situations is to provide multipurpose props that can be used to stand for many objects. For example, a cardboard box could be a computer in the office, a sink in the kitchen, or a baby crib for a doll in the nursery. An advantage of these nonspecific props is that children must use more descriptive language when interacting with their play partners: unless they describe what the object stands for and how it will be used, the other children will find it hard to follow the change in meaning of the object from one play use to the other.

Another alternative to providing realistic play props is to encourage children to make their own. For example, instead of using plastic hamburgers and fried eggs in a pretend restaurant, children can make their own play food with playdough and other art materials.

Some children may not be ready to make their own props or to play with unstructured objects. They will not play unless there are some realistic props available. For these children, teachers need to introduce symbolic use of objects gradually—both in the play area and outside of it. In the play area the teacher can start with realistic props to keep play going and then add other materials that are increasingly less realistic. For example, a pretend grocery store can combine realistic props (grocery cart, scale, cash register) with some that are generic (boxes, plastic bags) and some that are open-ended (pieces of paper that can be used for play money, coupons, or shopping lists).

Outside the play area, teachers can use additional strategies to help children create and maintain the imaginary situation. These can be used during group time or in a center with four or five children. For example, teachers can show the children common objects and brainstorm how they can use these things to stand for something different: a paper plate looks like a Frisbee to one child, a flying saucer to another, and a pizza to yet another.

After all the children learn how to transform real objects into pretend ones, the teachers could extend the game by limiting the choice of props to a specific play theme. The paper plate would become something that could be used in a spaceship: an instrument dial, a steering wheel, or a round window. When playing this game, it is important to encourage children to use both gestures and words to describe how they are using the object in a pretend way. In some cases, teachers can place the objects used for the game in the play area so children can use them in the new ways in later play.

Helping children act out various roles

In mature play the set of roles associated with a theme is not limited and stereotypical but is easily expanded to include supporting characters. Playing hospital does not mean the only roles are those of doctor and patient. A nurse, lab technician, dietitian, and pharmacist can also participate. Patients can bring their parents or children with them; they

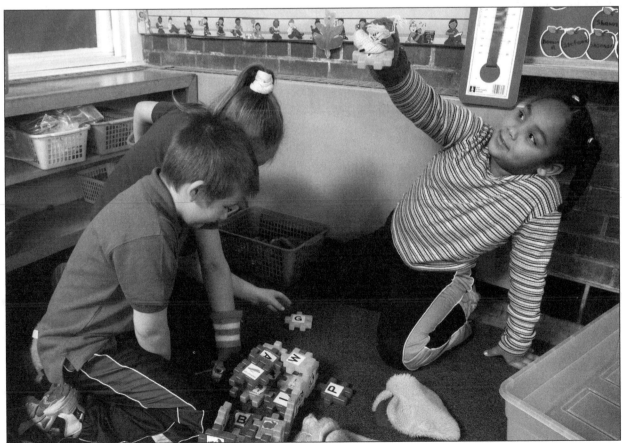

can be brought by an ambulance driver or the pilot of an emergency helicopter.

Being able to choose among a variety of roles decreases the number of disagreements that are common when several children want to be the doctor and nobody wants to be the patient. In addition, when children get to play different roles in different scenarios, they learn about social interactions they might not have in real life (following commands and issuing them; asking for help and helping others; being an expert and being a beginner).

The ability of young children to act out various roles depends on their familiarity with what people do in different settings, how they interact with each other, what kinds of tools they use, and so on. Children are not likely to gain all this knowledge on their own. Teachers can help children expand the number of themes in their play and the number of roles associated with different play themes.

Field trips, literature, and videos are wonderful sources for expanding children's repertoire of play themes and roles. However, taking children on a field trip does not necessarily ensure they will incorporate this new experience in their play scenarios. The most common mistake is to focus children's attention on the things part of a field trip or video—what is inside a fire truck or what happens to the letters when they arrive at the post office. Instead, teachers should point out the people part of each new setting—the many different roles people play in each setting and how the roles are related to each other.

Learning about new roles and the language and actions associated with each of them helps children reenact these new experiences in their play. For example, on a field trip to a historic train station, without the teacher's help, all the children notice is the large engine. But with the teacher's help, they can learn about the roles of engineer, stoker, and conductor. They can talk about the passengers boarding the train, stowing their luggage on the overhead rack, and giving their tickets to the conductor.

This attention to the people aspect of the field trip will translate into more complex play back in the classroom. When the focus is on the objects, children's play may be limited by the number of appropriate props—imagine the difficulty of sharing one engineer's hat! However, when the focus shifts to the people and their roles, children can easily make up for the missing objects by substituting others or simply by naming them: Vincent says, "I am the engineer," as he pretends to put on his engineer's hat and then makes gestures as if he were holding on to a steering wheel.

Helping children plan their play

In mature play, children can describe to each other what the play scenario is, who is playing which role, and how the action will happen.

> Marcie says, "Let's pretend that I'm the teacher and these will be the students and you'll be a student. Then we'll read a book and sing our song together. Maggie [pointing to a toy bear] will be bad." "No, I want to be the teacher," says Jason. "OK, I'll read the book first, and then you'll be the teacher," says Marcie.

During this planning period, Marcie and Jason discuss how to handle the fact that both of them want to be the teacher. To get children to the point where they can do this mature planning, teachers have to encourage children to discuss

- **the roles**—who they are going to be

- **the theme of the play**—what they are going to play

- **how the play will unfold**—what is going to happen

Teachers should set aside time to discuss this before the children enter the center. The children should focus on what will be played, who will be which person, and what will happen. At first the teachers will need to do some prompting, because children are used to discussing what they will play with or which center they will play in rather than the roles and themes of their play. Children who are going to the same center should discuss their plans with each other. We have found that children begin to use the discussion as a strategy for play itself. The planning helps children maintain and extend their roles.

Do play and foundational skills need to compete for the teacher's attention?

Our research shows that an emphasis on play does not detract from academic learning but actually enables children to learn. In classrooms where children spent 50 to 60 minutes of a two-and-a-half-hour program in play supported by teachers' use of Vygotskian strategies to enhance play, children scored higher in literacy skills than they did in control classrooms (Bodrova & Leong 2001).

Because children could play intensely during their center time, teachers had more time for meaningful one-on-one interactions with children. Group times were short and sweet because all the children were able to participate and pay attention. There was more productive time to learn, more time to be creative, and more time to have fun! Teachers commented that there was little fighting, a lot of discussion, and more friendships as children had many more positive interactions with each other than in previous years.

> Mr. Drews decides to promote mature play in his classroom by following up on the Chinese New Year. He finds a book on Chinese restaurants, and he plans a field trip to a local Chinese restaurant. He asks May's parents to come to school to share the food that the family cooks and eats at home. He helps the children brainstorm the different restaurant roles—the cook, the person who seats you, the busboy, the customers. Children make their own food out of paper. They brainstorm the props that work best. Children's play really begins to improve. The restaurant play spreads from housekeeping to other play centers as children call in their orders to the restaurant by phone.

Play does not compete with foundational skills: Through mature play, children learn the very foundational skills that will prepare them for the academic challenges that lie ahead.

Reprinted from *Young Children* 58 (3): 10–17. Copyright © 2003 NAEYC.

References

Berk, L.E. 1994. Vygotsky's theory: The importance of make-believe play. *Young Children* 50 (1): 30–39.

Berk, L.E., & A. Winsler. 1995. *Scaffolding children's learning: Vygotsky and early childhood education.* Washington, DC: NAEYC.

Bodrova, E., & D.J. Leong. 1996. *Tools of the mind: The Vygotskian approach to early childhood education.* Englewood Cliffs, NJ: Merrill/Prentice Hall.

Bodrova, E., & D.J. Leong. 2001. *The Tools of the Mind project: A case study of implementing the Vygotskian approach in American early childhood and primary classrooms.* Geneva, Switzerland: International Bureau of Education, UNESCO.

Bodrova, E., & D.J. Leong. 2004. Learning and development of preschool children: The Vygotskian perspective. In *Vygotsky's educational theory in cultural context,* eds. A. Kozulin, V. Ageyev, S. Miller & B. Gindis. New York: Cambridge University Press.

Bodrova, E., D.J. Leong, J.S. Norford & D.E. Paynter. 2003. It only looks like child's play. *Journal of Staff Development* 24 (2): 47–51.

Bodrova, E., D.J. Leong, D.E. Paynter & R. Hensen. 2002. *Scaffolding literacy development in a preschool classroom.* Aurora, CO: Mid-continent Research for Education and Learning.

Corsaro, W.A. 1988. Peer culture in the preschool. *Theory into Practice* 27 (1): 19–24.

Davidson, J.I.F. 1998. Language and play: Natural partners. In *Play from birth to twelve and beyond: Contexts, perspectives, and meanings,* eds. D.P. Fromberg & D. Bergen, 175–83. New York: Garland.

Elkonin, D. [1971] 1977. Toward the problem of stages in the mental development of the child. In *Soviet developmental psychology,* ed. M. Cole, 538–63. White Plains, NY: M.E. Sharpe.

Elkonin, D. 1978. *Psychologija igry* [The psychology of play]. Moscow: Pedagogika.

Fantuzzo, J., & C. McWayne. 2002. The relationship between peer-play interactions in the family context and dimensions of school readiness for low-income preschool children. *Journal of Educational Psychology* 94 (1): 79–87.

Howes, C., & C.C. Matheson. 1992. Sequences in the development of competent play with peers: Social and social pretend play. *Developmental Psychology* 28 (4): 961–74.

Krafft, K.C., & L.E. Berk. 1998. Private speech in two preschools: Significance of open-ended activities and make-believe play for verbal self-regulation. *Early Childhood Research Quarterly* 13 (4): 637–58.

Newman, L.S. 1990. Intentional and unintentional memory in young children: Remembering vs. playing. *Journal of Experimental Child Psychology* 50 (2): 243–58.

O'Reilly, A.W., & M.H. Bornstein. 1993. Caregiver-child interaction in play. *New Directions in Child Development* 59: 55–66.

Roskos, K. & J. Christie. 2001. Examining the play-literacy interface: A critical review and future directions. *Journal of Early Childhood Literacy* 1 (1): 59–89

Sigel, I. 2000. Educating the Young Thinker model from research to practice: A case study of program development, or the place of theory and research in the development of educational programs. In *Approaches to early childhood education,* 3d ed., eds. J.L. Roopnarine & J.E. Johnson, 315–40. Columbus, OH: Merrill/Macmillan.

Smilansky, S., & L. Shefatya. 1990. *Facilitating play: A medium for promoting cognitive, socio-emotional, and academic development in young children.* Gaithersburg, MD: Psychological and Educational Publications.

Vygotsky, L.S. [1966] 1977. Play and its role in the mental development of the child. In *Soviet developmental psychology,* ed. M. Cole, 76–99. White Plains, NY: M.E. Sharpe.

Vygotsky, L.S. [1930–35] 1978. *Mind in society: The development of higher psychological processes.* Cambridge, MA: Harvard University Press.

Carol Anne Wien with Bobbi-Lynn Keating,
Annette Coates Comeau, and Barbara Bigelow

7

Moving into Uncertainty:
Sculpture with 3- to 5-Year-Olds

"It's not playdough. It's sculpture,"

said Omar, one January day, when invited to put away the playdough before lunch. We found his comment intriguing. What could the term *sculpture* mean to him? Did other children in the room also think playdough creations were sculpture?

Bobbi teaches in the seniors classroom (children 3 to 5 years of age) at Peter Green Hall Children's Centre in Halifax, Nova Scotia, Canada. The center offers care for 91 children from infancy through school age. Situated in an apartment building for families of university students in the city, the center serves a group of children that is highly diverse both culturally and economically. During that year, I (Carol Anne) visited this classroom weekly as an educational consultant, listening, observing, and meeting with the staff—teachers Bobbi-Lynn Keating and Matthew Sampson, center artist/assistant director Annette Coates, and director Barb Bigelow.

The teachers thought Omar's comment was profound, and when Bobbi followed up, asking other children what they thought about sculpture, she found there was avid and startling interest. The following week I returned to find Omar's comment displayed on the documentation shelf, a place that shows and describes the children's work for families and others. The comment and several photos were accompanied by some lumpish play-dough animals—a cat, a turtle. What do 3- to 5-year-olds know about sculpture? What do they think it is? Where did their ideas come from? How do they differentiate between their usual playdough molding, which gets thrown back into the tub at the end of a session, and sculpture?

This article describes a six-month emergent curriculum project on sculpture in a child care center inspired by the Reggio Emilia approach (Edwards et al. 1998; Filippini & Vecchi 1996). The center has been working for 12 years to transform its curriculum into one that follows the minds of children—listening alertly to their ideas, desires, and hopes—and supports the children in expanding and developing their theories about the world with strong, purposeful curriculum activities embedded with rich learning (Wien et al. 2002; Wien et al. 2005). In addition to describing the sculpture project, we trace the thinking

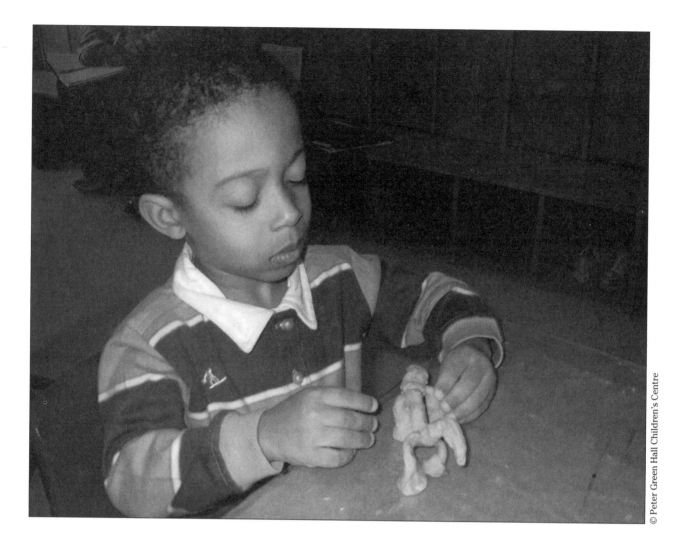

behind the decisions that teachers made to support the children's developing ideas.

First responses

For Bobbi and Matthew, the rash of new playdough animals and the children's insistence they were making sculpture was "this real scary discovery." The fear arose because neither knew anything about sculpture or how to make it, and the idea of embarking on an inquiry into the children's notions felt like "jumping without a net."

Carol Anne Wien is Full Professor in the Faculty of Education, York University in Toronto, Canada, and a board member of NAREA. **Bobbi Lynn Keating** is a preschool room teacher at Peter Green Hall Children's Centre in Halifax, Nova Scotia, Canada. **Annette Coates Comeau** is the director at Jubilee Road Children's Centre in Halifax. **Barbara Bigelow** is the executive director of the Peter Green Hall Children's Centre.

For several weeks, the teachers' response was to do more of the same—offer lots more playdough and begin to document what the children did with it. Pedagogical documentation is a teacher research process that educators use in the Reggio Emilia approach, and it is now widely adapted in early childhood settings in many countries (Fleet et al. 2006; Giudici et al. 2001; Hendrick 2004). Such documentation—in this case, taking photographs of children as they worked and noting their comments and conversations—helps to make children's theories and learning visible, both to themselves and to others (Edwards et al. 1998; Giudici et al. 2001). As a result of this documenting, Bobbi noticed the children's frustration with playdough as a medium. The children commented, "It won't stay together" and "It's breaking." Also, the children wanted to revisit their playdough sculptures to work more on them, but their works dried out and became fragile. The children seemed to hold the implicit notion that if it was sculpture, you kept it.

Problems open up a line of inquiry

Bobbi describes emergent curriculum as "like a road" she is on and sees a new problem arising as adding excitement to her work: "The problem gives me a direction." In this case, she went to Annette, an expert with materials, to discuss the children's frustrations. Annette thought immediately of potter's clay, but this material also dries out quickly and can be as fragile as playdough. She then suggested plasticine. Previously Bobbi had found plasticine unsuccessful: it was stiff and unyielding, and the children did only the most rudimentary rolling and sticking together with it. Annette suggested it might be more "sculptural" to keep the colors neutral—grays, black, white. This would focus attention on the tactile rather than the visual qualities of plasticine. Bobbi put aside her misgivings and agreed to try it, wondering what would happen.

During some small group times, when four or five children work together with a teacher on an activity, Bobbi would explore plasticine with the children. The children responded to the plasticine with increased focus on their work and experimented with added detail when Bobbi introduced real pottery tools, such as wedges, palette knives, and scribing tools. As they worked daily with the plasticine, the children's confidence with the material increased, and more and more children attempted ideas with the medium.

Through the ongoing documentation, the center staff and I saw that many children worked flat, creating their objects in two dimensions or attempted three-dimensional pieces without success. It is difficult to get three-dimensional materials to stand tall, and this property troubled the children. For example, five children were entranced by a basket of artificial sunflowers and tried to represent them in plasticine. Our documentation revealed repeated comments such as these:

"They are just lying down."

"Why won't they stand up?"

"They won't get up."

Bobbi noticed that the children's struggle to build vertically was constant as they worked with the plasticine.

The problem of vertical stability

Bobbi wondered whether to demonstrate how to make the children's work stand. Should the teachers show them what an artist might do? Malaguzzi, the former leader of the Reggio Emilia approach, talks about adults "loaning" their knowledge to children, but with the expectation that the loan will be "repaid" (1998). How far should the center staff go?

Annette suggested showing the children how an artist might use a wire armature as a framework for getting a sculpture to stand up in three dimensions. In several small group times, she wrapped rocks with wire and demonstrated how to add lumps of playdough to the wire and mold it on the armature. The children were enthralled. With their own wire-wrapped rocks, they explored bending the loose wire on top into shapes and adding clumps of gritty playdough (Annette had added coffee grounds for texture). These materials were highly effective for large-scale, three-dimensional work, and soon the children created a cat, a lizard, and a police dog with a worm on its back.

Sharing displays with the children

The teachers displayed six of the rock-and-wire-supported sculptures on a low shelf, a cloth underneath, with photos of each child working on his or her sculpture. Each was accompanied by a little card with the child artist's name and comment about the work. We found it interesting that even the 3-year-old children understood this arrangement *as a display*. While the children rearranged the items frequently, showing others the photos and labels and conversing about them, they did not play with the objects. They seemed to treasure the fact that their work was being kept and shown: some quality of permanence and visibility seemed central to their implicit notions of sculpture, though we can only hypothesize about the origin of their theories.

Four months earlier, a parent who worked at a kiln had donated leftover clay reclining figures. Several of these were on display around the classroom. These figures seemed a probable source for the children's theories, though we cannot be sure. If they were the source, it is an interesting example of the Reggio (and Montessori) notion of the power of the environment itself to teach. The idea is that resources and their organization in the room have the power to compel ideas and actions in the children (Malaguzzi 1998; Montessori 1964).

The children's evolving concepts of sculpture

One week I brought a box of wrapped objects, and Bobbi and I held a small group discussion with five children about whether each item could be sculpture or not. There was general consensus that a sculpture "has to be *hard.*" The children didn't consider a cloth otter to be sculpture, for instance, because it was soft. They clarified that sculpture might be soft first and then harden, like clay. They became confused by a stone polar bear carving, struggling with whether something made of "rock" occurred naturally. Scott said, for instance, "It's not sculpture because it's made of rock." Interestingly, the children referred to molding with playdough or clay as carving—"like carved out of playdough, carved out of clay."

The discussion astonished us because it lasted over an hour, long and intense. Did the children understand that sculpture is something that is human-made? They were confused by items they interpreted to be rock. At one point, when asked if an object was sculpture, Nicolas said, "I don't know. It's very mysterious."

Some of the 4-year-olds showed a clear sense of aesthetic evaluation of objects. Ike, for example, when considering a two-inch-high fuzzy teddy bear sitting on a miniature wooden chair, said no, it wasn't a sculpture "because it doesn't look beautiful." He said this with gentleness, even tenderness, as if it were a great sorrow for the bear not to be sculpture.

Walks in the community challenge the children's concepts

Teacher Matthew, who loves to do things outdoors with the children, thought it would be interesting to go on a sculpture walk to see if they could find any sculpture in the neighborhood. In March, they went on several walks, photographing and investigating objects the children claimed as sculpture. Sometimes there were disagreements, such as one about a boulder inlaid with a bronze plaque.

"It's not sculpture. It's a rock."

"Yes, but it's got writing on it."

One boy insisted that the clamshell carrier for skis on the roof of a car was sculpture, but couldn't say why he thought so. The carrier was indeed a streamlined shape easily described as sculpturesque. We found this presence of aesthetic sense in 4-year-olds notable.

Matthew organized the photographs from the sculpture walks on three panels, set low to encourage interaction among the children and parents, and much discussion occurred as the children revisited them. Many other activities were taking place in the classroom simultaneously, such as a study of faces led by Annette, an interest in building that moved from blocks on the carpet to miniatures with toothpicks and plasticine, as well as frequent play in housekeeping and story exploration in the library.

On another walk with Matthew, to a park bordering the ocean, the group of 16 children discovered an old military battery with concrete steps, platforms, and two strange iron structures like huge bolts with a hinge on one side and a latch on the other.

"It's a sculpture! It's hard."

"It's not a sculpture."

"No, it's broken." [*referring to the objects being rusty*]

"No, because it opens and closes."

Here the children appear to differentiate between objects that are practical and objects that are decorative. The concern for what is and what is not sculpture had captured the interest of most of the children in the classroom, and there was an implicit theory among them that if something had a practical function, then it was not sculpture.

Meanwhile, the classroom was flooded with images and discussion. Annette shared art books with sculptures by Michelangelo and others.

The defining characteristics

By late March, we could summarize the children's overall notions of sculpture as an object (1) made of hard material, (2) that has no functional purpose, and (3) is visible and permanently saved for others to see. Some children thought sculpture should be beautiful. There was confusion over whether naturally occurring shapes, such as rocks, are sculpture, and over how sculpture is made.

Further explorations in making sculpture

In late April, Tobias brought a "sculpture" from home and asked to have a small group with whom to share it. Five other boys were interested and formed a group, with Bobbi and me, to discuss the pair of painted plaster fighting dragons, wings wide and mouths stretched open in aggression.

Bobbi and I later realized that a new understanding was occurring for the boys during their discussion:

"But how did they make the eye good?"

"Maybe it's glass."

"Because they are artists."

"Maybe they cooked it." [*Perhaps he means firing in a kiln.*]

"Maybe they put it in the oven to dry up."

"It's not hot."

"Maybe they put it outside to cool."

"I was thinking about that."

When we reviewed the transcript of this conversation, we recognized how carefully the boys were thinking of "artists" in the process of making the dragons, hypothesizing intensely what might have happened to produce the sculpture, which had clear power for them. Reflecting on their conversation, we better understood Nicolas's remark, "Maybe we should make the same thing!"

This idea was immediately taken up by the group, infectious as wildfire, and propelled all of us to the art area, where Bobbi handed out chunks of plasticine. Much rolling of tails and pressing of bodies began. The boys worked furiously, with an urgency and concentration that had us paying close attention and almost breathless. What I call the "windhorse" effect in emergent curriculum had happened. I borrow this term from the secular Buddhist tradition of Shambhala (Trungpa 1987): it refers to raising a "wind" of energy and alertness, a sense of being alive in the moment. We could feel this energy all around the table, inside each of us—children and adults—a dynamic, positive, creative force.

The boys made long flat bodies with spikes down the back and used tools to make eyes and stretching mouths. Knowing their interest in having their sculptures stand, we commented that the sculpture Tobias had brought in stood up. "Ours are lying down," they said. But shortly after, Tobias wanted his creation to stand, and Bobbi found a spatula so he could pry it off the table. Pointing to a shelf, she offered him a choice of bases—rocks or

© Peter Green Hall Children's Centre

© Peter Green Hall Children's Centre

folded cardboard. Soon each boy chose a rock or cardboard base, attaching dragon bodies and long tails with spikes. The boys worked on their dragons without interruption for 80 minutes.

For days the boys did not touch their dragon work, sitting in view on a low table, but a week later they wanted to continue. We infer they needed an incubation period for their ideas to coalesce. On the next occasion, they worked with equally furious concentration, several of them for over an hour. They added a base of black plasticine "dirt," and skulls like those they noticed on the base of the sculpture. They also wanted to add horns on the dragons (Scott was having trouble making the horn stand up). Another child commented, "Everyone is working fabulously!"

Nicolas had made a two-foot long, pencil-thin roll with spikes all along it—"the green dragon," he said. Together we all studied the green dragon in the sculpture, how its head and neck curved up into the air. Nicolas attempted to lift his plasticine figure, but it was fragile, and broke.

Bobbi disappeared and quickly returned with wire and wire cutters. She demonstrated to Scott how to cut a length of wire the size of the horn he was working on. Together they folded the plasticine around the wire and placed the horn on the dragon's head. Scott saw that it worked beautifully. Nicolas stopped his work to watch several children constructing horns and finally said, "I need wire." After cutting a two-foot piece, he began to push the wire into the plasticine of his dragon. The coordination required to push the wire into the thin roll was so delicate that the task was very difficult for Nicolas. After 10 minutes, he was halfway; he wiped his forehead and went for a drink of water, fatigued by his intense effort. We wondered whether he could continue. He returned, and took another 10 minutes to complete his self-set task. When finished, he immediately lifted the dragon into the air like a trophy. He was very pleased, as were we.

We wondered whether he would think to bend the straight, pencil-thin dragon, but he didn't. The work of getting it up off the table into the air was itself a triumph.

One boy worked with ease and dexterity in three dimensions, but the others struggled, motivated to make their dragons three-dimensional but terrifically challenged by the problem. I speculate that they were trying to bring to plasticine the "language" of their expectations for drawing (Malaguzzi 1998; Steele 1998). The plasticine demanded they learn a new language, new ways of moving their hands and of thinking, the properties of a new material, and the discipline necessary to master those properties and develop a new "literacy." Such mastery requires the coordination of a third set of reference points compared to drawing: in addition to length and width, depth in space must be coordinated, requiring mathematical estimation.

Bobbi felt the task for her at this point was to support the children who were still working flat. What would help them understand the capacity of the material to work in three dimensions rather than two? What could she do so young children could be comfortable with the material and create to their satisfaction?

Next steps

In May, Bobbi and Annette brainstormed possible next steps in supporting the children's understanding of working in three dimensions. They decided to provide new materials and props for the children to explore—a wood plank base with three vertical rods plus soft and bendable wire, netting, hardware cloth, and ribbons. The children could wind, bend, fold, and wrap these around the rods, exploring vertical space. The wrapping board opened up new interests in the classroom, creating a kind of playscape that drew in different children, including several girls. But we focus here on something interesting that happened for Nicolas.

Nicolas enjoyed bending, folding, and wrapping the wire with an exploratory freedom. Suddenly it was more than a tool to allow his dragon to lift off the table. He cut a length of wire, coiled one end into a spiral, turned up the other end slightly, and said, "I think I'm making a chameleon. See, this is its tail. Isn't it fabulous!" His wire design was precise, succinct, expressed, as wire suggests, in two dimensions. He commented that he didn't remember "what a chameleon looks like" and asked for a reference book: "I need to look in that book to make my sculpture." He studied the photos of a chameleon and asked to do a sketch to "remember what it looks like." After several sketches he produced one he was pleased with.

We could see so much potential in these actions. Would Nicolas grasp that he could use the wire frame as an armature for a clay sculpture? Would he prefer to keep wire as the sculpture medium? We were impressed by his capacity to generate ideas and to follow through in developing them through study and through sketching. We saw that he had a sense of the preparatory work necessary for successful design. But what happened was one of those quirky unexpected things that has no clear explanation, except that it was unlikely it would have happened without everything that had occurred previously. It also shows how difficult it is to create nice, neat endings in a piece like this.

One day in June, Nicolas and Scott together decided to make an encyclopedia. It would show all the different penguins they had found in learning how to check out reference books. This work began during a noon hour and lasted several days, and the work went from tight, restricted drawing representations to a fluid expressivity that continues to astound us: how did Nicolas and Scott move from their previous drawings to this level of perceptual acuity and capacity to convey it? Who could have predicted that months of sculpture work would lead to fluent, graceful drawings? Yet the first principle of development in Copple and Bredekamp's summary of developmentally appropriate practice (2009) is that development in one domain affects development in other domains.

Teacher reflections

When a teacher sees a problem "as a direction," as Bobbi does, reflection becomes closely linked to planning the next step. Planning that is closely linked to a specific challenge, such as how to help children work in three dimensions, is suspenseful and uncertain, because the teachers do not know how the events will work out. Everyone gets excited to see what will happen.

The value of documentation

Documentation helps teachers study what children understand and plan what to do: we find it a crucial aid to reflection on teaching and learning. At our center, teachers use documentation as a habit of teaching. They alter displays weekly and provide a focus for conversation among children,

teachers, families, and visitors. The development of these skills has been part of the influence of the Reggio Emilia approach on the center (Cadwell 2003; Edwards et al. 1998; Wien 2008). Without such documentation, we might never have seen the children's initial frustration with playdough in a busy classroom.

In early June, we studied the documentation generated since January (36 pages of notes and transcripts, 100–120 digital images printed for individual portfolios and classroom documentation). It was only after we had reviewed the documentation from January to May, discussing what was most significant in terms of challenges to the children and tracing their development in those challenges as well as the teacher responses to those problems, that we saw clearly that Nicolas had shifted from using a straight wire in his dragon to working with wire with ease and facility to make a chameleon. Without the review of the documentation, we would not have seen the arc of development in his use of materials.

Teacher decision making

How do teachers decide what to plan, what resources to have available, and what to offer as supportive scaffolding when engaging in emergent curriculum? We found that the intriguing nature of the overall question—What do young children think sculpture is?—gave us direction. Our own sense of inquiry into what children think suggested possibilities for what to ask or try. Such inquiry engages us in problem solving. And a move that does not work well is not seen as an error, but rather as a step toward what will work: teaching is self-correcting.

Conclusion—Children learning, teachers learning

Throughout this project, the children understood that their ideas mattered and that they could participate in deciding what to do—such as offering a sculpture for discussion and deciding to re-create it. They understood they could trust teachers with their ideas, and that teachers would support their intentions—such as compiling a penguin encyclopedia. These are powerful learnings for children in a democracy; they will help the children learn how to participate in group decision making.

The teachers learned much about letting children explore and plan in an area they themselves scarcely knew about. We had no idea of the potential of sculpture for children this age. The fact that the children thought of their work as sculpture deepened their levels of exploration and conceptualization: it made their efforts more serious. The teachers learned as much as the children, and this joining of minds enlivens teaching and makes every move fresh and stimulating. The joy of a project is in its continual surprises and in the capacity of everyone involved to participate in this joy. The work was disciplined and focused, and it built skill in both children and teachers from week to week. It is the capacity of emergent curriculum to create joy that makes it memorable, sustainable, and unmatched in developing identity, culture, and attachment in both children and their teachers.

References

Cadwell, L.B. 2003. *Bringing learning to life: The Reggio approach to early childhood education.* New York: Teachers College Press.

Copple, C., & S. Bredekamp, eds. 2009. *Developmentally appropriate practice in early childhood programs serving children from birth through age 8.* 3d ed. Washington, DC: NAEYC.

Edwards, C., L. Gandini & G. Forman, eds. 1998. *The hundred languages of children: The Reggio Emilia approach—Advanced reflections.* Greenwich, CT: Ablex.

Filippini, T., & V. Vecchi, eds. 1996. *The Hundred Languages of Children: Narrative of the possible.* Catalog to the exhibit. Reggio Emilia, Italy: Reggio Children.

Fleet, A., C. Patterson, & J. Robertson, eds. 2006. *Insights: Behind early childhood pedagogical documentation.* Castle Hill, New South Wales, Australia: Pademelon.

Giudici, C., C. Rinaldi & M. Krechevsky, eds. 2001. *Making learning visible: Children as individual and group learners.* Reggio Emilia, Italy: Reggio Children; Cambridge, MA: Project Zero.

Hendrick, J., ed. 2004. *Next steps toward teaching the Reggio way: Accepting the challenge to change.* 2nd ed. Upper Saddle River, NJ: Pearson Merrill Prentice Hall.

Malaguzzi, L. 1998. History, ideas, and basic philosophy: An interview with Lella Gandini. In *The hundred languages of children: The Reggio Emilia approach—Advanced reflections,* 49–97. Greenwich, CT: Ablex.

Montessori, M. 1964. *The Montessori method.* New York: Schocken.

Steele, B. 1998. *Draw me a story: An illustrated exploration of drawing as language.* Winnipeg, MN: Peguis.

Trungpa, C. 1987. *Shambhala: The sacred path of the warrior.* Boston: Shambhala Books.

Wien, C.A., ed. 2008. *Emergent curriculum in the primary classroom: Interpreting the Reggio Emilia approach in schools.* New York: Teachers College Press.

Wien, C.A., A. Coates, B.L. Keating & B. Bigelow. 2005. Designing the environment to build connection to place. *Young Children* 60 (3): 16–22.

Wien, C.A., S. Stacey, B.L. Keating, J. Rowlings & H. Cameron. 2002. The doll project: Handmade dolls as a framework for emergent curriculum. *Young Children* 57 (1): 33–38.

Susan L. Golbeck

8

Building Foundations for
Spatial Literacy in Early Childhood

Words are only one way of symbolizing ideas.
We also use numbers, pictures, graphs, maps, diagrams, photographs, and other means to convey information. Researchers refer to notational systems such as graphs, diagrams, and maps as "inscriptions" (Lehrer & Schauble 2002). Inscriptions are tools that help us to perceive and to talk about our spatial worlds. For example, physicians use X-rays to talk about the body, and quilters use patterns to organize their stitching. The ability to use these nonlinguistic, graphic systems is useful in everyday life and vital for communications in the sciences, mathematics, the arts, engineering, and other professions.

Just as adults lay the groundwork for children to become proficient readers and writers of the English language, so too do they play a central role in teaching children to use spatial notational systems. By supporting children in making sense of and creating pictures, models, graphs, maps, and diagrams, they help children to become spatially literate.

Gestures, drawings, graphs, maps, models, photographs, images on a computer screen, and words (both oral and written) are all symbols. These symbols are cognitive tools that we use for learning new information, problem solving, and sharing ideas with others. All symbols, whether gestures, objects, or markings, can "stand for" something that is not present. Unlike written words, spatial symbols have a spatial relational correspondence to what they stand for.

A road map provides an example. Some of the markings on the map preserve the spatial relationships of the real world. Roads that intersect in the real world also intersect on the map. But maps contain other markings, such as lines of latitude and longitude, map legend, and compass, that do not correspond directly to any feature in the real world.

In another example, a photograph of a building might show a door with windows on either side of it. But the spatial symbol does not show a one-to-one correspondence in *all* aspects with what it represents. The image shows only one side of the building—three of the sides are not shown at all. Yet, even a preschool child looking at the photograph usually assumes that the building in the photograph has a back and sides.

Mastery of any spatial symbol system, like mastery of oral language, requires an understanding—sometimes an unconscious one—of a complex set of rules. This process begins during late infancy. As they become able to create and interpret pictorial and graphic symbols, such as a photograph on the outside of a box illustrating the contents, children have access to more information. Increased information helps children deal with more complex problems, communicate more effectively, and gain greater control over more of their social and physical worlds (DeLoache & Smith 1999; Liben & Downs 2001; Uttal 2000).

Success with using graphic symbols requires skilled imagining, drawing, and analysis of the spatial world. Such competence is complex. Many cognitive ability assessments, such as the Stanford Binet or the Weschler Intelligence Scales, include a spatial component. For young children these instruments might incorporate activities such as drawing, visual pattern recognition, and the reproduction of designs with unusual blocks. But spatial competence is also reflected in the visual motor skills required for bringing a spoon filled with cereal to the mouth, cutting with a knife and fork, tying a shoe, shooting a basketball through a hoop, weaving on a loom, folding Japanese paper patterns, interpreting an aerial photograph, sculpting a statue, or building a birdhouse. Indeed, spatial knowledge is a distinct aspect of human intelligence at the behavioral, cognitive, and neurological levels of analysis (Golomb 2004; Newcombe & Huttenlocher 2000; Shelton 2004).

Philosophers and cognitive psychologists have long debated the origins of spatial memory and spatial understanding. Contemporary researchers in neuroscience emphasize the importance of brain processes (Fischer & Rose 1996), while cognitive and educational psychologists focus on specific learning experiences (Allen & Huan 2004). Although the process is not fully understood, it seems clear that teachers and families play a central role in young children's emerging skills with spatial symbols.

Two broad trends can be identified from the research in cognitive and educational psychology. First, as they age, children become increasingly adept at aligning objects, or symbols of objects. Preschoolers easily organize objects with reference to the edge of a sheet of paper or a table top. As children become more experienced and can hold more information in mind at one time, they can organize representations by using two reference lines

Susan L. Golbeck is a former preschool teacher and currently an associate professor at Rutgers University.

at the same time. Children trying to reproduce an arrangement of pegs on a peg board usually need to think of a peg's placement with regard to both the horizontal lines of peg holes as well as the vertical columns of peg holes. Second, children also become better at understanding how the individual parts fit together to form a single coherent and integrated whole. For example, children can combine individual pieces in a puzzle and organize drawings of single "things" to create a picture filling a page. This process is called *part-whole integration*.

Findings "anchors in space"

Over the course of childhood, children become increasingly skilled at discovering how to anchor themselves and their ideas in space. Children's first "anchor" is their body. Infants and toddlers rely primarily on their body and the "axis" on which their bodies are oriented for remembering postions and for moving around their world. But even toddlers begin to make use of additional anchors outside the body. An anchor might be an object in space—the doorway or a distinctive corner. In combining the body anchor with the external anchor, a young child can remember how to move around, where things happened, and where to find things. By four or five, when children can think about more things at once, they become able to combine multiple reference points beyond their bodies.

Children also create an internal system of self-regulation that helps them see beyond conflicting or distracting cues in the environment. This internal system works with the external system to help structure the spatial world. A child also uses a mental system of self-regulation to manage a task in a poorly structured situation, such as writing a word on a blank, unlined sheet of paper. Maintaining letter orientation, letter placement, and horizontal alignment are not easy tasks for most beginning writers, and their struggles are evident in their early written products. (See **"Writing at the pre-axial level"** in the box on next page.)

Reproducing an arrangement, as in recreating an arrangement of blocks shown in a photograph or diagram, also calls for the coordination of external information with body-based references. In both the diagram and the new arrangement the child must locate corners, a baseline, and a top. In addition, internal features of the diagram must be properly identified (e.g., two triangular blocks, one pink and one green, combined to become a square and three more square blocks, all blue). Each block must be identified and then properly positioned in the child's re-creation.

According to cognitive developmental psychologists, children's spatial thinking appears to progress through several levels. Advances are determined by growing cognitive capacities and the child's specific experience in the world (Case et al. 1996; Case et al. 2001; Demetriou et al. 2002). Spatial thought in preschool-age children is typically *pre-axial,* which means that although children can represent objects and can remember location, they cannot coordinate these understandings with a stable reference point or line. They can represent individual items or objects, but they cannot keep track of, or symbolize, multiple items at once. Drawings by children at the pre-axial level depict objects floating in space weightlessly. (See **"Drawing at the pre-axial level."**)

Gradually, children develop a *uni-axial* system of spatial thinking in which their representations are organized along a single dimension. This shift usually occurs by age 6. Drawings at this level depict objects arranged along a single line, usually a horizontal ground line but sometimes along a vertical line. While these drawings are more organized than those at the earlier pre-axial level, the frame of reference remains simple and one dimensional. (See **"Drawing at the uni-axial level."**)

With experience and growing memory capabilities, children shift from a uni-axial to a *bi-axial* system for spatial representation. Children start to think about space in more precise terms and to encode more complex spatial relationships. They begin to organize drawings, mental images, and other representations along two dimensions simultaneously. (See **"Drawing at the early bi-axial level"** on next page.) In drawings, initial efforts to represent depth relations may appear, but since children have not fully coordinated or refined their understanding

Writing at the pre-axial level. A child's writing on unlined paper illustrates the child's difficulty in aligning letters. (Although the letters are not aligned, it is possible to "read" what the child wrote.)

Transition to uni-axial. Letters are arranged along a line but not aligned with the page.

Drawing at the pre-axial level.

Drawing at the uni-axial level.

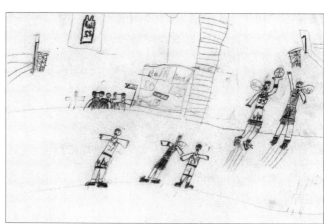

Drawing at the integrated bi-axial level

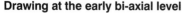

Drawing at the early bi-axial level

of how to use the two reference lines, they have difficulty representing three-dimensional space. Typically, the beginnings of a bi-axial system are evident around 8 or 9 years of age.

By age 10, most children have refined the bi-axial system to an *integrated bi-axial* level. They become capable of fully integrating two or more reference lines and they can connect the two in drawing. This can be seen in their depiction of depth relationships. (See **"Drawing at the integrated bi-axial level."**) While children do not precisely represent depth relationships, they display an intuitive understanding of them.

The box **"Children's Drawing and Spatial Conceptual Skill"** illustrates the developmental changes evident in children ranging in age from about 3 to about 10 years. Later, in adolescence, children become capable of still more advanced spatial reasoning as they integrate multiple reference systems. For example, they integrate a Cartesian-like coordinate reference system (the integrated bi-axial system just described) with a more developed understanding of perspective or point of view. At this time children can better understand linear perspective and depth relationships, especially if someone teaches them the conventions of their culture for drawing in this way. For example, Western art, from the 15th through the 19th centuries, placed a high priority on realism and a specific set of conventions for portraying it. Other cultural traditions prize

different features in drawing and sculpture, and children would learn about those instead.

Cognitive developmental psychologists point out that this sequence applies to activities besides drawing. Implicit frames of reference are used to organize written words on a page and to encode non-literal spatial arrays such as those shown in the box **"Seriation arrays"** on page 88. Look closely and see if you can find the pattern in each of the four arrays shown in the box. Children learn to anticipate the trajectory of a baseball or tennis ball and modify their actions accordingly. They may even try to depict such relationships in drawing, such as that shown in **"Representation of an imagined moving object"** on page 88.

Arrangements of three-dimensional models of familiar spaces provide further evidence of children's emerging spatial reference systems. In several studies (Golbeck 1995; Newcombe & Huttenlocher 2000; Siegel & Schadler 1975), young children were presented with a small-scale model of their classroom and asked to align model furniture pieces just as they were in the real classroom. The children placed items near walls, corners, and rug edges more accurately than items far from such reference frames. They also had difficulty coordinating the positioning and placement of many furniture items simultaneously.

When children create drawings and diagrams of the physical world, they also rely upon spatial reference systems. Trees on hillsides, chimneys on sloping roofs, water levels in tipped containers, and plumb lines illustrate invariant horizontals/verticals in the physical world that can be in conflict with the most immediate reference line. Children use mental reference systems to encode the physical position and orientation of objects and to track movement. For example, they explore how the cone-shaped block rolls down the incline or why water poured through the funnel turns the water wheel. In these situations, children's spatial awareness supports their ability to infer causality. Thinking about these events and drawing diagrams of the relationships among the objects also requires skill in perceiving the relationships between individual items in the array, imagining and representing that knowledge on a two dimensional surface.

An understanding of perspective or point of view is another type of spatial reference frame or reference system. Children are intrigued by the apparent distortions of projections (e.g., shadows cast at different times of the day), yet they are unlikely to understand the patterns and regularities of projective geometry. Projective systems of reference guide the cartographer creating maps, the scientist developing graphs, and the artist drawing in linear perspective. In each of these areas extensive cultural and societal knowledge about the particular disciplines and problem areas is integrated with experience on the part of the individual knower or worker. As children develop mental processing abilities, so too do they learn to effectively make use of spatial symbolic tools.

Children's Drawing and Spatial Conceptual Skill

The chart illustrates shifts in children's drawing, from about age 4 through about age 10. The drawings depict a still-life arrangement (right) and a landscape featuring a mother, father, and baby in a park, with a tree in the distance.

Landscape drawing	Still-life drawing

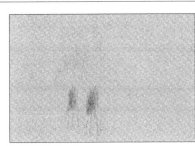 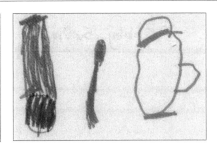

Spatial representational competence level: Pre-axial—about age 4

Spatial representational competence level: Uni-axial—about age 6

Spatial representational competence level: Bi-axial—about age 8

Spatial representational competence level: Integrated bi-axial—about age 10

Cognitive psychologists offering the explanation of emerging reference systems maintain that children's progress in spatial reasoning results from cognitive growth, experience with the world, instruction from adults, and opportunities to integrate all of these within enjoyable, meaning-making experiences such as play (Case et al. 2001). Importantly, progress in spatial thinking results both from interactions with others while thinking and talking about problems in the spatial world and from the child's overall social, emotional, and cognitive development (Demetriou et al. 2002; Rogoff 1990).

Part-whole integration

A second element of spatial thinking is the ability to integrate the parts and the whole in any spatial array or spatial experience. The gist of the part-whole integration problem is that young children often (although not always) have trouble simultaneously maintaining the integrity of parts and the whole that the parts compose.

Interest in this problem dates back many years. David Elkind studied part-whole integration in a series of studies using black-and-white line drawings (Elkind et al. 1964). He and his colleagues showed young children ambiguous pictures in which objects, such as fruit, were arranged to look like a recognizable whole, such as a man, and they were asked to describe what they saw. (See the box **"Ambiguous figures"** below.) Younger children initially reported seeing only global wholes (the man), whereas slightly older children reported that they saw parts (the fruit), but they were unable to see the picture both ways. Sometime during the early elementary school years, children begin to be able to offer fully integrated responses ("A man made out of fruit").

Difficulties were attributed to children's overall cognitive limitations and pre-operational intelligence (Elkind et al. 1964). However, later work suggests that this conclusion underestimates children's skills. A closer look at children's responses under controlled time conditions reveals a cognitive processing factor at work (Whiteside et al. 1976). When young children were given more time to view the pictures, they offered more complete responses, although they never explicitly stated that the whole was "made out of" the parts. Instead, they reported,

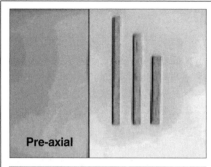

Pre-axial

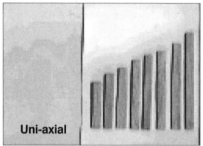

Uni-axial

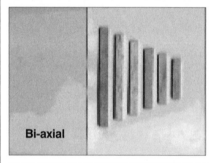

Bi-axial

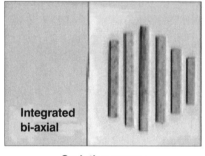

Integrated bi-axial

Seriation arrays

Representation of an imagined moving object

 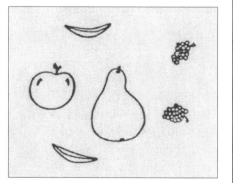

Ambiguous figures—Parts arranged to look like something else

"Apples, bananas, grapes—a *man!*" Older children simply said, "A man made out of fruit." In other words, young children seemed able to see the picture both ways, but it took them longer; they seemed uncertain how to describe the ambiguous pictures and they seldom used complex language.

Drawings illustrate the problems children have in integrating parts into a whole. For example, in the box "Children's Drawing and Spatial Conceptual Skill," children about 4, 6, 8, and 10 years of age were shown a still-life arrangement on a table and asked to draw what they saw. While older children organized the individual elements into a coherent whole, the younger children depicted objects floating freely in space. Along the same lines, Piaget ([1930] 1972) reported the difficulties children encountered when he asked them to draw a bicycle. Even if children looked at the bicycle while they drew, they seemed to find it extremely challenging to portray the various components in a connected, integrated fashion. Young children often portrayed the most salient parts in a disconnected manner or as a global whole lacking any detail. With age came greater attention to detail and varying strategies for integrating the parts into the whole. Piaget intriguingly pointed out that the drawings of bicycles and children's explanations of how bicycles worked were closely related.

Recently, Sophian (2004) examined the children's understanding of part-whole relations within the context of mathematical thinking. She finds that young children can make use of intuitive spatial reasoning to solve simple mathematical problems. Little attention has been devoted to such spatial reasoning in the context of mathematics instruction, and Sophian has designed an innovative preschool curriculum to partially address this deficit.

Children's work with small-scale models of familiar spaces, such as their classrooms, also shows the fragile nature of early part-whole integration (Golbeck 1995; Golbeck et al. 1986). Preschool-age children find it challenging to arrange items in a small-scale three-dimensional classroom model "so it looks like school." Most 4-year-olds can recognize and position individual items when other items are already in place. They also can locate clusters of furniture items correctly. However, they have difficulty integrating multiple clusters into the larger space of the model room. Children have greater success when their attention is directed to specific functional areas or "parts" of the room and the furniture it contains (e.g., the art area or the block area). This seems to help children break down the complexity of the task and integrate the parts (including both the individual furniture items and the functional groupings) within the whole (both the functional groupings and the larger classrooms space). Researchers in Britain studying young children's ability to create model landscapes of familiar spaces, such as their neighborhoods, report a similar pattern of findings (Blades et al. 2004).

Both interpreting professional maps and creating informal sketch maps present part-whole dilemmas. Sketch maps, or casual maps drawn by lay people, often show a single route or pathway between two familiar points, while failing to account for the larger context in which the route is situated. Integration problems also occur in sketch maps when adults are asked to "draw a map" of a familiar environment. Maps of familiar portions of the environment are often larger and contain more detail, overwhelming the representation of the less familiar spaces. Young children's early maps follow a similar progression.

Implications for teachers

Spatial literacy is embedded in nearly every discipline in the school curriculum, including mathematics, social studies, science, and the arts. Spatial competence and skill with spatial symbols is essential for careers in engineering, mathematics, science, graphic design and other arts, and many trades and professions, from carpentry to biomedical engineering. By promoting spatial understanding early in life, adults give children an important foundation for the future. Yet teachers do not need another topic in an already crowded curriculum. Rather, they need to understand how to enhance children's spatial reasoning within the context of the work they are already doing.

Mathematics

In its standards, the National Council of Teachers of Mathematics (NCTM) identifies geometry as an important area, often in need of more attention in current early childhood mathematics curricula (NCTM 2000). Within mathematics, geometry focuses specifically upon spatial relationships and measurement. Recognizing and naming common shapes is certainly a component of spatial thinking. But teachers extend children's mathematical understanding when they encourage children to compare, to transform, and to actively discover relationships within and between shapes. For example, a teacher might encourage children to discuss the different ways to create a block tower as "high as the window sill." Children can keep a record of the different block shapes and the orientation of the blocks they use. (For an in-depth review of research on children's mathematical thinking, see Ginsburg et al. 1998.)

Many math manipulatives draw upon children's spatial thinking. Montessori recognized the significance of spatial features in the design of her materials. She thoughtfully combined variations in a spatial feature, such as size or volume, and then kept all other physical features, such as color, constant or unchanged. So, children explore length and differences in length when they work with the "red rods." The set of large rods vary in length but are always red and made of wood. When children place them on the floor, differences in length are very obvious.

Teachers need to think carefully about how and why they are encouraging children to use manipulatives. Color and shape may not matter much for counting activities, but they are important for geometry. Combinations of color, shape, and volume can make the discovery of geometric characteristics more challenging and interesting or simply more difficult.

Spatial thinking enters into other areas of mathematics too. While teachers know that children make use of spatial thinking to solve math problems, some view these strategies as impediments to success (Bryant & Squire 2001). Children generate some remarkable explanations and solutions, drawing upon apparent relationships that adults have learned to ignore. There are times when reliance upon spatial cues can lead to errors. For example, the number conservation task, in which a child is asked to judge the equality of two rows of objects before and after a transformation, is frequently solved incorrectly by children who report that there are more objects in the row with end points further apart or in the "longer" row. Yet spatial

awareness can correct for this problem, too, when children recognize that not only is one row longer but there is also more empty space between the objects in that row.

Mathematics brings together spatial reference systems and part-whole integration. This begins with early experience in measurement, usually along a single line (single axis). Key to this early geometric thinking is the idea of using one *unit*, over and over again. A unit, if it is a standard size, is easy to talk about with other people; individual units can be organized into a larger whole. For example, an inch is a standard unit. Inches can be combined into feet.

Teachers can demonstrate the power of these ideas by having children apply them to a meaningful task, such as making a diagram of the classroom layout. The class begins with the idea that the walls of the room can be measured in feet. On the diagram, created on graph paper, one foot will equal one side of one square. (Large size graph paper helps here.) Measuring along one wall in the real room is measuring along one axis. As the class translates this information to the graph paper, the children are creating a symbol for the space (e.g., tracing the sides of 10 blocks to represent 10 feet of the wall). The next big task occurs when the class measures a wall that touches the first wall at a corner, forming a right angle. With the addition of measurement information for this wall, the class is beginning to create a second axis. The line symbolizing the second wall will be oriented at a right angle to the line of the first wall. The measurement unit, the foot, remains the same. With the addition of the second line (second axis) to the graph paper, the children have created a coordinate reference system. The lines representing the walls, meeting at a right angle, will work as good anchors for the rest of the diagram. The remaining items in the room can be located using these two lines. Within the context of early geometry, the notions of part-whole integration and frames of reference are powerful ideas with great practical utility for teaching and learning.

Many familiar early childhood practices foster spatial thinking, and many traditional materials serve this goal. Unit blocks are an excellent manipulative to support children's understanding of part-whole relations as well as a horizontal/vertical reference system. Unit blocks are rectangular blocks measuring about 5 x 1 x 2½ inches. They come in sets with half, double, and quadruple units. While children build and explore with unit blocks they solve problems in spatial visualization, spatial orientation, planning and problem solving, and implicit measurement; they make implicit judgments about length; and they recognize the importance of orientation and position. They also must become sensitive to horizontals and verticals in the environment as they struggle with balance and symmetry.

While some teachers acknowledge the value of blocks, they seem uncomfortable engaging with children in the block area. Yet learning can be enhanced when an adult converses about the activity, encourages building elaboration through modeling and questioning and hinting, and embellishes the overall activity with creative play.

In my own work, I have studied the complexity of unit block construction in relation to performance on other measures of spatial knowledge and graphic skill in writing and drawing. Block-building scores were related to every other measure of spatial thinking including problem solving, drawing, and writing (Golbeck 2003). There is every reason to believe that appropriately structured social interactions with adults and peers foster such abilities (Eberly & Golbeck 2004).

Teachers can also incorporate graphics and diagrams, such as those accompanying Lego blocks, to encourage spatial symbolization, part-whole integration, perspective-taking, and spatial visualization. Researchers have only begun to study the complexity of young children's interpretations of diagrams and illustrations (Gauvain et al. 2001; Szechter & Liben 2003). Lego blocks, Unifix cubes, and Cuisenaire rods can all be used with graphics and diagrams either prepared by the teacher (or publisher) or created by children.

Pattern blocks and parquetry blocks, with flat, colored shapes reminiscent of old-fashioned quilting, can be used both with and without frames. *Frame* used here means a card with a design that children cover with blocks, an actual physical frame that children fill with a design, or even hoops that might be used to define groups, as in a Venn diagram. These activities are especially good for promoting part-whole integration. Clements (2004) and colleagues (Sarama & Clements 2004) have

created an interesting math program integrating technology and computer images with traditional pattern blocks.

Social studies

Teachers can also promote spatial literacy and competence in social studies and early geography. Children are familiar with miniaturized and overhead views of a space; models and mats for miniatures depicting roadways, houses, and similar scenes are popular. Yet these commercially marketed models and schematics almost never correspond to the real places in which children live, and they are not symbols for a specific place or space. To foster children's thinking about space, symbols that correspond to the real environs children live in and move through are essential. Children need experience with meaningful symbols.

Blaut (1997) and colleagues showed that

© Anna Volk

kindergartners could identify locations within their communities on black-and-white aerial photographs. The photographs were of familiar places and taken close enough to the ground so children could identify specific buildings. Aerial photos share many features with maps, and they show us how competent children can be. The Internet now gives access to many kinds of images not readily available before, such as aerial views and satellite photos of specific locations. The U.S. Geological Survey website is one source of information. Teachers can use symbolized spaces such as a scale model of the school, playground, or classroom along with aerial views. With assistance and using maps as examples, children can create models of familiar spaces (Blades et al. 2004; Liben & Downs 2001).

Young children can understand such representations and enjoy the opportunity to create and work with them. With help from teachers, they can create a model of the school and neighborhood. As children play and talk about their everyday experiences, teachers can encourage questions about location and spatial organization and about what information to include in the model. Such activities also could include different symbolic representations of the same space. For example, an interesting playground space could be represented with a model, a mat for miniature objects and figures, photographs, maps at different viewing angles, and different kinds of drawings.

Science

Nearly all approaches to science include the close observation of physical phenomena. The activities of observing and recording draw upon spatial skills, as does the representation of information for oneself and for others. Consider for example children's emerging understanding of shadows and light.

Children find creating shadows intriguing, but they come to understand shadow phenomena through a progressive coordination of relationships among four elements: an object, a shadow, a wall or projection screen, and light (DeVries et al. 2002). Understanding how to effect changes in shadows requires coordinating representations of object position, distance, light projection, and shadow size and orientation. With experience, social interaction, and active exploration of the surprising shapes that shadows of objects in different positions create,

children come to understand the relationships among all four elements of the problem (DeVries et al. 2002). Using a balance scale, reading a thermometer, identifying physical transformations, and graphing and charting findings all build spatial thinking as well as scientific understanding (see Gelman & Brenneman 2004). These issues are also explored by Ginsburg and Golbeck (2004).

Literacy

Because most children express knowledge with gestures before words, an important part of the early literacy curriculum involves helping them to express spatial understanding with words. Appropriate language and vocabulary is needed to talk about the relationships of space. Adults can regularly name and reinforce shape, position, and directionality with children. Discussions of pictures in children's books have great potential to foster this knowledge (Szechter & Liben 2003).

Spatial knowledge is an important component of writing. Organizing language on a page—in the case of English, from left to right in a straight line—is no simple feat. The positioning of the shapes of specific letters within words also can be complex. Consider, for example, the word *gargoyle*. Its letters extend above and below the writing line, having horizontal, vertical, and diagonal components. Successful placement of these elements is difficult for early writers.

Awareness of the left-to-right movement across the line of text is also an important component skill in reading English. Skeen and Rogoff (1987), in a Vygotskian perspective, say such an orientation serves to direct children's attention in tasks other than reading, such as searching for a specific image in a complex photograph or locating an item on crowded shelves. Teachers can foster such attention to direction across a variety of classroom activities, for instance, by organizing objects on shelves, creating classroom displays, hanging objects on the walls, and devising interesting matrix activities.

Visual arts

The visual arts include numerous opportunities to promote spatial thinking, both through the process of creating and in an analysis of creations. An appreciation of aesthetic principles such as symmetry and balance is linked to frame of reference and part-whole integration.

There is general agreement among experts that the visual arts have an important place in the early childhood curriculum. However, many teachers are not even aware of the limitations of their own understandings of art. Harlan (1996) examined preservice elementary and early childhood teachers' ideas about art and found that teachers either viewed art as an opportunity for free self-expression or as an activity synonymous with crafts. They were largely unaware of the cognitive challenges in art making and had little idea of how to bring those ideas to the classroom. A visual arts curriculum is inherently centered around spatial ideas and helping children appreciate the power of spatial symbols and images. Harlan's work suggests that a great deal needs to be done to help teachers who are outside the arts field understand just how to bring this about.

Some teachers are hesitant to ask children to draw from observation. Yet work from the Reggio perspective suggests that such guided exploration is important for children and may help explain the wide cultural and contextual differences in their artistic productions (Winner 1989). Teachers may want to arrange interesting sets of objects and invite children to draw what they see—and to talk about the objects both before and after they draw. This type of activity is enriched by shared reading of children's books on and discussion of master artworks, both traditional and contemporary. Such interactions create an active meaning-making experience for young children. When teachers themselves feel comfortable with the arts, they will be more effective in discussing the art-making process with children and also in making use of the rich opportunities it provides for spatial literacy.

Conclusion

Research from cognitive and educational psychology provides direction for teachers interested in promoting children's spatial literacy. The ability to understand and use spatial symbols progresses over the course of childhood as children become better able to integrate information and make use of stable reference systems. This research also suggests strategies teachers can use to reach

these goals within the context of the early childhood curriculum.

References

Allen, G., & D. Huan. 2004. Proximity and precision in spatial memory. In *Human spatial memory: Remembering where*, ed. G. Allen, 41–66. Mahwah, NJ: Erlbaum.

Blades, M., C. Spencer, B. Plester & K. Desmond. 2004. Young children's recognition and representation of urban landscapes. In *Human spatial memory: Remembering where*, ed. G. Allen, 287–308. Mahwah, NJ: Erlbaum.

Blaut, J. 1997. Children can. *Annals of the Association of American Geographers* 87: 152–58.

Bryant, P., & S. Squire. 2001. Children's mathematics: Lost and found in space. In *Spatial schemas and abstract thought*, ed. M. Gaddis, 175–200. Cambridge, MA: MIT Press.

Case, R., S. Griffin & W. Kelly. 2001. Socioeconomic differences in children's early cognitive development and their readiness for schooling. In *Psychological perspectives on early childhood education: Reframing dilemmas in research and practice*, ed. S. Golbeck, 37–63. Mahwah, NJ: Erlbaum.

Case, R., K. Stephenson, C. Bleiker & Y. Okamoto. 1996. Central spatial structures and their development. In *The role of central conceptual structures in the development of children's thought*, eds. R. Case & Y. Okamoto. Monographs of the Society for Research in Child Development, vol. 61, nos. 1–2, serial no. 246. Oxford: Blackwell.

Clements, D. 2004. Geometric and spatial thinking in early childhood education. In *Engaging young children in mathematics: Standards for early childhood math education*, eds. D.H. Clements & J. Sarama, 267–97, Mahwah, NJ: Erlbaum.

DeLoache, J., & C.M. Smith. 1999. Early symbolic representation. In *Development of mental representation: Theories and applications*, ed. I.E. Sigel, 61–86. Mahwah, NJ: Erlbaum.

Demetriou, A., C. Christou, G. Spandoudis & M. Platsidou. 2002. *The development of mental processing: Efficiency, working memory, and thinking*. Monographs of the Society for Research in Child Development, vol. 67, serial no. 268. Oxford: Blackwell.

DeVries, R., B. Zan, R. Edmiaston & R. Wohlwend. 2002. Casting shadows. In *Developing constructivist early childhood curriculum*, eds. R. DeVries, B. Zan, C. Hildebrandt, R. Edmiaston & C. Sales, 77–101. New York: Teachers College Press.

Eberly, J., & S. Golbeck. 2004. Blocks, building and mathematics: Influences of task format and gender of play partners among preschoolers. *Advances in Early Education and Child Care* 13: 39–54.

Elkind, D., R.R. Koegler & E. Go. 1964. Studies in perceptual development II: Part-whole perception. *Child Development* 35: 81–90.

Fischer, K., & S. Rose. 1996. Dynamic growth cycles of brain and development. In *Developmental neuroimaging: Mapping the development of brain and behavior,* eds. R. Thatcher, G. Lyon, J. Rumsey, & N. Krasnegor. New York: Academic.

Gauvain, M., J.L. del Ossa & M. Hurtado-Ortiz. 2001. Parental guidance as children learn to use cultural tools: The case of pictoral plans. *Cognitive Development* 16: 551–75.

Gelman, R., & K. Brenneman. 2004. Science learning pathways for young children. *Early Childhood Research Quarterly* 19 (1): 150–59.

Ginsburg, H., & S. Golbeck. 2004. Thoughts on the future of research on early learning in math and science. *Early Childhood Research Quarterly* 19 (1): 190–200.

Ginsburg, H., P. Starkey & A. Klein. 1998. The development of children's mathematical thinking: Connecting research with practice, In *Child psychology in practice,* eds, I.E. Sigel & K.A. Renninger, 401–78. Vol. 4 of *Handbook of child psychology,* 5th ed., ed. W. Damon. New York: Wiley.

Golbeck, S. 1995. The social context and children's spatial representations: Recreating the world with blocks, drawings and models. *Advances in Early Education and Care* 7: 213–50, Greenwich CT: JAI Press.

Golbeck, S. 2003. Promoting young children's thinking with blocks. Unpublished final report to the Spencer Foundation, Grant # SG 200100262.

Golbeck, S., M. Rand & C. Soundy. 1986. Constructing a model of a large-scale space with the space in view: Effects of guidance and cognitive restructuring. *Merrill Palmer Quarterly* 32: 187–203.

Golomb, C. 2004. *The child's creation of a pictorial world.* Mahwah, NJ: Erlbaum.

Harlan, S. 1996. Exploring early childhood education students' beliefs about art education. PhD diss., Graduate School of Education, Rutgers University, New Brunswick, New Jersey.

Lehrer, R., & L. Schauble. 2002. Symbolic communication in mathematics and science: Co-constituting inscription and thought. In *Language, literacy and cognitive development: The development and consequences of symbolic communication,* eds. E. Amsel & J. Byrnes, 167–92. Mahwah, NJ: Erlbaum.

Liben, L., & R. Downs. 2001. Geography for young children: Maps as tools for learning environments. In *Psychological perspectives on early childhood education,* ed. S. Golbeck, 220–52. Mahwah, NJ: Erlbaum.

NCTM (National Council of Teachers of Mathematics). 2000. *Principles and standards for school mathematics.* Reston, VA: Author. Online: http://standards.nctm.org.

Newcombe, N., & J. Huttenlocher. 2000. *Making space: The development of spatial representation and reasoning.* Cambridge MA: MIT Press.

Piaget, J. [1930] 1972. *The child's conception of physical causality.* Totowa, NJ: Littlefield, Adams.

Rogoff, B. 1990. *Apprenticeship in thinking: Cognitive development in social context.* Cambridge, MA: Harvard University Press.

Sarama, J., & D. Clements. 2004. Building blocks for early childhood mathematics. *Early Childhood Research Quarterly* 19: 181–89.

Shelton, A. 2004. Putting spatial memories into perspective: Brain and behavioral evidence for representational differences. In *Human spatial memory: Remembering where,* ed. G. Allen, 309–28. Mahwah, NJ: Erlbaum.

Siegel, A.W., & M. Schadler. 1975. The development of young children's spatial representations of their classrooms. *Child Development* 48: 388–94.

Skeen, J.A., & B. Rogoff. 1987. Children's difficulties in deliberate memory for spatial relationships: Misapplications of verbal mnemonic strategies? *Cognitive Development* 2: 1–9.

Sophian, C. 2004. Mathematics for the future: Developing a Head Start curriculum to support mathematics learning. *Early Childhood Research Quarterly* 19: 59–81.

Szechter, L.E., & L.S. Liben. 2003. Parental guidance in preschoolers' understanding spatial-graphic representations. *Child Development* 75: 869–85.

Uttal, D. 2000. Seeing the big picture: Map use and the development of spatial cognition. *Developmental Science* 3: 247–64.

Whiteside, J., C. Elkind & S. Golbeck. 1976. Effects of exposure duration in part-whole perception in children. *Child Development* 47: 498–501.

Winner, E. 1989. How can Chinese children draw so well? *Journal of Asestheic Education* 23 (1): 41–63.

Executive Function and the Development of Self-Regulation

The ability to analyze situations, plan, focus and maintain attention, and adjust one's actions to complete a task is known to neurologists and psychologists as *executive function*. To early childhood educators the more familiar term is *self-regulation*. We should bear in mind that executive function or self-regulation is more than just impulse control; it is the managing and orchestration of many cognitive functions. A growing research base links this ability strongly to school success; in fact, the level of executive function is more predictive of school achievement than is IQ (Blair 2002). In the social arena as well, the ability to pause and think through the possible consequences before acting promotes positive relationships and peer acceptance.

On this important topic the first selected article is **"Recognizing and Supporting the Development of Self-Regulation in Young Children"** by Martha Bronson, the author of *Self-Regulation in Early Childhood: Nature and Nurture*. She begins by outlining the child's development of self-regulation and summarizing the place of self-regulation in five theoretical perspectives—psychoanalytic, behavioral, social learning, cognitive-developmental, and information processing. Bronson then turns to how caregivers and teachers can support children's development of self-regulation at each life stage from infancy through the early school years, emphasizing that the social-emotional context is critical throughout this course of development. Indeed, the cognitive and social-emotional aspects of self-regulation are so intertwined that looking at self-regulation virtually compels us to look at both together, as Bronson does here.

A major way that children are able to regulate their own behavior is through private speech—"thinking out loud," as the authors of the next selection call it. Eventually this outloud speech becomes internalized as thought. Using Vygotsky's work, educational consultants and authors Becky Bailey and Carolyn Brookes trace the evolution of private speech in early childhood and provide teaching guidance for supporting its use in **"Thinking Out Loud: Development of Private Speech and the Implications for School Success and Self-Control."** The authors note, for example, that preschoolers tend to blurt out their comments and responses, and adults often see this behavior as rude and immature. But when they understand that children need to verbalize their ideas on the spot and are not yet able to "hold that thought," teachers can alter their practice in activities such as story reading. Instead of requiring children to wait and respond one at a time to a question or something in the story that grabs their attention—and usually forgetting during the wait what they were going to say—the teacher pauses to give them a chance to exchange their thoughts with assigned buddies before she moves on with the story.

Bailey and Brookes' article is an excellent illustration of how increased knowledge of children's cognitive development helps teachers to do their job better. Without such knowledge—in this case, understanding of the function and maturation of private speech—teachers tend to misinterpret child behaviors (such as blurting) and thus react in ways that frustrate children and hinder development instead of optimizing it. The insights and strategies offered here will enable teachers to view private speech as an important stepping stone to self-regulation and treat it accordingly.

Children's development of both symbolic thinking and self-regulation in early childhood enables them to plan and reflect. Experience with planning and reflection, in turn, strengthens children's symbolic and self-regulatory abilities. Ann Epstein, senior director of curriculum development at the HighScope Foundation, describes proven methods for promoting these abilities in **"How Planning and Reflection Develop Young Children's Thinking Skills."** The approach she describes involves development of both symbolic thought (the mental representations needed to plan and to reconstruct events) and self-regulation with its "stop and think" component. I could have flipped a coin to determine whether to place her article with those on symbolic thought or those on self-regulation. I chose the latter because the self-regulatory activities of planning and reflecting back on one's experiences are both pervasive and fundamental in this educational approach.

The Tools of the Mind model (which has elements in common with the HighScope approach described by Ann Epstein in her article) derives from Vygotskian theory and places self-regulation front and center. Its founders and directors, Deborah Leong and Elena Bodrova, authored the next selection, **"Developing Self-Regulation in Kindergarten: Can We Keep All the Crickets in the Basket?"** In section 1, their "Chopsticks" article focuses on promoting high-level play with its many contributions to learning and development, which include both symbolic development and self-regulation. In the selection here, the lens rotates a few degrees to a direct focus on self-regulation and all the ways that Tools of the Mind promotes it (including but not limited to play). Classrooms around the country that use the Tools of the Mind approach have shown impressive success with children growing up in poverty and other difficult life circumstances, even though these children often enter the program significantly lacking in self-regulation. Visiting a Tools classroom, one is struck by the way children are working and playing with engagement, focused attention, and cooperation. The crickets indeed are in the basket, and learning is under way.

Reference

Blair, C. 2002. School readiness: Integrating cognition and emotion in a neurobiological conceptualization of child functioning at school entry. *American Psychologist* 57 (2): 111–27.

Martha B. Bronson

9

Recognizing and Supporting the Development of Self-Regulation in Young Children

Distressing headlines and teachers' own experiences in homes and classrooms point to the need for children to develop self-control, self-direction, and positive strategies for coping with life situations. Teachers want to help children develop these skills—to help them learn to control their emotions, interact with others in positive ways, avoid inappropriate or aggressive actions, and become self-directed learners. Each of these abilities has been investigated as a form of what is termed *self-regulation*.

There has been a striking increase in both public and academic interest in self-regulation in recent years (Barkley 1997; Baumeister & Vohs 2004; Bronson 2000; Gross 2007; Shonkoff & Phillips 2000). In order to support the development of self-regulatory skills, teachers need to understand how the skills develop and how psychological theory and research suggest that social and physical environment can help.

Research suggests that the capacity to develop self-regulatory functions is present from birth (Barkley 1997), is somewhat affected by innate factors such as temperament (Rothbart et al. 2004), and is highly influenced by the environment (Calkins & Hill 2007; Grolnick & Farkas 2002). It is related to both social competence (Eisenberg & Fabes 1992) and success in school (McClelland et al. 2006; Zimmerman & Schunk 1989). There is also evidence that early self-control is related to self-control in later childhood (Eisenberg et al. 1996; 1997) and throughout life (Sroufe et al. 1993).

During the early childhood years, there is a great increase in self-regulation. This increase is a "central and significant" developmental hallmark of this period (Flavell 1977) and a "cornerstone" of early development that cuts across all domains of behavior (Gillespie & Seibel 2006). During these years, the child makes tremendous progress toward regulating emotional responses (Eisenberg & Fabes 1992; Eisenberg et al. 2004; Fox 1994) and is increasingly able to comply with external requests (Kopp 1982; 1989), control behavior in familiar settings (Luria 1961; Mischel & Mischel 1983), control attention (Barkley 1997; Holtz & Lehman 1995; Rueda et al. 2004; 2005), and engage in self-directed thinking and problem solving (Brown & Deloache 1978; Deloache & Brown 1987; Friedman et al. 1987; Hudson & Fivush 1991; Rueda et al. 2005).

A classic summary by Kopp (1982) described the developmental progression—from control of arousal and sensory motor functions in the early months of life, to a beginning ability to comply with external suggestions at the end of the first year, to emergence of internal impulse control in the second year. Kopp notes that increasingly sophisticated forms of self-regulation develop from age 3 or 4 onward. With maturation and appropriate experiences, the child becomes increasingly capable of deliberate action, planning ahead, and conscious control.

Self-regulation is described in a number of different ways. The terms *impulse control* and *self-control* (Barkley 1997; Logue 1995) are usually used to describe the ability to inhibit inappropriate responses, delay engagement in an activity, or wait for rewards. Terms such as *self-direction* and *independence* (Ryan et al. 2006) are used to describe the ability to control and manage ongoing activities.

Self-regulated learning and problem solving require higher-level regulatory skills such as planning, using strategies, monitoring progress, correcting errors, and persisting until the (social or cognitive) goal is reached successfully. These higher-level abilities are often called *executive skills* by researchers interested in cognitive control functions in the brain (Barkley 1997).

Perspectives on the development of self-regulation

In addition to differences in terminology and emphasis, a variety of theoretical explanations for the origins and growth of self-regulation have contributed to early childhood professionals' understanding of regulatory development. This section gives a brief overview of the major theoretical perspectives on how children develop the capacity for self-regulation, as well as how theorists and researchers suggest the social and physical environment can nurture it. A final section discusses applications for caregivers and teachers.

Martha B. Bronson is retired from Boston College, where she was a professor of developmental and educational psychology. She has also been a teacher of young children.

The psychoanalytic perspective

In the psychoanalytic tradition, the development of self-regulation has been related to the development of a strong ego (Block & Block 1980). Freud (1920; 1923) defined *ego* as that part of the mind that channels basic drives into goals and behaviors acceptable to society, thus keeping internal control over behavior. More recently, psychologists in the psychoanalytic tradition view the ego as more active and autonomous and suggest other ego goals such as competence, control, and positive relationships with others (May 1969; Rogers 1963; White 1960; 1963).

From the psychoanalytic perspective, self-regulation increases as the child develops ego strength. The ego is strengthened when the child is successful in coping with the social and physical world around her and feels competent and accepted by others. The development of a strong ego has been related to warm and responsive relationships with caregivers (Sroufe 1995) and support for autonomous and effective interactions with the social and physical environment (Ryan et al. 2006; White 1960).

The behavioral perspective

Behavioral theorists focus on the power of the environment to shape behavior. They stress aspects of self-control that are learned through reward and punishment (Skinner 1938; 1974) and link the growth of emotional and behavioral control to learned strategies for controlling impulses (Logue 1995). Self-control is described as the ability to choose larger but more delayed rewards and is contrasted with impulsiveness, which is choosing smaller but more immediate rewards. Effective control also includes being able to use behavior strategies to obtain rewards.

From the perspective of behavioral theory, a child needs to learn to: (1) assess the relative value of different rewards ("If I take Jake's truck, he won't play with me anymore"); (2) choose appropriate goals (for the setting and the child's own level of skill); (3) give himself previously learned instructions ("I have to wait till it's my turn," "I have to put the toys away"), or successfully follow instructions provided by others; and (4) monitor his own actions (noticing when he is doing something successfully and when he has made a mistake).

Behavioral psychologists also suggest teaching children to reward themselves in the short term, with statements to themselves about their progress and competence (e.g., "I am listening to the teacher," "I am waiting in line quietly"), for behaviors that will ultimately be rewarded or that will keep them from being punished in the external environment (Baldwin & Baldwin 1998; Meichenbaum 1984; Mischel & Mischel 1983; Mischel et al. 1989).

The social learning perspective

Social learning theorists focus on children's ability to learn through observation as well as through the rewards and punishments they experience (Bandura 1977; 1997). They note that children learn through observation, even when that learning is not demonstrated in behavior (Bandura et al. 1963). For instance, a child may learn what not to do from observing a behavior that has negative outcomes (e.g., seeing another child fall when running down too steep a slope) or is punished (e.g., seeing a child removed from the block area when he knocks down another's structure).

However, the ability to imitate comes before the ability to learn from the consequences of observed behaviors. Toddlers and young preschoolers may see another child fall off a high wall and still may climb the same wall themselves. They may imitate observed hitting behaviors although they have witnessed negative consequences for hitting.

Social learning theorists (i.e., Bandura 1997) argue that self-evaluation is more powerful than external rewards and punishments in supporting self-regulation. They propose that the ability to observe and evaluate one's own behavior provides both motivation to engage in independent activities and guidance in carrying them out. Children gradually develop performance standards for self-evaluation from their own experiences of receiving rewards and punishments and from observing others.

These standards are being developed during the early childhood years and become the basis for self-regulated learning and behavior (Bandura 1997; Zimmerman 1995; Zimmerman et al. 1996). As the standards become clearer and more internalized during the primary school years, children may begin to reward themselves (with feelings of self-efficacy) for meeting the standards or punish themselves (with feelings of self-contempt) for failing to meet them.

From the social learning theory perspective, the development of self-regulation depends on having good models, on being rewarded for appropriate behavior or seeing others rewarded for it, and, ultimately, on internalizing appropriate performance standards. If a child has inappropriate or inaccurate expectations about the outcomes of behavior in a particular environment, she may not direct behavior adaptively in that setting. If a child's internalized standards are too high for his age and skills, self-reward will be unlikely because he will rarely be able to meet the standards. If internalized standards are too low, they will be reached too easily, and the child may not make independent efforts that match her potential.

Cognitive-developmental perspectives

Cognitive-developmental theorists such as Piaget (1952; 1954) and Vygotsky (1962; 1978) suggested that young children construct their understanding of the world and the ability to act effectively in it. Both theorists assumed that children have an innate interest in controlling themselves and aspects of the environment, and both assumed that the ability to exercise control effectively develops in interaction with the environment. While Piaget focused more on the child's individual efforts to construct a model of the world that was predictive enough for effective action, Vygotsky emphasized the role played by the social environment in assisting that construction.

Both Piaget and Vygotsky associated the development of control over emotions and behavior with overall cognitive development. Piaget (1952; Piaget & Inhelder 1969) proposed that self-regulatory mechanisms, in the form of assimilation and accommodation, are innate to the child's mental functioning and that development proceeds in stages as the child progressively reorganizes her understanding of objects, the physical world, and the perspectives of others. Piaget considered that, as higher levels of understanding of the social and physical world are reached, the child is able to regulate behavior and thought more effectively in these areas.

Vygotsky (1962; 1978) emphasized social supports for development and, particularly, the role of language in developing internal control of action and thought. Vygotsky considered language the primary means for developing both understanding and self-regulation. The child internalizes the instructions given by others and begins to give himself audible directions (e.g., "The green ones go there," "That piece doesn't fit"). Later, at age 6 or 7, this private speech becomes inaudible as the child learns to think the directions without speaking (Berk 1992; 1994). From this perspective the child can be helped to learn to direct his own activities by providing verbal directions he can use later in independent thinking and problem solving.

Vygotsky (1977) also underlined the importance of sociodramatic play in supporting the development of self-regulation. In play, children can practice both regulating and being regulated by others. The roles and rules of dramatic play help children control their activities in a more advanced way by providing supports ("scaffolds") for internal control. High levels of sociodramatic play are related to self-regulatory behavior (Berk et al. 2006; Elias & Berk 2002).

Information processing perspective

Information processing theorists focus on the mental processes that support thinking, decision making, and problem solving, using the computer as a metaphor for cognitive functioning (Sternberg 1984). They relate the development of self-regulation to the development of executive processes that control thinking and action, and suggest that what develops in children is the ability to engage in more organized, efficient, and effective cognitive processing. From this perspective, children develop by actively organizing information in their minds and by making use of feedback from the environment to modify these organizations or the way information is handled (i.e., "processed") as they think.

With maturation and experience children are better able to take in (i.e., "encode") information from the environments, organize it, and retrieve it more effectively from memory (Case 1985). They develop more complex strategies for mentally manipulating information and making decisions (Siegler & Jenkins 1989), and they learn to monitor their ongoing activities, modifying the strategies they are using if necessary (Sternberg 1984).

Toward the end of the early childhood period, children begin to be aware of and able to control their own thinking processes (Brown 1978). Support for the development of self-regulated thinking and problem solving can be provided by suggesting useful strategies and making children aware of strategies they are already using (Brown & Campione 1981).

How caregivers and teachers can support the development of self-regulation

Supporting and nurturing the development of self-regulation in young children requires an integrated approach that considers the whole child and the developmental level of each child. Young children cannot separate their feelings, actions, and thoughts as older children and adults learn to do. Caregivers need to consider the physical, emotional, social, and cognitive aspects of control required in a given situation. In addition, the requirements for supporting self-regulation change somewhat with age.

Infants

Infants need to discover their capacity for understanding and influencing the activities of objects and other people. They need enough predictability in their environments that they can begin to connect events and anticipate what will come next (Barkley 1997). When infants can anticipate events, they learn to expect order in the world and begin to look for it.

Through their interactions with caregivers and the cycles and changes in their environments, infants begin to regulate their own arousal (waking and sleeping cycles) and their emotional responses to internal and external stimulation (Kopp 1982). In order to support development, caregivers can arrange routines and events in the environment so that the infant can discover regularities. These regularities help the child learn when it is time to be awake and alert for interesting things and when it is time to sleep. They help her learn to recognize the signals that mean food or comfort or stimulation is coming and then regulate her emotions and arousal accordingly.

Infants also discover their own ability to affect or control the environment in interaction with people and objects. When caregivers are responsive to infants' signals, infants learn that they are capable of influencing others. When infants can create interesting effects by their own actions, they learn that they can have an impact on their environment and that their explorations will be interesting and rewarding (Sroufe 1995). Infants are rewarded by evidence of their own effectiveness and show their pleasure by smiles and persistent efforts to increase this effectiveness. They begin to expect to be successful in interaction with people and objects, and their confidence and motivation for competence in these areas grow.

Toddlers

Toddlers love to exercise their developing skills and are very interested in independent action. There is a strong push for autonomy during these years, but toddlers also use imitation as a means of acquiring new behaviors. Caregivers can model appropriate behavior sequences that toddlers can carry out independently (Crockenberg et al. 1996). Toddlers are able to engage in more active exploration than infants and are beginning to use simple self-regulated routines or strategies when they are interacting with people or objects (Jennings 1993). Caregivers can provide materials that support these play activities and allow appropriate choices that help children learn how to choose.

Toddlers are beginning to be able to carry out simple requests and may get upset if they violate known rules (especially if a caregiver is present). To support developing impulse control, caregivers can use responsive guidance techniques that emphasize individual control over behavior, provide simple cause and effect reasoning for desired behaviors, use suggestions rather than commands, and use language to assist self-control (Sroufe 1995).

Language is developing quickly during this period, and toddlers are using it to label their own actions as well as aspects of the social and physical world around them. Language also helps the children remember routines and rules and provides categories for organizing information (Berk 1992). Caregivers can use it to highlight important

aspects of the environment, including cause and effect and other connected sequences or routines.

Preschool and kindergarten children

Preschool and kindergarten children are increasingly capable of voluntary control of their emotions, their interactions with others, and their problem-solving activities. They can focus attention for longer periods, follow more complex directions, and comply with rules more reliably. They are increasingly able to interact cooperatively with peers and engage in sociodramatic play.

Caregivers can support growing self-regulation by giving children age- and skill-appropriate responsibilities, allowing choices among appropriate social and cognitive activities, supporting the growth of complex dramatic play with roles and rules, and encouraging independent learning and problem solving (Berk et al. 2006). Teaching strategies that help children feel competent and give

© Susan Woog Wagner

them the tools to carry out tasks independently are also important.

During these years, children are also internalizing the values and the standards of behavior and achievement of those around them (Sroufe 1995). To assist internalization of positive and appropriate standards, caregivers can model positive behaviors, minimize exposure to violent or antisocial models, expect and encourage independent and responsible effort, and use guidance strategies that provide reasons for rules and help children understand the consequences of their actions (Katz & McClellan 1997; Zahn-Waxler et al. 1992).

School-age children

School-age children have more advanced self-regulatory skills and are becoming more consciously aware of their ability to control their actions and thoughts (Berk 1992). Support for self-regulation in learning tasks can now include providing more complex strategies for problem solving, such as decoding strategies for reading (Zimmerman et al. 1996). Teachers can also help children become consciously aware of when and how to use specific strategies.

School-age children's growing awareness makes them more vulnerable to external events and judgments that threaten their feelings of competence and control. They are beginning to compare themselves with others and to use internal standards for judging their behavior and achievements (Zimmerman et. al 1996). The challenges posed by formal schooling can lower the child's perceived control and willingness to try if there is an over-emphasis on competition or external standards that he cannot reach. Teachers can support self-regulated learning by allowing individual choices among appropriately challenging alternatives and providing assistance in ways that support the child's independent effort and perceived control over the outcome (Barkley 1997).

School-age children are also more interested in and affected by influences outside the family and school environments than younger children are. Peer judgments and standards are becoming more important. A history of positive, trusting, and mutually respectful relations with adults; guidance strategies that promote mutual respect and problem solving; and continuing positive expectations

for responsible behavior help children direct their behavior appropriately and resist negative influences (Berk & Winsler 1995; Katz & McClellan 1997).

Conclusion

Children learn self-regulatory skills in a responsive social and material environment that provides opportunities for effective action, and is predictable enough to allow children to recognize the effects of their efforts. They develop internal control of emotions and behavior in a warm and trustworthy environment where responsible action is modeled, approved, and expected and where guidance strategies involve clarifying the effects of actions and a problem-solving approach to difficulties or disagreements. Opportunities to make meaningful choices and assistance in developing strategies for carrying out independent social and learning activities also support the growth of self-regulation in young children.

Reprinted from E.L. Essa & M.M. Burnham, eds., *Informing our practice: Useful research on young children's development* (Washington, DC: NAEYC, 2009), 50–58. Copyright © 2009 NAEYC. Originally published in the March 2000 issue of *Young Children*.

References

Baldwin, J.D., & J.I. Baldwin. 1998. *Behavior principles in everyday life*. Upper Saddle River, NJ: Prentice-Hall.

Bandura, A. 1977. *Social learning theory*. Englewood Cliffs, NJ: Prentice Hall.

Bandura, A. 1997. *Self-efficacy: The exercise of control*. New York: W.H. Freeman.

Bandura, A., D. Ross, & S.A. Ross. 1963. Imitation of film-mediated aggressive models. *Journal of Abnormal and Social Psychology* 66: 3–11.

Barkley, R.A. 1997. *ADHD and the nature of self-control*. New York: Guilford.

Baumeister, R.F., & K.D.Vohs, eds. 2004. *Handbook of self-regulation: Research, theory, and applications*. New York: Guilford.

Berk, L.E. 1992. Children's private speech: An overview of theory and the status of research. In *Private speech: From social interaction to self-regulation*, eds. R.M. Diaz & L.E. Berk, 17–53. Mahwah, NJ: Lawrence Erlbaum

Berk, L.E. 1994. Why children talk to themselves. *Scientific American* 271 (November): 78–83.

Berk, L.E., T.D. Mann & A.T. Ogan. 2006. Make believe play: Wellspring for development of self-regulation. In *Play = learning: How play motivates and enhances children's cognitive and social-emotional growth*, eds. D.G. Singer, R.M. Golinkoff & K. Hirsh-Pasek, 77–100. New York: Oxford University Press.

Berk, L.E., & A. Winsler. 1995. *Scaffolding children's learning: Vygotsky and early childhood education.* Washington, DC: NAEYC.

Block, J.H., & J. Block. 1980. The role of ego-control and ego-resilience in the organization of behavior. In *Minnesota Symposia on Child Psychology, vol. 13: Development of cognition, affect, and social relations*, ed. W.A. Collins, 39–101. Minneapolis, MN: University of Minnesota Press.

Bronson, M.B. 2000. *Self-regulation in early childhood: Nature and nurture.* New York: Guilford.

Brown, A.L. 1978. Knowing when, where, and how to remember: A problem in metacognition. In *Advances in instructional psychology, vol. 1*, ed. R. Glaser. Hillsdale, NJ: Lawrence Erlbaum.

Brown, A.L., & J. Campione. 1981. Inducing flexible thinking: A problem of access. In *Intelligence and learning*, eds. M. Friedman, J. Das, & N. O'connor, 515–529. New York: Plenum.

Brown, A.L., & J.S. Deloache. 1978. Skills, plans, and self-regulation. In *Children's thinking: What develops?*, ed. R.S. Siegler, 3–35. Hillsdale, NJ: Lawrence Erlbaum.

Calkins, S.D., & A. Hill. 2007. Caregiver influences on emerging emotion regulation: Biological and environmental transactions in early development. In *Handbook of emotion regulation*, ed. J.J. Gross, 229–48. New York: Guilford.

Case, R. 1985. *Intellectual development: Birth to adulthood.* Orlando, FL: Academic Press.

Crockenberg, S., S. Jackson & A.M. Langrock. 1996. Autonomy and goal attainment: Parenting, gender and children's social competence. In *New directions for child development, no. 73: Children's autonomy, social competence, and interactions with adults and other children: Exploring connections and consequences*, ed. M. Killen. San Francisco: Jossey-Bass.

Deloache, J.S., & A.L. Brown. 1987. The early emergence of planning skills in children. In *Making sense: The child's construction of the world*, eds. J. Bruner & H. Haste, 108–30. London: Methuen.

Eisenberg, N., & R.A. Fabes. 1992. Emotion, regulation, and the development of social competence. In *Review of personality and social psychology, vol. 14: Emotion and social behavior*, ed. M.S. Clark, 119–50. Newbury Park, CA: Sage Publications.

Eisenberg, N., R.A. Fabes, I.K. Guthrie, B.C. Murphy, P. Maszk, R. Holmgren & K. Suh. 1996. The relations of regulation and emotionality to problem behavior in elementary school children. *Development and Psychopathology* 8: 141-162.

Eisenberg, N., R.A. Fabes, S.A. Shepard, B.C. Murphy, I.K. Guthrie, S. Jones, J. Friedman, R. Poulin & P. Maszk. 1997. Contemporaneous and longitudinal prediction of children's social functioning from regulation and emotionality. *Child Development* 68: 642–64.

Eisenberg, N., C.L. Smith, A. Sadovsky & T. Spinrad. 2004. Effortful control: Relations with emotion regulation, adjustment, and socialization in childhood. In *Handbook of self-regulation: Research, theory, and application*, eds. R.F. Baumeister & K.D. Vohs, 259–82. New York: Guilford.

Elias, C.L., & L.E. Berk. 2002. Self-regulation in young children: Is there a role for sociodramatic play? *Early Childhood Research Quarterly* 17 (2): 216–38.

Flavell, J.H. 1977. *Cognitive development.* Englewood Cliffs, NJ: Prentice-Hall.

Fox, N.A. 1994. *The development of emotion regulation: Biological and behavioral considerations.* Monographs of the Society for Research in Child Development, vol. 59, nos. 2–3, serial no. 240. Chicago: University of Chicago Press.

Freud, S. 1920. *General introduction to psychoanalysis.* New York: Washington Square Press.

Freud, S. 1923. *The ego and the id.* London: Hogarth Press.

Friedman, S.L., E.K. Scholnick & R.R. Cocking. 1987. Reflections on reflections: What planning is and how it develops. In *Blueprints for thinking: The role of planning in cognitive development*, eds. S.L. Friedman, E.K. Scholnick, & R.R. Cocking, 515–34. Cambridge, England: Cambridge University Press.

Gillespie, L.G., & N. Seibel. 2006. Self-regulation: A cornerstone of early childhood development. *Young Children* 61 (4): 34–39.

Grolnick, W.S., & M. Farkas. 2002. Parenting and the development of children's self-regulation. In *Handbook of parenting, vol 5: Practical issues in parenting*, 2d ed., ed. M.H. Bornstein, 89–110. Mahwah, NJ: Lawrence Erlbaum.

Gross, J.J. 2007. *Handbook of emotion regulation.* New York: Guilford.

Holtz, B.A., & E.B. Lehman. 1995. Development of children's knowledge and use of strategies for self-control in a resistance-to-distraction task. *Merrill-Palmer Quarterly* 41: 361–80.

Hudson, J.A., & R. Fivush. 1991. Planning in the preschool years: The emergence of plans from general event knowledge. *Cognitive Development* 6: 393–415.

Jennings, K.D. 1993. Mastery motivation and the formation of self-concept from infancy through early childhood. In *Mastery motivation in early childhood: Development, measurement and social processes*, ed. D.J. Messer. London: Routledge.

Katz, L.G., & D.E. McClellan. 1997. *Fostering children's social competence: The teacher's role.* Washington, DC: NAEYC.

Kopp, C.B. 1982. Antecedent of self-regulation: A developmental perspective. *Developmental Psychology* 18: 199–214.

Kopp, C.B. 1989. Regulation of distress and negative emotions: A developmental view. *Developmental Psychology* 25: 343–54.

Logue, A.W. 1995. *Self-control.* Englewood Cliffs, NJ: Prentice-Hall.

Luria, A.R. 1961. *The role of speech in the regulation of normal and abnormal behavior*. London: Pergamon.

May, R. 1969. *Love and will*. New York: Norton.

McClelland, M.M., A.C. Acock & F.S. Morrison. 2006. The impact of kindergarten learning-related skills on academic trajectories at the end of elementary school. *Early Childhood Research Quarterly* 21: 471–90.

Meichenbaum, D. 1984. Teaching thinking: A cognitive behavioral perspective. In *Thinking and learning skills, vol. 2*, eds. J. Sigal, S. Chipman, & R. Glaser. Hillsdale, NJ: Lawrence Erlbaum.

Mischel, H.N., & W. Mischel. 1983. Development of children's knowledge of self-control strategies. *Child Development* 54: 603–19.

Mischel, W., Y. Shoda & M.L. Rodriguez. 1989. Delay of gratification in children. *Science* 244: 933–38.

Piaget, J. 1952. *The origins of intelligence in children*. New York: International Universities Press.

Piaget, J. 1954. *The construction of reality in the child*. New York: Basic Books.

Piaget, J., & B. Inhelder. 1969. *The psychology of the child*. New York: Basic Books.

Rogers, C.R. 1963. Actualizing tendency in relation to motives and to consciousness. In *Nebraska Symposium on Motivation*, ed. M.R. Jones. Lincoln, NE: University of Nebraska Press.

Rothbart, M.K., L.K. Ellis, & M.I. Posner. 2004. Temperament and self-regulation. In *Handbook of self-regulation: Research, theory and applications*, eds. R.F. Baumeister & K.D. Vohs, 357–70. New York: Guilford.

Rueda, M.R., M.I. Posner & M.K. Rothbart. 2004. Attentional control and self-regulation. In *Handbook of self regulation: Research, theory, and applications*, eds. R.F. Baumeister, & K.D. Vohs, 283–300. New York: Guilford.

Rueda, M.R., M.I. Posner & M.K. Rothbart. 2005. The development of attention: Contributions to the emergence of self-regulation. *Developmental Neuropsychology* 28: 573–94.

Ryan, R.M., E.L. Deci & W.S. Grolnick. 2006. The significance of autonomy and autonomy support in psychological development and psychopathology. In *Developmental psychopathology, vol. 1: Theory and method*, 2d ed., eds. D.C. Ciccetti, & D.J. Cohen, 795–849. Hoboken, NJ: John Wiley & Sons.

Shonkoff, J.P., & D.A. Phillips, eds. 2000. *From neurons to neighborhoods: The science of early childhood development*. Washington, DC: National Academies Press.

Siegler, R.S., & E. Jenkins. 1989. *How children discover new strategies*. New York: Lawrence Erlbaum.

Skinner, B.F. 1938. *The behavior of organisms: An experimental analysis*. Englewood Cliffs, NJ: Prentice-Hall.

Skinner, B.F. 1974. *About behaviorism*. New York: Knopf.

Sroufe, L.A. 1995. *Emotional development: The organization of emotional life in the early years*. Cambridge: Cambridge University Press.

Sroufe, L.A., E. Carlson & S. Schulman. 1993. Individuals in relationships: Development from infancy through adolescence. In *Studying lives through time: Personality and development*, eds. D.C. Funder, R.D. Parke, C. Tomlinson-Keasey & K. Widaman, 315–42. Washington, DC: American Psychological Association.

Sternberg, R.J. 1984. Mechanisms of cognitive development: A componential approach. In *Mechanisms of cognitive development*, ed. R.J. Sternberg, 163–86. New York: Freeman.

Vygotsky, L.S. 1962. *Thought and language*. Cambridge, MA: MIT Press.

Vygotsky, L.S. 1977. Play and its role in the mental development of the child. In *Soviet developmental psychology*, ed. M. Cold. White Plains, NY: M.E. Sharp.

Vygotsky, L.S. 1978. *Mind in society: The development of higher psychological processes*. Cambridge, MA: Harvard University Press.

White, R.W. 1960. Competence and the psychosexual stages of development. In *Nebraska Symposium on Motivation, vol. 8*, ed. M.R. Jones, 97–141. Lincoln, NE: University of Nebraska Press.

White, R.W. 1963. *Ego and reality in psychoanalytic theory: A proposal regarding independent ego energies*. New York: Independent Universities Press.

Zahn-Waxler, C., M. Radke-Yarrow, E. Wagner, & M. Chapman. 1992. Development of concern for others. *Developmental Psychology* 28: 126–36.

Zimmerman, B.J. 1995. Self-efficacy and educational development. In *Self-efficacy in changing societies*, ed. A. Bandura, 202–32. New York: Cambridge University Press.

Zimmerman, B.J., S. Bonner, & R. Kovach. 1996. *Developing self-regulated learners: Beyond achievement to self-efficacy*. Washington, DC: American Psychological Association.

Zimmerman, B.J., & D. Schunk. 1989. *Self-regulated learning and academic achievement: Theory, research, and practice*. New York: Springer-Verlag.

Becky A. Bailey and Carolyn Brookes

10

Thinking Out Loud: Development of Private Speech and the Implications for School Success and Self-Control

Imagine going to a family reunion where scientists place electrodes on each person's head. The electrodes continually broadcast people's internal dialogues. Imagine the noise and confusion as everybody's private thoughts spill out for all to hear. As you greet your cousin, you hear, "Did I pick up the dry cleaning?" It sounds ridiculous, yet children verbally express their inner thoughts in this manner all the time.

Every teacher has a humorous story of a child blurting out a surprisingly candid opinion to create a delightful moment. However, the blurting out and constant chatter can also be a source of teacher frustration. In reaction, teachers and caregivers sometimes rebuke young children for lack of impulse control. Some parents and educators may misinterpret children's chatter as a sign of disobedience, inattentiveness, or even emotional instability. In fact, use of private speech is an essential part of cognitive development for all children.

Chatter is one of the ways children process their learning and monitor and guide their actions. In its earliest stages private speech is thought spoken out loud that accompanies ongoing action and provides self-stimulation (for example, making car noises). As young children's use of private speech develops, it functions as a source of self-guidance (like the preschooler who says "No hitting" to a doll) by assisting with the formulation of plans and the inhibition of inappropriate actions. Most children do not gain the ability to internalize private speech until the age of 7 or 8.

The 4- to 8-year-old children in the following situations have not yet developed the private speech skills that would allow them to process, retain, or delay information internally:

> A teacher says, "Today we are going to read a story about Sam the dog." Hands shoot up and unsolicited comments abound, like "I have a dog!" "My granny has a dog!" and "My grandma is picking me up today!"

> A child waves his arm frantically, trying to get the teacher to call on him to answer her question. When she calls his name, he looks confused, as if to say, "Where did it go?"

A teacher continually reminds children to read silently to themselves during independent reading time.

An early childhood teacher suggests that a young child spend some time alone thinking about ways to handle a situation differently, only to find her fidgeting and making popping sounds with her lips.

The good news is that teachers can support children's gradual internalization of private speech, which is vital to academic and social success. They can adopt certain classroom strategies and more thoroughly understand the process of speech internalization.

The purpose of private speech

Human language has unique properties that distinguish it from the communication patterns of other animals. Human language is distinctive because we don't use it solely as a means of communication; we also use it to reflect. Reflection, in turn, allows people to propose, test, and apply different plans of action. People have the ability to think through the consequences of their actions and choose the most effective course. We can reflect because there is a delay between the arrival of a stimulus or event and our response to it. The seemingly automatic pause allows each person to

1. focus and sustain attention to a certain situation

2. think through a course of action

3. organize actions into a plan

4. inhibit emotional reactions, delay gratification, and self-motivate to obtain a goal (Barkley 1997)

The event/reaction pause is vital to success in school and in life. In neuropsychological terms, the thought processes that occur during the critical pause are referred to as the executive functions of the brain (Goldberg 2001). The internalization of speech—the ability to talk silently in one's head—is critical to the executive functions. The private speech conducted during the event/reaction pause permits rule-governed behavior, contributes to the ability to delay gratification (Berkowitz 1982; Mischel et al. 1989), assists in problem solving (Berk

1985; 1994), supports self-control (Kropp 1982), and improves moral conduct (Kochanska et al. 1995). The event/reaction pause develops over time in young children from birth to about age 10 and is closely linked to their development of private speech.

Development of private speech

An infant learns to sit up, crawl, and cruise before walking. Like learning to walk, the emergence of self-directed private speech seems to follow a predictable developmental sequence. Children by the age of 3 to 5 years develop outer speech that is especially noticeable during problem-solving tasks. Self-speech becomes increasingly silent—spoken in the child's mind but unheard by others—during the primary grades. Most children have predominantly internalized private speech by ages 9 to 12 years (Diaz & Berk 1992). According to Vygotsky (1987), private speech develops from social interaction and seems to follow a developmental timetable. However, this said, the reader is cautioned that the field of research on private speech is not fully developed (Diaz 1992).

Based on the work of Vygotsky, stages in the development of private speech have been hypothesized. These stages provide an effective tool for caregivers and families to use in enriching the lives of young children.

Stage 1: Vibrations and rhythms (conception–toddler)

In stage one, the child moves from distinguishing vibrations and rhythms from within the womb to true hearing as a newborn. The rhythms of speech, music, and movement work together to connect sensory and motor areas in the infant's brain. Parents' and other caregivers' social interactions with the newborn form the basis for this phase of brain development. Caregivers can play a variety of music (especially classical), sing songs, chant rhymes, and conduct lively conversations to support children's sensory-motor connections.

Stage 2: Imitation and sound play (newborn–toddler)

In stage two, children delight in imitating the cadence and intonation of language before utter-

Becky A. Bailey is an author, teacher, expert in childhood education and developmental psychology, and the creator of Conscious Discipline. **Carolyn Brookes** is a consultant working with schools across the country to help them increase academic achievement for all of their students.

ing their first words. After they learn to speak, they continue to delight in repeating and imitating. Infants' and toddlers' imitations lay down neural connections in the brain. When children begin to play with sounds, they create nerve connections to the muscles of the larynx (voice box). As children continue this play, the nerves become myelinated. (Myelin is a substance that increases the speed of nerve impulse transmission, protects the nerve, and assists in nerve regulation if the nerve is damaged [Kotulak 1997]). A child must play with sounds, even crying sounds, in order to create the motor connections that are critical to learning language.

Caregivers can support this process by playing interactive social games (I Love You rituals [Bailey 2000], peekaboo, patty cake, and such), talking, singing, moving, and describing the child's actions. Describing the child's actions ("You placed the green block on the blue block") supports the child's eventual use of language to track his own actions.

Stage 3: Naming and functions (15 months–4 years)

In stage 3, children between the ages of 15 months and 4 years gain a greater understanding of the functions of objects and people. The language that adults model for children is very important during this time. At this stage, children name and crudely classify objects. If we assist a child in reaching beyond the object's label ("This is a bus") to the object's function ("The bus brings children to school"), we can enhance the child's creative thought processes (Coulter 1986). A relational language approach of this nature fosters the optimal development of the neural system that searches out relationships. It facilitates the child's development of a sense of time. As children name and classify items, they create a file called past that they can unconsciously search in the pause between stimulus and response.

© Ellen B. Senisi

Stage 4: Stream of consciousness (4–7 years)

Children younger than age 8 chatter about their world, constantly thinking out loud. A teacher who tells a 5-year-old, "Sit quietly and do not talk while I read this story," is essentially telling the child, "Sit quietly and do not think while I read this story." The endless broadcast of thoughts from a child at this age is called stream of consciousness talking. Stream of consciousness talking is the problem-solving tool of children from about 4 to 7 years of age. Private speech is spoken aloud and typically becomes more abbreviated and less understandable to others as the child ages. Also, children are more likely to use stream of consciousness talking when they work on challenging tasks than when they work on simple tasks. Think of this in terms of your own life. When a task is extremely challenging, even as adults we talk ourselves through it by speaking out loud to ourselves.

When a task is overly difficult, a child is likely to display disorganized behavior or disengage from the task rather than use stream of consciousness talk to help them succeed (Berk 1994). Teachers can support children's development during this stage by depicting sequenced routines visual-ly. Children can easily identify routines if teachers

- post them on bulletin boards in picture form
- create class books that clearly show routines
- sing songs to indicate transition procedures

One teacher took photos of the classroom's healthy routine for blowing the nose and created a class book showing how to use and dispose of tissues and wash hands. The children delight in reading the blowing-the-nose book to each other as well as to their families.

Stage 5: Internal private speech (7–8 years)

The frontal lobe of the brain, the final lobe to mature, begins a growth spurt at about age 8. As children's speech centers in the frontal lobe advance, internal private speech begins to occur naturally. When this happens, children gain rudimentary abilities to process information and think through options before acting. They begin to rehearse information to be remembered later and reflect on their own behavior (Diaz & Berk 1992). Providing developmentally appropriate classrooms and knowing which children have or have not obtained mature private speech (see "Informal Assessment

Informal Assessment of Children's Private Speech

Development of private speech is progressive, much like cutting teeth. While most children develop mature, internal private speech by age 8, some develop sooner and others later. There are several quick and easy ways to assess the progress of a child's private speech.

Singing. Have children sing a song in which the words are sung softer and softer until eventually the children are soundlessly lip-synching. Songs such as "Bingo" and "John Jacob Jingleheimer Schmidt" are good. When they get to the point where singers silently mouth the words, watch the children's mouths. The children who are beginning to acquire the skill of internal private speech will be able to silently mouth the words. If the skill is not present, children will just open and close their mouths randomly because they are not cognitively tracking the words silently in their heads.

Counting. Lay a number of items on a table for children to count. Make sure the quantity is greater than they can count easily by sight. Ask the children to count the items. Many will touch each object and say the number aloud. Change the number of items and then ask the children to count again without touching the objects or speaking aloud. If the children cannot perform the task, internal private speech has not fully emerged.

When a teacher asked a child to count objects, she observed that he deliberately pointed to each object and counted out loud. The teacher changed the number of objects and asked him to count them in his head. He pointed to the first object and looked up at her in frustration and said, "I can't hear myself!"

Reading. Many children cannot read silently to themselves until they develop internal private speech. Observe children as they are reading; if they tend to read aloud, their inner voice has not yet fully developed.

of Children's Private Speech") will help teachers to support this connection.

Implications for the classroom

Having looked at the importance of private speech to children's behavior, and at children's development of private speech over time, let's consider the implications for teachers' classroom practices.

Anticipating children's thinking

A teacher reading aloud to children who have not yet developed internal private speech would be more effective if she anticipated the children's stream of consciousness thinking. The teacher might say, "Boys and girls, today we are reading a story about Sam the dog. Tell your buddy about a dog you know." The students will turn and talk to each other. They are each able to think out loud with their buddy.

Younger children may need more structure than simply "Tell your buddy." A plain "Tell your buddy" might erupt into a chaotic scene with children trying to talk all at once and some seeing only the back of another's head. For the tell-a-buddy approach to be successful with younger children, the teacher must assign buddies ahead of time. The buddies will sit together at their table and during circle time. Each buddy is given an identifier such as A or B. Then the teacher must organize the actual sharing. The teacher might say, "Buddy A, tell Buddy B about a dog you know." After a few seconds the teacher would then say, "Stop. Now, Buddy B tell Buddy A about a dog you know." A teacher using this structure, called the pair-and-share system, ensures that everyone has the opportunity to think without the frustration associated with stream of consciousness chatter.

Asking children to answer questions

For teachers, calling on young children after they raise their hands can be another source of frustration. A child cannot rehearse the answer prior to being called on if she has not acquired the skill of internal private speech. Therefore, the teacher must call on the child the moment she raises her hand, otherwise the answer is literally gone. A teacher who calls on one child at a time creates an obstacle

for young learners. The one-question-one-answer system allows only one child the opportunity to think. Using the pair-and-share buddy system helps the teacher engage all the children in making predictions, giving opinions, and answering questions. Pair and share is a necessary tool for teachers to use with stream of consciousness talkers in order to involve the entire class in the learning process.

Expectations for children's silent reading

Silent reading is another common task in many classrooms; however, it is ineffective for developing reading skills and is simply not possible for some children under the age of 7 (Coulter 1986). Teachers must encourage children to read out loud. It may be surprising to many adults, but verbalizing text during independent reading time or in a guided reading group is not distracting to most children. Most children are able to focus on their own reading. If a child does have a problem focusing while the others are reading, teacher intervention is helpful.

If a child is distracted by other children's verbalizing during independent reading, the teacher can allow her to move away from others who are reading out loud. She may also provide a PVC pipe connector, often called a phonophone, for the child to hold up to her ear and mouth into like a telephone. The phonophone amplifies the child's voice and helps her to focus. If a child has difficulties during a guided reading group, the teacher can have him sit next to her to provide a quiet side and have him hold the phonophone to the opposite ear to block out the sound of the rest of the class reading.

Classroom management

When it comes to classroom management, teachers who expect children to sit quietly and contemplate their misbehavior are creating needless frustration for both themselves and the children. Because private speech is important in social control of one's behavior (Hannaford 1995), young children who have yet to develop internal private speech do not possess the proper self-control systems to regulate their behavior. They cannot reflect on their choices and arrange a plan for future behavior on their own. Teachers must assist them with this process.

Teachers may use the following strategies to aid a child in choice and consequence recognition:

Establish a safe place in the classroom. The function of the safe place is to help a child regain composure during upsetting times. Children do not go to the safe place to reflect. Instead, the teacher instructs the students to use the safe place as a location to calm down. Teachers must think of the safe place as an anger and frustration management center for children. It should be filled with focused activities to help students actively regain their composure (Bailey 2001). Teachers must explain calming strategies and relaxation skills like deep breathing as part of the safe place curriculum.

Guide the child in the reflection process. People automatically engage the fight-or-flight response when they feel upset or stressed. Once the child has established composure and turned off her fight-or-flight response, the teacher might say, "You wanted everyone to know how angry you felt about not getting a turn, so you screamed and stomped your feet just like this. [Teacher demonstrates.] Did the screaming and stomping help get you a turn?" The teacher waits for the child's response and then says, "When you want a turn, say, 'May I have a turn please?' Say that now for practice, making your voice match mine."

Summary

Once internal private speech skills emerge, children are able to read silently, think without verbalizing, and rehearse an answer as they raise their hand in class. Children develop a pause between the event or stimulus ("He hit me") and the response ("I hit him back") as the executive functions of the brain develop. The ability to think through options, solve problems, and delay gratification comes with the event/reaction pause. The pause provides the soil to plant the seeds of reflection, critical thinking, problem solving, compassion, and empathy in a young child's mind.

Reprinted from *Young Children* 58 (5): 46–52. Copyright © 2003 NAEYC.

References

Bailey, B.A. 2000. *I Love You rituals*. Oviedo, FL: Loving Guidance.

Bailey, B.A. 2001. *Conscious discipline: Seven basic skills for brainsmart classroom management*. Oviedo, FL: Loving Guidance.

Barkley, R.A. 1997. *ADHD and the nature of self-control*. New York: Guilford.

Berk, L.E. 1985. Why children talk to themselves. *Young Children* 40 (5): 46–52.

Berk, L.E. 1994. Why children talk to themselves. *Scientific American*, November, 78—83.

Berkowitz, M.W. 1982. *Self-control, development, and relation to prosocial behavior: A response to Peterson*. Merrill-Palmer Quarterly 28: 223–36.

Coulter, D.J. 1986. *Children at risk: The development of drop-outs. Longmont*, CO: Coulter, Sound Cassette.

Diaz, R.M. 1992. Methodological concerns in the study of private speech. In *Private speech*, eds. R.M. Diaz & L.E. Berk, 55–84. Mahwah, NJ: Erlbaum.

Diaz, R.M., & L.E. Berk. 1992. *Private speech: From social interaction to self-regulation*. Mahwah, NJ: Erlbaum.

Goldberg, E. 2001. *The executive brain: Frontal lobes and the civilized mind*. New York: Oxford University Press.

Hannaford, C. 1995. *Smart moves: Why learning is not all in your head*. Arlington, VA: Great Ocean.

Kochanska, G., N. Aksan & A.L. Koenig. 1995. A longitudinal study of the roots of preschoolers' conscience: Committed compliance and emerging internalization. *Child Development* 66: 1752—69.

Kotulak, R. 1997. *Inside the brain: Revolutionary discoveries of how the mind works*. Kansas City, MO: Andrews McMeel.

Kropp, C.B. 1982. Antecedents to self-regulation: A developmental perspective. *Developmental Psychology* 18: 199–214.

Mischel, W., Y. Shoda & M.l. Rodriguez. 1989. Delay of gratification in children. *Science* 244: 933–38.

Vygotsky, L.S. 1987. Thinking and speech. In *Problems of general psychology*, Vol. 1 of *The collected works of L.S. Vygotsky*, ed. R.W. Rieber. New York: Plenum.

Ann S. Epstein

How Planning and Reflection Develop Young Children's Thinking Skills

Last night Tatiana, age 4, was telling us [her parents] her plan for the evening as we were eating dinner. She told us she planned to watch her new video, play her memory game with her mom, give her baby doll a bath, and have me read her some books. When I asked her when she was going to brush her teeth and go to bed, she told me that wasn't part of her plan!

Today after choice time, 3-year-old Eric told me [his teacher] he had watched Goober, the hamster. He reported that at first Goober was asleep, then he woke up and started drinking his water and eating his food. I said Goober must have been hungry. Eric agreed, then added that Goober wanted to get out of his cage "'cause he kept looking at the roof and standing up." Eric further observed, "I think he's lonely. You need to get another hamster to keep him company."

Young children ages 3 to 6 are capable of making thoughtful decisions about their behavior and keen observations about their environment (as the vignettes above show). Like Tatiana and Eric, they have insight into their desires, form mental images of the past and future, and attempt to explain their behavior and that of others.

Although today's early childhood educators often focus on enhancing reading and mathematics skills to meet ever increasing academic expectations, we must also remain committed to promoting broader thinking abilities. They are the foundation upon which children learn to make decisions, regulate their own behavior, meet complex challenges, and take responsibility for their actions.

Eager to Learn: Educating Our Preschoolers, the noted National Research Council report (2000), reminds us that "key concepts involved in each domain of preschool learning must go hand in hand with information and skill acquisition" (p. 8). It cites research showing that metacognition—higher-level thinking and problem-solving skills—develops when children are encouraged to reflect, predict, question, and hypothesize. How can adults help children exercise these capabilities?

Vignettes above adapted with permission from N. Vogel, *Making the most of plan-do-review: The teacher's idea book #5* (Ypsilanti, MI: High/Scope, 2001), 11 and 141.

There is empirical and practical evidence that we can promote the development of thinking and reasoning in young children in the early years by providing two curriculum components—*planning* and *reflection*. Both are thoughtful activities that encourage children to consider what they are doing and what they are learning. They also promote a broad range of other academic, social, and artistic competencies. This article summarizes the research in support of these claims and offers strategies teachers and caregivers can use to encourage planning and reflection in their programs.

Definitions

Both the accreditation criteria of the National Association for the Education of Young Children (NAEYC 2007) and the Head Start Performance Standards (U.S. Department of Health and Human Services 2002) indicate that young children should have opportunities to plan and make choices. However, the guidelines, and in fact most early childhood programs, do not differentiate between these two activities. Planning is more than making choices. Planning is *choice with intention.* That is, the chooser begins with a specific goal or purpose in mind that results in the choice.

First we must differentiate real choices in which teachers offer multiple options ("What colors do you want to use in your painting?") from pseudochoices in which teachers direct children to a limited number of adult-selected options ("Do you want to use red or blue?") But planning goes further than selecting from open-ended choices. When we engage children in planning, we encourage them to identify their goals and consider the options for achieving them. For example, they might consider what they will do, where they will do it, what materials they will use, who they will do it with, how long it will take, and whether they will need help. Planning thus involves deciding on actions and predicting interactions, recognizing problems and proposing solutions, and anticipating consequences and reactions.

Ann S. Epstein is Senior Director of Curriculum Development at the HighScope Foundation and the author of many publications, including the NAEYC bestseller *The Intentional Teacher.*

Most early childhood practitioners also recognize the importance of developing memory skills in young children. Teachers might ask children to remember something they learned earlier in the day or to recall an event that occurred earlier in the week. Reflection, however, is more than memory or a rote recitation of completed activities. Reflection is *remembering with analysis.*

When we engage children in reflection, we encourage them to go beyond merely reporting what they've done. We also help them become aware of what they learned in the process, what was interesting, how they feel about it, and what they can do to build on or extend the experience. Reflection consolidates knowledge so it can be generalized to other situations, thereby leading to further prediction and evaluation. Thus planning and reflection, when they bracket active learning, are part of an ongoing cycle of deeper thought and thoughtful application.

Supporting research

Evidence establishing the importance of planning and reflection comes from studies conducted by the HighScope Educational Research Foundation and other researchers. In one large national study, trained independent observers collected data on early childhood programs serving children from a wide range of socioeconomic, ethnic, linguistic, and geographic backgrounds (Epstein 1993). (The programs used many different curriculum approaches, not just the HighScope plan-do-review sequence.)

Across all settings, children who were given more opportunities to plan and reflect on their own activities scored higher on measures of language, literacy, social skills, and overall development. Independent investigations in the United Kingdom (Sylva 1992) and the Netherlands (Veen et al. 2000) confirmed that when children plan, carry out, and review their own learning activities, their behavior is more purposeful and they perform better on language and other intellectual measures.

Using words to plan and reflect are examples of language that is *decontextualized* (focused on nonimmediate events), which in turn is related to later reading success (Dickinson & Smith 1994). As they help children elaborate on their plans and think back on their activities, adults add complexity to the children's language, providing adjectives, adverbs, and new or rare words. This richness of vocabulary is also a critical component of subsequent literacy development (Snow et al. 2001).

Further, making predictions (planning) and assessing outcomes (reflection) lie at the heart of mathematical and scientific thinking. These processes are central to meeting the early childhood standards of the National Council of Teachers of Mathematics (2000). Planning and reflection also play a role in social problem solving. For example, effective strategies for conflict resolution encourage children to reflect on their feelings, plan alternative solutions and predict the consequences, and assess the efficacy of their ideas (Evans 2002).

Finally, studies of discipline-based art education (which emphasizes the intellectual as well as the expressive components of the arts) demonstrate the importance of these thoughtful processes as children not only make art, but also develop an appreciation for the artwork created by others (Arts Education Partnership 1998). In all these ways, the development of higher order thinking skills in young children can prepare them to master skills across multiple content areas.

Developmental notes

Before applying the strategies that follow, bear in mind that the ability to plan and reflect develops gradually and with practice during the early childhood years. Here are two general principles that will help you apply these strategies to children ranging in age from 3 to 6 years.

As they grow older, children are increasingly able to form mental images that allow them to anticipate and remember objects, people, and events that are not there. Children younger than three understand the world on a concrete, physical level. They may need to look at materials to devise a plan or reimmerse themselves in a setting to recall what happened. Older children, with greater language and cognitive abilities, begin to function at a more conceptual level. They can rely on verbal and visual representations, including abstract images and printed words, to think through, carry out, and reflect on their ideas.

Planning and reflection become increasingly detailed as children age. Younger children

devise simple plans and focus on one or two salient objects or events as they ponder their experiences. They express intentions or reactions with gestures and limited vocabularies. Older children develop multipart sequenced plans and enrich their recollections with layered explanations and hypotheses. As they plan and reflect on a daily basis, they develop the linguistic and conceptual structures that allow them to formulate and share complex thoughts.

Observe the children in your program and note where they are along these developmental continua. As you generate a collection of anecdotes, you will gain an understanding of how children's thinking develops in these intertwined areas. By adding your own observations to the examples presented on the following pages, you will be able to support and extend children's emergent thinking skills.

For more information on developmental progressions and strategies in planning and reflection with young children, see Hohmann and Weikart (2002) and Vogel (2001).

Strategies to promote planning

Here are some strategies teachers and caregivers can use to encourage children to think about their intentions as they indicate choices and make plans throughout the day.

1. **Make planning a regular part of the program day.** Planning should be a regular classroom activity so children will automatically begin to think in terms of what they want to do and how to carry it out. Do it at the same time(s) each day, for example, after morning greeting, during breakfast, or following nap. You can plan with children in small groups or pairs, as well as individually, making sure each child gets to express his or her intentions. In fact, children benefit from planning in small groups because the thoughts and elaborations of others often spark their own ideas. In the following example, Meredith, the teacher, is planning around a table with a group of 4- and 5-year-olds.

> **Jason:** I'm going to make a racetrack in the block area.
>
> **Meredith:** You made a racetrack yesterday that stretched all the way to the bookshelf.
>
> **Mike:** Me and him made it together. Today we're gonna make a longer one.

Meredith: It sounds like Jason and Mike are planning to work together today. [The boys go to the block area.]

Darya: I'm going to work together too.

Meredith: Who are you planning to work with?

Darya: With Mei Lin.

Mei Lin: Let's fill all the jars with water and make them sing.

Darya: First let's make the water orange. I'll mix the paint while you get the jars.

Meredith: Let me know when the jars are ready to sing. I want to hear them. [The girls head for the art area and water table, respectively. Meredith continues to plan with the rest of the group.]

Children should begin implementing their plans immediately or soon after they make them. Allow enough time—10 or 15 minutes total should be sufficient to give everyone in the group a chance—and don't rush children when they plan. If they

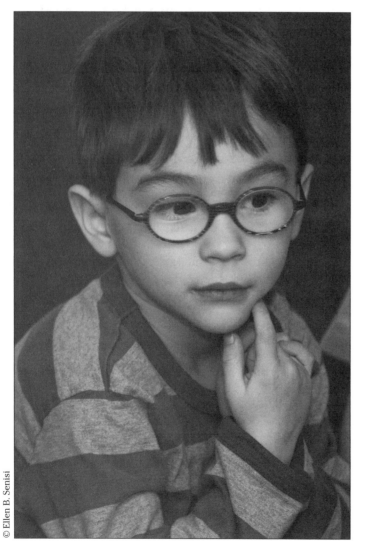

© Ellen B. Senisi

are struggling for words or ideas, wait and listen patiently. Let them know their intentions are as important to you as they are to them.

2. Make sure children can see the areas and materials in the room when they are planning. Visibility is important for younger planners whose mental representations are limited. Even older planners cannot keep in mind all the possibilities of a well-stocked room. Tour the room before or during planning and point out new materials or things the children have not used for a while. Avoid high shelves or other barriers that block a full view.

Being able to see everything not only enhances planning, it also means children will incorporate a wider variety of materials into their ongoing play. When they encounter a problem carrying out their plans, they will also have a better idea of the alternatives available to help them solve it. Knowing what is in the room also minimizes the chance that children will plan activities they cannot carry out with existing materials. If they do, however, this presents an opportunity for you to say something like, "We don't have any arm casts. What could you use instead to wrap your doll's broken elbow?"

3. Ask children questions. It isn't sensible to ask adults questions to which you already know the answers. The same applies to conversations with children. Ask them open-ended questions to seek genuine information about their intentions and how they plan to carry them out. "How will you build your tower?" will elicit more detail than "Will you use the big blocks?"

4. Listen attentively to children's plans. Share conversations with children, don't direct them. By paying attention to their words and gestures, you will learn about their ability to anticipate and think about the details of their plans. Then you can choose the most appropriate support strategies to help them elaborate their ideas and consider the options for implementing them.

5. Support, accept, and extend all the ways children express their plans. Never force children to express their plans in a certain way. If they gesture (e.g., bring you a book), don't insist they verbalize their idea before being allowed to proceed. Accept the gestured plan, but reflect it back in words to make sure you've understood the intention and to supply the vocabulary they can use when they are ready ("You want me to read you this book, *The Snowy Day*").

Don't negate a plan or offer children an alternative to their plans. This defeats the whole purpose of encouraging them to express their own intentions. Avoid the temptation to say, "You've gone to the house area every day this week. How about painting in the art area for a change?" Instead, observe what interests the child in the house area and think of ways to extend it: "You took Tamika's order for lunch yesterday. You might want to use these menus that I brought from the diner."

6. Encourage children to elaborate on their plans. Children at all stages of planning can be helped to extend their ideas. For beginners, try simple follow-up questions: "What will you need to do that?" Comments about what children are doing may elicit more details than questions. When his teacher observed, "You're barking like a dog," Mitch replied, "I'm a lost dog and I want you to find me."

In your eagerness to assist younger children, don't overlook opportunities to scaffold older students' learning. Encourage them to give details about where they will work, the materials they intend to use, the sequence of their activities, and the outcomes they expect to achieve. For example, when Rachel announced she was going to draw the family dog, her teacher said, "I wonder how you're going to show the puppies growing inside Daisy's tummy." This encouraged Rachel to consider such issues as size and spatial relationships as she planned her drawing.

7. Write down children's plans. If you record their plans, children get the message that their ideas are valuable. For example, you might label a drawing a child has made or the tracing of objects he or she intends to use. Take dictation when children describe what they will do and how they will go about it. Write the child's name on the plan. With older children, encourage them to begin writing down their names and ideas themselves. Documentation—including writing, drawing, and photography—helps children become more conscious of the process and value of planning. They are more likely to think through and elaborate on their ideas as they formally record them. Children can also review their documented plans as they reflect on their experiences and compare their intentions with the actual outcomes.

8. Use encouragement rather than praise. Another way to support planning is to avoid praising children's ideas. If you say "great idea" on one day or to one child, you may inadvertently convey disapproval if you forget to say those words to another child or on the following day. Praise also tends to end the conversation, cutting off the possibilities for children to elaborate their plans. Instead, use the other strategies listed here—listening, asking questions, commenting, recording their ideas—to encourage children to think about and follow through on their intentions.

Strategies to promote reflection

Many of the strategies that support planning also apply to promoting reflection. Remember too that planning and reflection are iterative processes. Encouraging children to think about what they did enables them to use this information as they plan what they will do next.

1. Make reflection an ongoing part of the program day. It is valuable to have a set time each day when children gather in a small group to share what they have done. For example, this can occur immediately after free play or center time, during snack, or before going outside. Schedule a period for reflection soon after children have completed their planned activities. In addition to these set times, however, reflection can and should happen whenever children are actively engaged in learning. Using the other strategies listed here, you can encourage children to ponder the what and why of their actions with a temporal immediacy that makes reflection especially relevant and meaningful to them.

2. Ask open-ended questions. As with planning, questions about what a child did should be asked sparingly and only to obtain information that is not trivial or already known. Open-ended queries such as "What happened when you added the third block?" will invite more observation on the part of the child than something obvious like "Did you add another block?" Questions that begin with "How did you . . . ?" or "Why do you think . . . ?" also encourage children to reconstruct and create meaning from their experiences.

3. Interpret and expand what children do and say. Nonverbal children, or those with limited language, may gesture or present materials to indicate what they did. You can add words to their actions, checking with them for cues to verify you understand their message. Your explanations will provide them with vocabulary for future reflection. Here, for example, John, a teacher, attaches sentences to the physical reenactment and simple words of Naomi, an older toddler:

John: What did you do at free play today, Naomi?

Naomi: [Points to block area.]

John: I saw you and Latoya playing in the block area.

Naomi: [Lifts her hands high.]

John: You built a high tower.

Naomi: [Bangs her hands down on the table.]

John: Did the tower fall down? [Naomi nods.] I wonder why that happened.

Naomi: More block.

John: You put another block on the tower?

Naomi: All fall down.

John: You put a big block on top, but it was too heavy so the tower fell down.

With children who are already verbal, use body language and conversation to show you are listening. Introduce new vocabulary words. Ask them to re-create an event or imitate their actions so you can observe and discuss the experience together. For example:

Teacher: [Sits next to child who is painting.] How did you make these swirly marks?

Child: I dipped my fingers in the paint and rubbed 'em all around. It's a tornado and it blowed down this house.

Teacher: [Bends to look.] That sure was a gigantic tornado. It blew down the whole house. What's this spot right here? It has a rougher texture.

Child: It's where the kitty scratched to get out of the house. It was scared.

Teacher: A tornado is very scary! How did you make that scratchy mark?

Child: I went like this. [Demonstrates with fingernail.]

Teacher: You drew a line with your fingernail in the paint. [Takes a piece of paper and imitates child's action.] Did you get paint underneath your fingernail too? [They compare nails.]

4. Accept conflicting viewpoints and interpretations. Children's recollections and explanations sometimes differ from one another or from those of

adults. It is important to acknowledge and accept each child's version, not to correct them or take sides. The point of reflection is not to arrive at some absolute truth but rather to encourage children to think about what happened and why. Even if the conversation goes far afield or heats up, it is important to find ways to support the thinking processes going on. In the following example, the adult acknowledges each child's observations about what animals like to eat:

Caregiver: [Whispers.] Bethany played with the [stuffed] animals and put them all to sleep.

Bethany: And I gave them peaches. [Pretends to feed a cat.]

Joey: Cats don't like peaches. They like cat food.

Bethany: Peaches!

Erika: My dog likes bananas.

Joey: That's dumb. Dogs aren't supposed to eat bananas. They like bones.

Margo: My dog likes chicken bones, but my mom says he'll choke. He coughs up hair, like this. [Demonstrates.]

Joey: Yech! That's gross.

Caregiver: Some cats like peaches, some like cat food. Some dogs like bananas, some like bones.

Margo: And chicken bones.

Caregiver: And chicken bones. Some cats like chicken bones.

Bethany: Peaches.

Joey: Oh brother!

5. Comment on what you see children doing as they play. Making comments while children are engaged in an activity serves two purposes. It encourages them to attend to and evaluate the experience as it is happening, and makes it easier for them to recall the event later. The more specific the comment, the more likely the child will remember and add his or her own details. For example, when Yusef's caregiver said "I saw you in the writing area using the markers," Yusef elaborated, "I invited Carlos to my party. Now there are five children and I'm 5 years old."

6. Write down what children say. Recording children's remarks as they reflect on their activities tells them their thoughts are worth preserving. You can label their drawings or take dictation

---

Dialogue in number 4 (above) adapted with permission from M. Hohmann & D.P. Weikart, *Educating young children: Active learning practices for preschool and child care programs,* 2d ed. (Ypsilanti, MI: High/Scope, 2002), 238.

as they dramatize something that happened. For older children, encourage them to write letters and words that capture their experiences and what they learned and thought while engaging in them. Written accounts—as well as drawings, photographs, and other forms of documentation—are also something concrete you and the children can share with their families.

7. Help children connect their plans and activities with their reflections. Having children recall their intentions in light of their actual behavior helps them establish causal relationships and a sense of efficacy and responsibility regarding their actions. You might say, "I remember you planned to make a superhero cape. Is that what you did?" The goal is not to hold children accountable for carrying out their plans—changing plans is perfectly acceptable—but rather to have them think about how and why their actions did, or did not, follow their intentions.

If children do change plans, going off in a new direction or even abandoning their original idea entirely, you might ask them, "Why did you make a different plan?" or "What made you think of doing that instead?" Again, the idea is not to force them to stick to one idea, but to encourage them to ponder their options, preferences, and problem-solving strategies.

8. Encourage children to carry over their activities to the next day. As children reflect on their experiences, they may recall problems they encountered or spin-offs they had not anticipated. These observations create a perfect opportunity for them to try different solutions or build on newly discovered interests the following day.

You can encourage children to use their reflections in future planning in several ways. Write a note, or ask the child to write a note, that will serve as a reminder. Put an item or set of materials from the relevant area in the child's cubby. A favorite device in the HighScope Demonstration Preschool is a Work in Progress sign. When children want to continue an art or construction project, this sign alerts others not to touch the unfinished work. It also acts as a visual memory aid when the children make plans the next day. Finally, it encourages children to share with teachers and families a description of what they have already done and their ideas

for adding to the detail and complexity of their undertaking.

Conclusion

Engaging children in planning and reflection makes them more than mere actors following prescribed roles. It turns them into artists and scientists who make things happen and create meaning for themselves and others. As you implement the strategies suggested here, you will discover that the complexity of children's planning and reflection parallels the development of their play.

Young children play in simple ways for short periods of time. As the school year progresses, their play becomes more elaborate in its use of materials, language accompaniment, and range of social interactions. It also lasts longer and is more likely to be resumed at a later point. Similarly, children's plans reflect the growing depth and range of their intentions. In fact, sometimes just telling the story of what they intend to do is as satisfying as actually carrying it out.

Likewise, children's ability to remember and explain what happened during play becomes increasingly intricate. Their speculations may not even be limited to what occurred during class, but may extend to related events or people at home or in other settings. Observing and tracking these changes allow teachers a window into how children think about their surroundings, the impact of their actions, and the implications of the past and present for their subsequent behavior.

The research and examples presented here show that planning and reflection are highly effective mechanisms for developing thinking skills in young children. Planning is making a choice with the added ingredient of intentionality. It incorporates a mental process that is fundamentally different from merely indicating a preference with no thought as to how the chosen item will be put to use. Reflection is remembering accompanied by evaluation. It transforms a simple exercise of memory into a thoughtful procedure that explores means-ends connections.

Planning and reflection thus involve decision making and problem solving. They encourage children to take the initiative in pursuing their interests, engendering a sense of control over the environment and one's ability to transform it. As children make plans and review their experiences, they enhance their predictive and analytical abilities, harness self-regulatory mechanisms, and develop a sense of responsibility for themselves and the choices they make. By encouraging these twin processes—expressing intentions and evaluating actions—we can equip young children with the thinking skills they need for later schooling and adult life.

Reprinted from *Young Children* 58 (5): 28–36. Copyright © 2003 NAEYC.

References

Arts Education Partnership. 1998. *Young children and the arts: Making creative connections—A report of the Task Force on Children's Learning and the Arts: Birth to Age Eight.* Washington, DC: Author.

Dickinson, D.K., & M.W. Smith. 1994. Long-term effects of preschool teachers' book reading on low-income children's vocabulary and story comprehension. *Reading Research Quarterly* 29 (2): 105–22.

Epstein, A.S. 1993. *Training for quality: Improving early childhood programs through systematic inservice training.* Ypsilanti, MI: High/Scope.

Evans, B. 2002. *You can't come to my birthday party! Conflict resolution with young children.* Ypsilanti, MI: High/Scope.

Hohmann, M., & D.P. Weikart. 2002. *Educating young children: Active learning practices for preschool and child care programs.* 2d ed. Ypsilanti, MI: High/Scope.

NAEYC. 2007. *NAEYC early childhood program standards and accreditation criteria: The mark of quality in early childhood education.* Washington, DC: Author.

National Council of Teachers of Mathematics. 2000. *Principles and standards for school mathematics.* Reston, VA: Author.

National Research Council. 2000. *Eager to learn: Educating our preschoolers.* Washington, DC: National Academy Press.

Snow, C.E., L.B. Resnick, G.J. Whitehurst & J. Daniel. 2001. *Speaking and listening for preschool through third grade.* Washington, DC: New Standards.

Sylva, K. 1992. Conversations in the nursery: How they contribute to aspirations and plans. *Language and Education* 6 (2): 141–48.

U.S. Department of Health and Human Services, Administration for Children and Families, Head Start Bureau. 2002. Program performance standards and other regulations. Online: www2.acf.dhhs.gov/programs/hsb/performance/index.htm

Veen, A., J. Roeleveld, & P. Leseman. 2000, January. *Evaluatie van kaleidoscoop en piramide eindrapportage.* SCO Kohnstaff Instituut, Universiteit van Amsterdam.

Vogel, N. 2001. *Making the most of plan-do-review: The teacher's idea book #5.* Ypsilanti, MI: HighScope.

Elena Bodrova and Deborah J. Leong

12

Developing Self-Regulation in Kindergarten: Can We Keep All the Crickets in the Basket?

When asked to describe her job, a kindergarten teacher said that teaching 5-year-olds is like trying to keep crickets in a basket: When you open the lid to put in a few more crickets, the others jump out. Anyone who teaches kindergarten can relate to this description; sometimes it seems that just managing a roomful of kindergartners takes up almost all the teacher's energy, leaving little for teaching academic skills.

In today's kindergarten classrooms, where demands for academic learning are on the rise, teachers can no longer wait until their "little crickets" simply outgrow their hard-to-manage behaviors. In fact, teachers rate "difficulty following directions" as their number one concern about children, indicating that more than half of their students experience this difficulty (Rimm-Kaufman et al. 2001). Teaching 5-year-olds to **regulate** their own behaviors becomes one of the major goals, adding yet another "R" to the list of basic skills children learn in kindergarten.

What is self-regulation?

Self-regulation is a deep, internal mechanism that enables children as well as adults to engage in mindful, intentional, and thoughtful behaviors. Self-regulation has two sides: first, it involves the ability to control one's impulses and to **stop** doing something, if needed—for example, a child can resist his immediate inclination to blurt out the answer when the teacher poses a question to another child. Second, self-regulation involves the capacity to **do** something (even if one doesn't want to do it) because it is needed, such as awaiting one's turn or raising one's hand. Self-regulated children can delay gratification and suppress their immediate impulses enough to think ahead to the possible consequences of their action or to consider alternative actions that would be more appropriate. While most children **know** that they are supposed to "use their words" instead of fighting, only children who have acquired a level of self-regulation are actually able to **use** them.

This ability to both inhibit one behavior and engage in a particular behavior on demand is a skill used not just in social interactions (emotional self-regulation) but in thinking (cognitive self-regulation) as well. For example, to read the word *cat* when it appears under a picture of a dog, a child must overcome the desire to pay more attention to the picture and instead focus on the word (Bialystok & Martin 2003). In fact, research shows that children's self-regulation behaviors in the early years predict their school achievement in reading and mathematics better than their IQ scores (Blair 2002; Blair & Razza 2007).

How does self-regulation develop?

Emotional self-regulation and cognitive self-regulation seem to have the same neural roots; thus, as children grow older and their brains develop, they can increasingly take control of both their thinking and their feelings. Furthermore, if a neural system is repeatedly exercised, it will continue to develop, as with exercising a muscle. Conversely, if children **do not** systematically engage in self-regulatory behaviors at a young age, the corresponding brain areas may not develop to their full potential.

There is growing evidence that self-regulation can be taught in the classroom (Blair & Razza 2007; Diamond et al. 2007). Let's look at some strategies for doing so.

How can kindergarten teachers promote children's development of self-regulation?

Although children come to kindergarten with different levels of ability to self-regulate, there are four simple strategies teachers can use to help all children develop this critical ability.

• **Teach self-regulation to all children, not just those thought to have problems.** All young children benefit from practicing deliberate and purposeful behaviors, such as repeated switching from one set of rules to another or resisting the tempta-

tion to function on autopilot. For example, during a calendar activity, instead of having children recite the dates as a memorized sequence, a teacher can alert students to the fact that two numbers are out of order. This way, children have to follow the number sequence *and* monitor the order the numbers are in to be sure it is correct.

• **Create opportunities for children to practice the rules of a certain behavior and to apply those rules in new situations.** When children are constantly regulated by adults, they may appear to be self-regulated, when in fact they are "teacher regulated." To be able to internalize the rules of a certain behavior, children can practice them in three ways:

First, children can **follow the rules** that are established and monitored by somebody else (most often by an adult, and sometimes by another child). It is a typical occurrence in a classroom when a teacher, for example, tells children that they can get up and leave only after their names are called.

Second, children need to be able **to set rules** for each other and **monitor** how those rules are followed (something that happens on the playground, e.g., when children set rules for taking turns when jumping rope and make sure nobody breaks those rules; violators who jump out of turn are not invited to play next time).

Finally, they need to **apply the rules to themselves**—for example, a child who wants to join some classmates playing a game but remembers that she needs to finish the book first and stays in the listening center.

The good news is that teachers can view a healthy amount of tattling in kindergarten as evidence of children's growing self-regulation!

• **Offer children visual and tangible reminders about self-regulation.** Learning to regulate one's own behavior is in many ways similar to learning other competencies, such as literacy or numeracy. For young children, early stages of learning to read or to count involve the use of hands-on activities and manipulatives like magnetic letters or Unifix cubes. Similarly, early stages of learning self-regulation involve the use of visual and tangible reminders that support children's memory and attention. For example, kindergartners who have

---

Elena Bodrova is Principal Researcher at Mid-Continent Research for Education and Learning. **Deborah Leong** is Professor Emerita of Psychology and Director of the Tools of the Mind Project.

trouble remembering to put their name on their papers will become much more attentive when they put on "editor's eyes"—that is, a pair of eyeglasses with the lenses removed—to remind themselves to check their work before turning it in. For example, an effective way to settle or avoid a fight about turn taking is to give young children a tangible tool—such as choosing the short straw, tossing a coin, or rolling dice—to determine who goes first in playing a board game or who has the next turn on the computer.

• **Make play and games important parts of the curriculum.** Not only should play and games *not* be pushed out of the kindergarten classroom to make room for more "academic" learning, they need to be taken very seriously. Kindergartners learn self-regulation best through activities in which children—and not adults—set, negotiate, and follow the rules. These include make-believe play as well as games with rules. Further, to engage in games like the ones many kindergarten teachers use to teach math or phonics, children have to first have the ability to follow rules that are quite abstract and

arbitrary. Children acquire and develop this ability during make-believe play, when they learn to follow concrete and simple rules such as not grabbing the stethoscope when pretending to be the patient. Instead of getting rid of blocks and dress-up clothes, kindergarten teachers need to primarily focus on improving the quality of make-believe play, ensuring that children have numerous opportunities to engage in acting out complex pretend scenarios—practicing self-regulation (Bodrova & Leong 2005; 2007).

Conclusion

Addressing gaps in knowledge and skills alone cannot guarantee success in learning for all children; we must also address the development of self-regulation as the underlying skill that makes learning possible. Kindergarten classrooms present an important opportunity to influence self-regulation in young children. In fact, for many children, school becomes the first and only place where they can learn to regulate themselves. Thus, instruction in self-regulation in the early years deserves the same, if not more, attention as the instruction in academic subjects.

References

Bialystok, E., & M.M. Martin. 2003. Notation to symbol: Development of a child's understanding of print. *Journal of Experimental Child Psychology* 86: 223–43.

Blair, C. 2002. School readiness: Integrating cognition and emotion in a neurobiological conceptualization of children's functioning at school entry. *American Psychologist* 57 (2): 111–27.

Blair, C., & R.P. Razza. 2007. Relating effortful control, executive function, and false belief understanding to emerging math and literacy ability in kindergarten. *Child Development* 78 (2): 647–63.

Bodrova, E., & D.J. Leong. 2005. Self-regulation as a key to school readiness: How can early childhood teachers promote this critical competence? In *Critical issues in early childhood professional development*, eds. M. Zaslow & I. Martinez-Beck, 223–70. Baltimore: Brookes.

Bodrova, E., & D.J. Leong. 2007. *Tools of the Mind: The Vygotskian approach to early childhood education.* 2nd ed. Columbus, OH: Merrill/Prentice Hall.

Diamond, A., W.S. Barnett, J. Thomas & S. Munro. 2007. Preschool program improves cognitive control. *Science* 318 (5855): 1387–88.

Rimm-Kaufman, S., R.C. Pianta & M. Cox. 2001. Teachers' judgments of problems in the transition to school. *Early Childhood Research Quarterly* 15:147–66.

Higher-Order, Complex Thinking

Classifications of goals for student learning (e.g., Bloom et al. 1956) often include the concept of *higher-order thinking skills*, which require more cognitive processing than other kinds of learning and also have broader benefits. Higher-order thinking skills are more valuable because we can use them in a wide range of situations. Yet, these more complex skills—analysis, critical thinking, problem solving, and the like—require different learning and teaching methods than does the learning of facts and concepts. The three selections that follow provide a picture of what these teaching methods look like in the early childhood setting.

Also discussed in this section is *metacognition*—higher-order thinking that involves active control over the thinking processes involved in learning. Processes such as planning how to approach a learning task, monitoring one's comprehension, and evaluating progress toward task completion are metacognitive. Students with greater metacognitive abilities, evidence suggests, are more successful thinkers.

While higher-order, complex thinking skills have always been important, arguably they are even more so in this technological, global economy. Sometimes called "21st century skills," these abilities are now strongly emphasized in the education goals of the highest-performing countries. With the growing concern about American students' lagging performance, especially in science, technology, engineering, and mathematics (STEM), education leaders today are urging greater attention to higher-order thinking skills at all age levels.

"Let's SQUiNK about It! A Metacognitive Approach to Exploring Text in a Second Grade Classroom," authored by classroom teacher and teacher educator Karen Capraro, illustrates how high-level cognitive processes such as metacognition play a role in literacy activities, in this case in journaling and reading nonfiction text. Until children develop the capacity and habit of stopping to look ahead as they approach text, they will simply plunge in and thus get less from the material than they would if they adopted a more deliberate, strategic approach. Capraro describes useful and engaging methods for helping children become more deliberate. As they prepare to read nonfiction material, for example, children can ask themselves what they already know about the topic and what questions they have about it. When they do so, students are more alert for key information as they read. Use of metacognitive processes is a skill that children need to continue developing throughout the elementary grades and beyond.

A number of authors represented in this volume have a strong interest in improving the learning of poor and minority children and in helping the United States to close the achievement gap between these students and their more advantaged peers. A focus on this goal is evident in **"From High Chair to High School: Research-Based Principles for Teaching Complex Thinking"** by researchers and educators Roland Tharp and Susan Entz. In their work at the Center for Research on Education, Diversity and Excellence (CREDE) and the research centers that preceded it, the authors conducted and reviewed studies on children including Latinos, Native Americans, Native Alaskans and Hawaiians, Asian and Caribbean immigrants, and African Americans and Whites growing up in poverty in urban and rural settings. Based on this extensive array of studies, Tharp and Entz list five evidence-based principles for pedagogy to enhance higher-order thinking skills and explain each principle and proven methods, such as teaching through conversation and involving students and teachers in working jointly in productive activity.

The various cognitive abilities and dispositions described throughout *Growing Minds* play essential roles in children's learning of subject areas across the curriculum, such as literacy and language arts, mathematics, science, social studies, and the arts. I have included the selection **"Science in Kindergarten"** by Boston-based researchers and educators Ingrid Chalufour and Karen Worth in order to convey how reasoning, problem solving, mental representation, and other cognitive processes come into play in children's learning within an academic area. Active, engaging pedagogy (in this case, in the teaching of science) also strengthens children's positive approaches to learning such as curiosity, flexibility, self-direction, and persistence—critical skills for scientists and for the rest of us as we seek to understand and use science in our daily lives.

Reference

Bloom, B., M. Englehart, E. Furst, W. Hill & D. Krathwohl. 1956. *Taxonomy of educational objectives: The classification of educational goals. Handbook I: Cognitive domain*. New York, Toronto: Longmans, Green.

Karen Capraro

13

Let's SQUiNK about It! A Metacognitive Approach to Exploring Text in a Second Grade Classroom

The children are excited. We are about to begin a classroom study of butterflies as part of our science unit on insects. I had carefully selected nonfiction texts at a variety of reading levels and assigned students to small reading groups based on their reading skills.

I call over a group of children, reminding them to bring their reader journals. The children eagerly gather around the table with journals and pencils in hand. As we get ready to explore the book *Butterflies*, by Karen Jo Shapiro, I suggest, "Let's begin by SQUiNKing about it."

Without missing a beat, the second-graders open their reader journals to clean pages and begin to design a recording format of columns so they can keep track of their thinking while reading about butterflies. In our classroom, we now call the format SQUiNK. It has become a useful tool in interacting with text for all children and at varying levels and abilities.

SQUNK (which later became SQUiNK)

happened quite out of the blue! We were about to read *If You Traveled on the Underground Railroad,* by Ellen Levine, in a small, guided reading group in my second grade classroom. Having recently studied African American heroes, including Harriet Tubman, the students had some background knowledge about the Underground Railroad. Because the text held a lot of information, I wanted to be sure that the children were prepared to understand the content.

I planned to have the children record in their reader journals what they already knew about the Underground Railroad; questions they thought of before, during, and after reading; and their new learning. Readers use their schema to activate prior knowledge and to make connections from the text they are reading to their own lives, other texts, and the world. Asking questions helps readers clarify meanings in the text and focus their attention on specific text components (Miller 2002). Using schemas and questioning allows the readers to further enhance their understanding and to increase overall learning when working with nonfiction texts.

I instructed the children to divide their journal pages into three columns and to label the first column "S" for *schema* (the children knew that this term means "what they already know"), the second column "Q" for *questions*, and the last "NL" for *new learning*. I had thought a lot about my teaching practices and goals for children's learning. What I hadn't thought about was what I might learn from the children.

Taking a new approach in the reader journals

Out of mistakes often come the best inventions.

"Oops! I made a mistake," Peter said as he labeled his reader journal columns.

"What is it?" I asked.

"I labeled the last column 'NK' instead of 'N.'"

I sat unmoving, momentarily puzzled. Peter must have sensed my confusion.

"NK . . . for *new knowledge*," he explained.

"Oh . . . oh, that's okay," I replied. "It's really the same thing, isn't it?"

Peter sat back and thoughtfully surveyed his work.

"SQUNK," he announced, grinning. Again, I was confused.

"SQUNK," he repeated. "See, if you put the letters together, and usually the letter *Q* would have a *U* with it, they spell SQUNK (rhyming with *think*)."

His reading group partner, Marla, responded quite happily: "Oh yeah! I get it! SQUNK! I'm going to change my journal so I can SQUNK too!"

Supporting children's metacognition

A reading teacher's crucial role is to help students become aware of their own reading comprehension abilities and needs and to learn specific strategies to address those needs at any given time (Reutzel & Cooper 2004). As a primary teacher, I take this responsibility very seriously. I wanted my students to become more metacognitive—more aware of and more knowledgeable about their own thinking (Flavell et al. 2001). When children pay attention to

Karen Capraro is an associate professor at the Henry Barnard Laboratory School at Rhode Island College (RIC). Karen works primarily as a second grade classroom teacher but also is a practicum instructor in RIC's early childhood teacher education program.

their thinking while reading, notice questions that pop into their head and attempt to answer them, conjure up mental images based on the words they are reading, and think about what certain words mean, they gain a deeper, richer understanding of the text.

Using the reader journals to activate prior knowledge, keep track of thinking, and record new learning seemed like a good way for children to develop their metacognitive skills and monitor their comprehension of the text, even if the format was teacher directed. Initially we designed a SQUNK entry together. We sat down to read and began to think out loud about what we already knew and recorded the information (the S column).Then we considered questions we had and wrote these down (the Q column). Next, we began to read. As we read, we continually added questions as they arose, and we also added new knowledge (the NK column).

Why not the KWL method?

In the past, when reading a nonfiction text with students, I often started with a KWL chart. But I wanted more. The KWL chart starts out by encouraging children to think about what they already *know*. After this step, I felt it stopped being interactive. We listed our "I *wonders* . . ." or "What we want to know . . ." and then began the text, often reading straight through without considering any new "I wonders . . ." or noting the *learning* taking place during the reading.

After a typical read-aloud session, we closed the book and looked back at the KWL chart. Next, I asked the students what they had learned. They told me a few facts they remembered, I wrote them on the KWL chart, and then we were done. With the book then put away and the chart rolled up, I worried that many of the children's "I wonders . . ." would remain unanswered and most children would forget what they learned.

My goal was for the children to mentally interact with text before, during, and after reading. The SQUNK method differs from KWL in that students use the format *throughout* their reading or *during* the process, not just before and after. This expectation leads children to a greater awareness of their own thinking—the metacognitive—enabling them to have a deeper understanding of the text. For example, while reading the introduction to *If You Trav-*

S	Q	NK
It wasn't a rail-road.	I wonder if it's telling about someone or what it is like?	Before 1860 there were about 4,000,000 slaves.
It was a "rail-road" to free-dom.		I didn't know runaway slaves were called fuge(i)tives.
It wasn't under-ground.		The majority of them ran away between 1830 and 1860.
The conductor of it was Harriet Tubman, and		I didn't know about Tice Davis (Davids).
she never lost a "passenger."		The underground got it's name because it was secret.
They knew witch (which)		The first slaves were brough(t) to America in 1619.
house to got (get) to be-cause there		I didn't know being a slave was that hard.
was a candle in the window.		I didn't know slaves ran to othe(r) places besides the north.
		The slaves were very clever.

Transcription of a page from Peter's reader journal

I think It was a great mistake and every body should use it.

Marla's opinion of SQUNK

eled on the *Underground Railroad,* Marla wondered about the number of slaves who reached freedom and recorded her question (the Q column). She was excited and then saddened to learn the answer just a page or two later. She recorded what she learned (the NK column).

Developing a new view on teaching reading

How and why did I change my approach? Several years ago at a science workshop, a fellow partici-

pant introduced me to Debbie Miller's *Reading with Meaning: Teaching in the Primary Grades* (2002). The text completely changed my thinking about teaching reading.

As a primary educator, I often felt that much of what I knew about reading instruction, as specifically related to comprehension strategies, was not applicable to teaching primary age children. In particular the instruction failed to honor children's thinking and instead emphasized what the teacher considered important.

I previously designed a list of questions to ask small groups of children upon the completion of their reading. If the students answered the questions, I considered their comprehension of the text adequate. If they were unable to answer the questions, I worked with them as we reread the text to search for the answers. One result of this approach was that it gave students a false impression that the teacher's ideas were more important than their own. Further, I felt I was not teaching the children about the different comprehension strategies available to them and was not addressing different learning styles and abilities. In contrast, the SQUiNK method (as later renamed) is accessible to all and honors what students consider important.

Miller's book gave practical advice in simple language and techniques a teacher could implement immediately. The comprehension strategies range from inferring meaning to determining importance in nonfiction to synthesizing information. Using these strategies let me explore reading with my students in ways neither I nor the children had experienced before. We learned to approach reading more thoughtfully, with an awareness of our thinking and an expanded ability to grow. The initial development of the SQUNK format depended on explicit instruction, based on Miller's ideas and particularly as they relate to schema theory and questioning. The acronym SQUNK would have gone unnoticed, had I not encouraged the children to be reflective thinkers.

Steps in reading comprehension— S to Q to NK

In September I introduced the second-graders to the term *schema* and talked with them about how it is "all the stuff already in your head" and how readers use schema as they read. With this understanding, they learned to make connections from their schema to the text, which allowed them to enhance their understanding. Classroom discussions often began with the questions, "What schema do you have that will help you when you are reading this? What do you already know?"(Miller 2002). For example, prior to beginning an author study of Tomie dePaola, I asked the children what they already knew about him. They'd had some previous exposure to the author during whole-class read-alouds and recalled that Tomie dePaola was also an

illustrator, wrote folktales, and had written a series of books about the character Strega Nona.

I also encouraged children to ask themselves questions along the way before, during, and after reading, to increase their comprehension of the text. If the children found the answers to their own questions, I asked them to explain how they discovered them. For example, was the answer explicitly stated in the text? Did the student have to infer the answer? Did the child consult an outside source, such as a dictionary or other resource (Miller 2002)?

The children knew from hearing me say it over and over again that it is not enough just to read the words; a reader has to read and think and think and read. Noticing the questions that pop into our heads and then trying to discover the answers while reading helps the reader understand and learn from the text. Further, answered questions become new knowledge, which in turn becomes part of our schema, better preparing us as we navigate through more complex texts in the future.

The children's reader journals, fixtures at their sides during whole group and small group reading instruction, are an easy way to record and assess thinking. Each day, during our readers' workshop, children independently read and worked in small groups, and kept track of their thinking in their journals. At certain times, the style of the children's journal recording was teacher directed, as was the case in the Underground Railroad lesson. However, children also used their journals spontaneously, independently, and creatively as they encountered new ideas while reading or as they discovered something about themselves as readers, such as "I like to study the illustrations on each page before I read the words." At the end of each day, I can now easily grab four or five journals from the book bins to learn more about how the students are thinking.

SQUNK as a word with meaning and action

What did I learn from Peter and Marla about teaching for comprehension in the primary grades? They taught me about coining a term that children can remember and, as a result, use autonomously. SQUNK, as it turns out, is an amusing word to say when you are in second grade. And because it

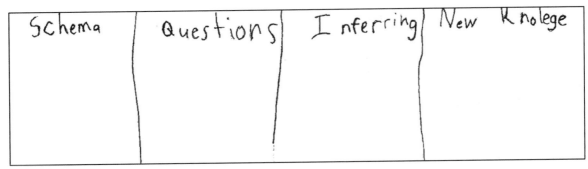

Peter's revised SQUiNK

conveniently rhymes with the word *think*, children are able to use the terms interchangeably, allowing them access to their own metacognition. Soon children were suggesting it as an active verb and that we "SQUNK about it" whenever we read something new and pull together everything we are learning.

Back to Peter

Peter, a thoughtful and reflective student, frequently led me to think about things differently. As we continued reading *If You Traveled on the Underground Railroad*, Peter used his reader journal along with the newly developed term.

> One day, near the end of the book, Peter said, "I think we missed something. SQUNK, because it rhymes with *think*, should really have an *i* in it."
>
> "Hmmm . . . What do you think the *i* should stand for?" I asked.
>
> "I don't know yet," he replied. "But I will let you know."
>
> Weeks later, Peter did let me know. "Infer!" he exclaimed. The *i* should stand for *infer* and we should divide our journals into four columns!"
>
> "Smart thinking!" I responded, smiling.
>
> "Maybe you should try that next year," Peter added.
>
> "Maybe I will, Peter. Maybe I will."

Conclusion

Initially I sought to address the needs of readers with strong skills by more fully engaging them with expository text. But through the introduction to a strategy for addressing the needs of *all* readers for *all types* of text, I saw how eagerly and successfully children took to SQUiNK and learned. The second-graders, regardless of their reading level, no longer had to rely exclusively on me to remind them to think and read at the same time. Using the easy-to-remember (and fun-to-say) SQUiNK acronym, they reminded themselves, and their classmates, to use their schema, ask questions, draw inferences or conclusions, and notice their new knowledge.

Reprinted from *Young Children* 66 (5): 14–18. Copyright © 2011 NAEYC.

References

Flavell, J.H., P.H. Miller & S.A. Miller. 2001. *Cognitive Development.* 4th ed. Englewood Cliffs, NJ: Prentice Hall/Pearson.

Miller, D. 2002. *Reading with Meaning: Teaching Comprehension in the Primary Grades.* Portland, ME: Stenhouse.

Reutzel, D.R., & R.B. Cooter. 2004. *Teaching Children to Read: Putting the Pieces Together.* 4th ed. Upper Saddle River, NJ: Prentice Hall/Pearson.

Roland Tharp and Susan Entz

14

From High Chair to High School: Research-Based Principles for Teaching Complex Thinking

Imagine a classroom—or if you are fortunate, remember one—like this:

> Teachers and students work together on real products, real problems. Activities are rich in language, with teachers encouraging students to develop their capacities to speak, read, listen to, and write English and the special languages of mathematics, science, the humanities, and art. Curriculum is taught through meaningful activities that relate to the students' lives and experiences in their families and communities. Teachers challenge students to think in complex ways and to apply their learning to solve meaningful problems. The classroom is full of talk; the basic teaching interaction is conversation. A variety of activities take place simultaneously (individual work; teamwork; practice and rehearsal; mentoring through side-by-side, shoulder-to-shoulder teacher-student work). Students have systematic opportunities to work with all their classmates. They learn and demonstrate self-control and common values: hard work, rich learning, and helpfulness to others.

This classroom description is an enactment of the research-based practices demonstrated to be most effective for all populations we have studied (Tharp et al. 2000), kindergarten through middle school. Four decades of research in the field of education and diversity have produced a clear and solid body of evidence strong enough to guide teachers, regardless of the languages, ethnicities, race, or prosperity of their communities. No matter children's cultures, races, individual interests, or abilities, these findings apply and thus are particularly appropriate for fully inclusive classrooms.

The authors both work with the national Center for Research on Education, Diversity and Excellence (CREDE) and the senior author worked with its predecessors, the National Center for Research on Cultural Diversity and Second Language Learning and the Kamehameha Early Education Program (KEEP). There we conducted 200 studies of children considered to be potentially at risk of academic failure due to cultural and linguistic diversity, race, poverty, and geographic isolation. The children we studied include Latinos, Native Americans, Native Hawaiians and Alaskans, Asian and Caribbean immigrants, and African Americans and Whites living in poverty in inner cities and rural mountain settings. These are the children who frequently have been left behind and who continue to be left behind, although knowledge is available for reforms that would bring them all along into school success.

The research work has been slow, laborious, and careful. Drawing from our own work and from all our colleagues', we used analytic deduction to discover five elements present in all successful programs for at-risk students:

- joint productive activity
- language and literacy development across the curriculum
- contextualization
- challenging activities
- instructional conversation

These elements lead to improved academic performance, school attendance, dropout rates, student engagement, and/or parental and community satisfaction. Regardless of grade level, cultural or racial group, or subject matter, two or more of these elements were present in successful programs.

We then spent five years seeking exceptions to these universals, urging colleagues (through print, Internet, television, speeches, focus groups) to help us find them. We found none. For the next 12 years, we systematically studied these universal five elements, separately and in combination. Finally, we refined the elements into Five Standards for Effective Pedagogy.

The word *standard* was selected for its more traditional use, that of a banner or flag around which to rally and that guides the way, rather than its usage as a criterion that establishes levels of performance. "As banners, the pedagogy standards convey ideals, not templates" (Dalton 1998). In this paradigm, standards provide general guidance for teachers, schools, and teacher educators interested in pedagogy and its effects on learning (Tharp et al. 2000). Now we are able to measure the degree to which teachers are enacting the standards and to assist them through training and coaching (Doherty et al. 2002).

Roland Tharp is Emeritus Professor of Psychology and Education at the Universities of Hawaii and California. **Susan Entz** teaches at Hawaii Community College and works with Hawaii P-20 Initiative through the W.K. Kellogg Foundation to improve literacy skills for children.

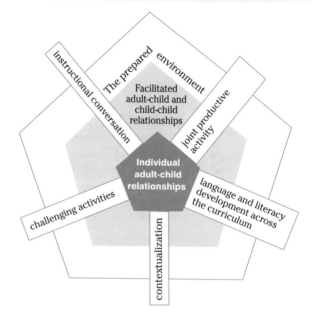

Creation of a Community of Early Learners through Implementation of the Five Standards for Effective Pedagogy

The evidence is clear. Using all appropriate methods, from ethnography to experimental random-assignment trials, in kindergarten through middle school, the findings are uniform. These elements have been tested on special education populations as well (Gallimore et al. 1989). The more the five standards are present in a classroom, the higher the student scores on standardized tests of academic achievement (Doherty et al. 2002, 2003; Hilberg et al. 2000; Tharp 1982; Tharp et al. 2003).

The five standards

1. **Joint productive activity: Students and teachers producing together.** Working together toward a common goal is the ideal setting for encouraging mutual assistance and for developing language in meaningful contexts. It is especially valuable for teachers to participate with children during activities; there they can see, evaluate, assist, and be most responsive to each child's strengths and needs.

2. **Language and literacy development: Developing language and literacy across the curriculum.** In every activity, throughout every domain of instructional goals, the teacher has a metagoal: developing children's language and literacy.

3. **Contextualization/making meaning: Connecting school to students' lives.** Every major theory of

human development—from cognitive science to sociocultural theory—assumes that understanding develops by connecting new information to things already known. Embedding the abstract goals of school in the knowledge, experiences, and values of children and their families increases retention and comprehension more than any other single strategy.

4. **Challenging activities: Teaching complex thinking.** Children learn what they are taught, and the more the teacher challenges them to use ever more complex thinking, the more they grow into it. The human brain is designed to seek new experiences and incorporate them into its developing structures (Shonkoff & Phillips 2000). Since learning changes the physical structure of the brain, compelling cognitive challenges have a decisive and long-term impact on the actual architecture of the brain (Bransford et al. 2000; Shore 1997).

5. **Instructional conversation: Teaching through conversation.** At times children do need to listen in large groups, to hear instructions and follow them, and to practice some routines together, with teacher leading and children chorusing. But this is not the ideal context for learning, and there is no warrant in research or theory for allowing whole-group instruction to increasingly dominate classrooms, from preschool through high school. Rather, individual and small group dialogues, pervasive in the quality preschool classroom, offer the ideal model for learning. Only in dialogue, an instructional conversation, can a teacher assess and assist in maximum responsiveness to children's development.

Although we discuss each standard in turn, all five are integrated facets of a unified classroom experience, just as in the ideal classroom described in the opening and the effective learning environment presented on the pages that follow. Each standard is important and even when used alone can enhance teaching and learning. However, when used in combination, the five provide a powerful teaching approach. When teaching and learning are organized in these ways, research consistently shows higher student achievement, engagement, pleasure, and harmony. But *why* is that so?

Key adult-child interactions at home

A clue lies in the ways families prepare their infants and children in the first three years of life for the greatest success in school (Shonkoff & Phillips 2000). Infants and children who *will* one day be successful in school are immersed in conversations with their mothers and fathers and families, beginning with infant babble. When a baby notices something, the mother talks to her about it. The mother also draws the baby's attention to interesting people, things, and books and begins to read stories when the child can only point to the letters and pictures. These conversations are always more complex than a learning child can fully comprehend, but the parent leads the child into the challenging zone of new vocabulary and new thoughts (Hart & Risley 1995). The five teaching standards describe teacher-child interactions that maximize those same interactions. This is perhaps the best explanation of why the CREDE standards, like the parent-child interactions in Hart and Risley's research, lead to higher child academic readiness and achievement (Doherty et al. 2003).

Learning in the context of the natural environment promotes inquisitiveness and persistence because the issues are meaningful to the child. Minds are fundamentally developed in relationship-based activities. How better can adults create comfort and confidence than by enacting their love through listening, conversing, assisting, and doing things together with their children?

Children prepared in this way are given the tool kit of language, thought, and love of learning that is school readiness. Children who hear far less language, see far less text, and receive verbal communications consisting primarily of directions and warnings from their caregivers lack the necessary skills for success in the classroom. Many schools do not offer this tool kit to children; they presume that families have provided it. And so the achievement gap is evident on the first day of school and widens every day thereafter.

Teachers in schools that transform their classrooms—under the **Five Standards for Effective Pedagogy**—do not assume that children have these language and thinking skills; they *teach* them. So the most likely explanation for the effectiveness of the standards is that they create the nearest possible school equivalent of a family environment filled with conversation and opportunities to engage in complex thinking. Because the continuity of effective learning environments at home and school is most obvious at the point of the transition—preschool—we draw our examples from there.

Developmentally appropriate practice and the five standards in action

The congruence between CREDE's five research-based standards and NAEYC's developmentally appropriate practices (Copple & Bredekamp 2009) is evident in a literature-based unit presented by early childhood teacher Sheri Galarza at the Kamehameha Preschool on the Island of Hawaii (Tharp et al. 2002). The preschool serves 4- and 5-year-olds of Native Hawaiian heritage, from families of modest means, whose first language is largely Hawaiian Creole. When planning any new unit, Ms. Galarza reflects on her individual preschoolers and on the rural lifestyle of the community, where wild boars roam the mountains and some families keep livestock.

Making meaningful connections

The 4-year-olds recently embraced the story of the Three Little Pigs and are now enthusiastically reenacting it. They talk about family experiences with wild pig hunting, and the class visits a high school animal-husbandry project to see pigs in a farm setting. Drawing upon their own firsthand experiences with both wild and domesticated pigs makes the story more meaningful to the children. The teacher guides a conversation about experiences with real animals and those in storybooks, stressing the difference between things that are real and those that are pretend. Ms. Galarza realizes that the pig activity presents a solid base for future learning. She also knows that one family has a goat, so she builds a Five Standards unit around the traditional tale of the Three Billy Goats Gruff.

Ms. Galarza introduces this new book at circle time, teaches the group a song about a troublesome troll, and then involves the children in planning a field trip to a coffee farm where a goat resides. The children benefit from the firsthand experiences of touching the goat's beard, watching it feed on grass, and hearing the *trip-trap-trip-trap* of its hooves on the driveway, just like in the book. For the children with no previous experience with goats, such sensory explorations provide the cognitive structures needed to make the literary experience more meaningful.

Each member of the class, including those with language and other developmental delays, can make the connection between the fictional characters in the story and the habits of real animals that live in their community. An important home-school-community connection is forged, and both the story and the field trip create a common context for subsequent activities.

Teachers and students producing together

Later in the week Ms. Galarza works with small groups to plan a reenactment of "The Three Billy Goats Gruff" using large stick puppets and a building block bridge. Each child learns all the roles in the play. For example, the teacher reminds the group that the troll in the story bellows, "Who's that walking on my bridge?" They discuss the tone of voice and decide that the troll would say his part in a mean voice. Then the children in the small group all practice the troll's lines. After learning the parts, the group decides by consensus who will portray each character. Ms. Galarza agrees to narrate the story and serve as the informal director.

Digital photographs are taken during each group's dramatization and used to make group books in which the children sequence the events in the story and dictate captions for the pictures. Ms. Galarza reads the stories to the whole group, and the books become popular selections in the library corner (Entz & Galarza 2000; Rivera et al. 2002).

Complex thinking and language and literacy through instructional conversation

After reenacting the story, each small group talks about the troll's behavior. The children decide that he's mean and a bully. They think he probably doesn't have any friends. Because forming friendships is very important to these 4-year-olds, they consider this a serious problem. The teacher suggests that the children use their own experiences in making and keeping friends to write an advice column to the troll. In the process, the children practice listening carefully as others speak, comment on and reinforce suggestions made by their classmates, and volunteer their own solutions. The group moves from suggestions on personal hygiene, such as "Brush your teeth," to more sophisticated

© Susan Entz

advice on social interaction, such as "Use your words" and "Don't butt heads."

The teacher records each suggestion and then encourages children to sign their names next to their ideas. The 4-year-olds decide to read their advice column to the rest of the class during the second circle time, then post it on the door for their parents to see at the end of the day.

The process of meaningful and sustained dialogue is not always easy. The more verbal children offer their suggestions quickly and their words flow smoothly. For other children, the process of taking in the question, contemplating it, and then organizing a response is slow and labored. The teacher sets a warm, supportive tone for these children, giving each one plenty of time to participate. The children learn that waiting for a child whose verbal skills are less developed sometimes yields keen insights that contribute to the strength of the overall product.

Each small group dramatizes the story and participates in a small-group project. In addition to the advice column, small groups explore different ways to confront a bully and other approaches the troll could have used to get what he wanted.

Extended activities

When the small-group activities are over, Ms. Galarza puts the props in the dramatic play center, which becomes a popular activity choice during center time. Because each class member learned all of the story roles and participated in the informal plays, the story takes on changes of plot and additional characters as the experienced thespians improvise their own story lines.

A variety of activities related to goats and trolls are added to the learning centers, across the curriculum, to reinforce key concepts of the story. Because Ms. Galarza identified specific content and developmental objectives for the class and for individuals before the unit began, the learning center activities are designed to offer theme-related opportunities to reinforce emerging skills.

Some children develop math concepts by sorting objects into sets of small, medium, and large and making color and size patterns with small plastic goats. Others improve motor skills by creating goat pictures using a negative painting technique at the easel. Pop-up troll cards encourage writing, games built on the story's *trip-trap* sounds promote phonological awareness, and two-part word-picture matching games are popular additions to the literacy center. Among a host of other activities, the children assemble a goat puzzle, eat goat cheese for snack, and fashion troll characters out of playdough. The library center features a variety of fiction and nonfiction books about goats as well as the child-made books created throughout the unit.

Class progress is measured against the group objectives identified at the beginning of the unit, and the Work Sampling System (Meisels et al. 1995) is used to document individual progress.

Culminating activity

The culminating activity for the unit gives the 4-year-olds a chance to don billy goat headbands and go trip-trapping along the sidewalk to enjoy a picnic in a grassy meadow. During the extended unit, the children are exposed to developmentally appropriate activities built around strong, research-based instructional principles. They develop into a strong, supportive community of eager learners. And they have as much fun as gamboling goats.

Reprinted from *Young Children* 58 (5): 38–44. Copyright © 2003 NAEYC.

References

Bransford, J., A. Brown & R. Cocking, eds. 2000. *How people learn: Brain, mind, experience, and school.* Washington, DC: National Research Council.

Copple, C., & S. Bredekamp, eds. 2009. *Developmentally appropriate practice in early childhood programs serving children from birth through age 8. 3d ed.* Washington, DC: NAEYC.

Dalton, S.S. 1998. *Pedagogy matters: Standards for effective teaching practice.* Santa Cruz: University of California, Center for Research on Education, Diversity and Excellence.

Doherty, R.W., R.S. Hilberg, G. Epaloose & R.G. Tharp. 2002. Standards Performance Continuum: Development and validation of a measure of effective pedagogy. *Journal of Educational Research* 96 (2): 78–89.

Doherty, RW., R.S. Hilberg, A. Pinal & R.G. Tharp. 2003. Five standards and student achievement. *NABE Journal of Research and Practice* 1 (1): 1–24.

Entz, S., & S.L. Galarza. 2000. *Picture this: Digital and instant photography activities for early childhood learning.* Thousand Oaks, CA: Corwin.

Gallimore, R.R., G. Tharp & R. Rueda. 1989. The social context of cognitive functioning of developmentally disabled students. In *Cognitive approaches in special education,* ed. D. Sugden, 51–82. London: Falmer.

Hart, B., & T.R. Risley. 1995. *Meaningful differences in the everyday experience of young American children.* Baltimore: Brookes.

Hilberg, R.S., R.G. Tharp & L. DeGeest. 2000. Efficacy of CREDE's standards-based instruction in American Indian mathematics classes. *Equity and Excellence in Education* 33 (2): 32–40.

Meisels, S.J., J.R. Jablon, D.B. Marsden, M.L. Dichtelmiller, A.B. Dorfman & D.M. Steele. 1995. *The Work Sampling System: An overview.* Ann Arbor, Ml: Rebus Planning Associates.

Rivera, H.H., S.L. Galarza, S. Entz & R.G. Tharp. 2002. Technology and pedagogy in early childhood education: Guidance from cultural-historical-activity theory and developmentally appropriate instruction. *Information Technology in Childhood Education* 1: 1 73–96.

Shonkoff, J., & D. Phillips, eds. 2000. *From neurons to neighborhoods: The science of early childhood development.* Washington, DC: National Academy Press.

Shore, R. 1997. *Rethinking the brain: New insights into early development.* New York: Families and Work Institute.

Tharp, R.G. 1982. The effective instruction of comprehension: Results and description of the Kamehameha Early Education Program. *Reading Research Quarterly* 17 (4): 503—27.

Tharp, R.G., S. Entz & S. Galarza. 2002. *The Sheri Galarza preschool case: A video ethnography of developmentally appropriate teaching of language and literacy.* CD-ROM. Provo, UT: Brigham Young University. Available online: www.crede.org.

Tharp, R.G., P. Estrada, S.S. Dalton & L.A. Yamauchi. 2000. *Teaching transformed: Achieving excellence, fairness, inclusion and harmony.* Boulder, CO: Westview.

Tharp, R.G., P. Estrada, S. Dalton & L. Yamauchi. 2003. Research evidence: Five Standards for Effective Pedagogy and Student Outcomes. *Technical Report No. GJ, March. Center for Research on Education, Diversity & Excellence.* University of California, Santa Cruz, CA 95064. Available online: www.crede.org.

Science in Kindergarten

Ingrid Chalufour and Karen Worth

It's Monday morning. Twenty kindergarten children are sitting in a circle as their teacher, Derek, presents them with an interesting challenge:

"I'm wondering how many ways you can think of to change the size and shape of your shadows. You'll all have a chance to work in our shadow theater this week, and then we'll talk about what you've discovered. There are paper and markers for you to keep track, and I'll be around to record your ideas, as well."

The children have been exploring shadows for three weeks—outdoors on the playground, indoors with flashlights and different objects, and with a small shadow box. A shadow theater, a sheet hung from the ceiling with a gooseneck lamp on one side, was introduced the week before. The children are very excited to use their bodies and puppets to make shadows. This week, Derek wants the experimentation to be more intentional, so he gives the children this challenge at the beginning of choice time.

During the week, the children explore the shadows they can make. Derek spends quite a bit of time with them observing, commenting, and asking questions. "How do you think you could make your shadow very small?" "What do you think would happen if we moved the lamp over to this side?" "Might your shadow look like a rock, just sitting there?" "You might like to draw what your shadow looks like when you stand sideways like that." "Let's write down what you did and where the lamp was."

By the end of the week, there are many pictures with captions on the wall near the theater—pictures the children have drawn and photographs Derek has taken with his digital camera. These images become the focus for the science talk at the end of the week, after the children have pursued some of their ideas about shadows and how they change.

Over the weekend, Derek will produce a documentation panel with the pictures, the children's captions, and the ideas they have come up with. Derek plans to wrap up the shadow work the following week with a shadow theater presentation for families and other classes.

In another classroom, in the spring, Katie and her kindergartners have been studying plants and how they grow:

While they watch grass sprouting and trees budding on the playground, they're growing a variety of things in the classroom. Windowsills and shelves are covered with potted plants, narcissus bulbs, garlic pieces, and carrot tops. The 21 children are gathered on the rug for their morning meeting, and 11 small foam trays are placed around the circle so the children can closely inspect the seedlings while they talk. The children are talking about what has been happening to the seedlings.

Katie begins by reviewing the chart of observations from the previous week and then asks, "How have our seedlings changed since last week?" The children are eager to share their observations. "They're longer."

"There are green leaves coming out on these." "This one is getting lots of things at the bottom." Katie writes their comments down on a chart with the date as she encourages specifics. "How do you know they're longer?" "Let's look at those leaves. The leaves on the kidney beans look different from the leaves on the lentils, don't they? How would you describe the difference?" "Does anyone know what we call the growth at the bottom of a plant? . . . Yes, it's called 'the roots.'"

Jamal is very interested in the growth of the seedlings. Katie decides it's time to begin measuring them. She asks Jamal to get the measurement basket, which has string, tape measures, and rulers in it. She quickly makes a chart they can use to record length over time. The children start filling in the chart by measuring three of the seedlings, then marking their length in inches on the chart in a column with the date on it. "I wonder how long these will be the next time we measure them?" "Do you think the kidney bean will always be the longest one? . . . What other changes do you think will happen?"

At the end of the discussion, Katie sets the stage for the day's choices. "There are several things you can do with these seedlings during choice time today. I'd like you to do a drawing in your journal. Draw the same seedlings you drew last time. I'll place the word cards at the table with your journals so you can use them to label your drawings. I'd also like some of you to do more charting of the seedlings' lengths. I think we could chart the growth of the bulbs, garlic, and carrots, as well." The children eagerly choose activities and choice time begins.

These examples give brief glimpses into the world of science teaching and learning that can and should take place in kindergarten classrooms. Three important questions must be answered in order for this teaching and learning to take place: What science should be taught? How should science curriculum be structured? How should it be taught? These questions lead to other questions: How much science should children do? What are the key instructional strategies teachers can use to promote learning? How can science fit into a program, given the typical kindergarten focus today on mathematics and literacy? The answers to some of these questions will be found in the following pages.

Ingrid Chalufour is currently a consultant, working with teachers and programs interested in providing a richer science program for young children. **Karen Worth**, faculty member at Wheelock College, consults nationally and internationally in science education at the early childhood and elementary levels.

What science should we teach?

The National Science Education Standards (National Research Council 1996) and the *Benchmarks for Science Literacy* (AAAS 1993) describe what students should know and be able to do in science. These documents have provided guidance to many educators for a decade, but neither one addresses the kindergarten year; both start with first grade. Since the publication of these documents, a growing number of states have developed standards both for the preschool years and for kindergarten. However, given the current emphasis on mathematics and literacy, and the reality that science has never been a significant part of programs for young children, many of these standards do not include science. With little guidance for teachers and few expectations from the school system, the science teaching in kindergarten is often just a science table in a corner of the room with a few objects for children to look at or individual activities that they can do during choice time. The science that happens is often focused on the study of living things—classroom pets, plants, and nature walks—and it neglects the physical sciences. In too many classes science is not taught at all.

What follows is a framework for thinking about science content in the kindergarten classroom. There are many ways to organize the content of science for any level. We have chosen to turn to the national documents, the research on cognitive development, the practice of expert educators, and our own experience in the development of science curriculum materials. We have based the framework on five content areas: inquiry, life science, physical science, earth science, and space science.

Inquiry

Perhaps the most important area of science content is inquiry. In science, *inquiry* refers to the diverse ways in which scientists study the natural world and propose explanations based on the evidence derived from their work. Inquiry also refers to the activities of students in which they develop knowledge and understanding of scientific ideas, as well as an understanding of how scientists study the natural world (National Research Council 1996).

The box opposite lists important inquiry skills that kindergarten children must be given the opportunity to develop. They should be able to perform these skills at a simple level by the end of kindergarten. The two vignettes that opened this chapter include many examples of children using these skills as they explore shadows and the growth of seedlings.

One often sees such lists of inquiry skills in science programs and frameworks. They are frequently accompanied by the suggestion that the simpler skills of exploration, observation, and description and simple tool use are the most appropriate for younger children, and that the skills of investigation and experimentation and the more analytic synthesizing skills can only be learned as children get older. We suggest that kindergarten children can and do use *all* of the inquiry skills, but at a kindergarten level.

This is not a list of skills to be taught in isolation. Instead, it provides a practical guide for teachers to use as they design science experiences for children. Whatever the topic of study, all of the skills are used in the process of pursuing that study. In the flowchart on the next page, the inquiry skills are placed in a context, demonstrating that children's inquiry is a process, or a set of stages. The stages follow one another, with the arrows in the diagram suggesting that children will move back and forth between different stages depending on their interests, the challenges that arise, and the guidance of teachers.

Inquiry is about questions—but it is hard for children to ask questions about something if they haven't had a chance to get to know the thing or the event, whether it is shadows, seeds, snails, or water flow. So the first stage in the framework is to *notice, wonder, and explore.* This is a time for children to play, to see what they already know, to mess about in a rich environment with little direct guidance or structure. As children explore, they ask questions through words or actions. They may be struck by a particular idea or question, such as, "I wonder what will happen if I shine the flashlight on the car from the block corner?" These questions may lead them to *take action and extend questions,* the second stage in the framework.

It may not be possible to investigate many of the questions children raise. "Why does the seedling come out of the seed?" cannot be explored directly. "What is the name of this plant?" will not lead to lengthy discussion. But "What does the seedling

need to grow?" has the beginnings of a rich investigation. At this stage, children often need adult guidance to begin to *focus observations and raise/clarify questions.* They need to be encouraged to make some predictions about what might happen.

When children *engage in more focused explorations,* they are entering the experimental phase of inquiry. Given the right materials and teacher support and guidance, kindergarten children can do focused investigations. The framework presents this as a circular process, one that can go around and around. Children may explore a question for a long time, with their explorations leading to new questions and new investigations.

Important Inquiry Skills

As a result of their science experiences, kindergarten children should develop their abilities to:

- Raise questions about objects and events around them

- Explore materials, objects, and events by acting upon them and noticing what happens

- Use all senses to make careful observations of objects, organisms, and events

- Describe, compare, sort, classify, and order in terms of observable characteristics and properties

- Use a variety of simple tools to extend their observations (a hand lens, measuring tools, eye droppers, a balance)

- Engage in simple investigations including making predictions, gathering and interpreting data, recognizing simple patterns, and drawing conclusions

- Record observations, explanations, and ideas through multiple forms of representation including drawings, simple graphs, writing, and movement

- Work collaboratively with others

- Share and discuss ideas and listen to new perspectives

Source: From K. Worth & S. Grollman, *Worms, shadows, and whirlpools: Science in the early childhood classroom* (Portsmouth, NH: Heinemann; Newton, MA: EDC; Washington, DC: NAEYC, 2003), 18. Reprinted with permission.

YOUNG CHILDREN'S INQUIRY

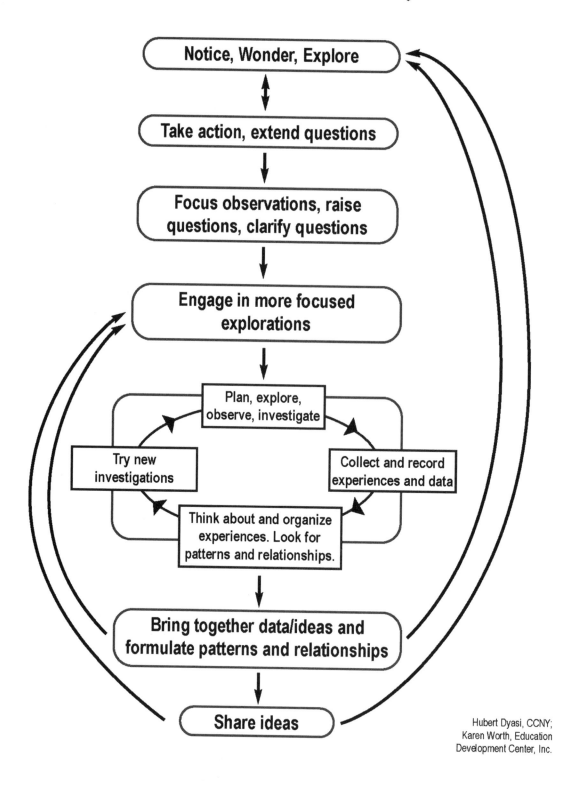

Notice, Wonder, Explore

Take action, extend questions

Focus observations, raise questions, clarify questions

Engage in more focused explorations

Plan, explore, observe, investigate

Collect and record experiences and data

Think about and organize experiences. Look for patterns and relationships.

Try new investigations

Bring together data/ideas and formulate patterns and relationships

Share ideas

Hubert Dyasi, CCNY;
Karen Worth, Education
Development Center, Inc.

When children have a good deal of experience and begin to form some ideas, they need to step back from their hands-on investigative work, review and reflect on what they have done, and *bring together data/ideas and formulate patterns and relationships.* Young children's explanations and generalizations may be quite simple and naïve. What is important is that they draw from the experiences they have had and the data they have collected. New ideas in science are built on the knowledge of others.

The important last step of the framework is to *share ideas.* This is a time when children are encouraged to share what they have done, relate it to what others have done, discuss, and debate.

Yet inquiry skills cannot be acquired in a vacuum. Children need to inquire into something. So we turn to a list of basic ideas and topics in the four remaining content areas—life science, physical science, earth science, and space science.

Subject matter

Educators do not completely agree on the appropriate science subject matter for the kindergarten year. The criteria we use in developing science curriculum materials follow below. We include concepts or topics if they are:

• Drawn from the life, physical, and earth/space sciences as they are experienced by children in their daily lives

• Based on important science ideas

• Developmentally appropriate

• Accessible to children's direct exploration

• About things/events that children can explore deeply and over time

• Engaging, challenging, and fun

Topics such as dinosaurs, the solar system, or rain forests do not meet all of these criteria and are not appropriate for kindergarten science study. They are examples that are not drawn from children's lives and are not accessible to children's direct exploration. In addition, the underlying science of the history of the Earth, the structure of the solar system, and the complex interactions of the rain forest require a level of abstract thinking more appropriate for older students.

Applying the criteria yields the concepts and topics shown in the box on the next page. This list, however, is not intended to dictate what content must be covered in kindergarten. Rather, its purpose is to guide teachers, schools, or districts in choosing topics for a strong year-long program. Such a program must:

• Reflect the nature of the local environment and community

• Provide experiences drawn from the different content areas (not just from life science)

• Be limited enough to allow for in-depth inquiry in each topic

Further, the questions accompanying each topic or concept are simply to suggest the kinds of questions that children might explore. In many cases, especially in life science, a number of concepts might be part of a single study.

State standards may be more numerous and specific than the broad ideas outlined here but most will fit within one or another of these very basic ideas and topics. If state standards include other content, teachers will need to use the criteria provided to determine the most age-appropriate topics.

The big ideas

A carefully designed science program includes more than specific content. There are major understandings or ideas in science—sometimes called its *unifying concepts* or *big ideas.* These may not be taught directly, but should be the basis for curriculum planning. For kindergarten children, these big ideas include looking for patterns, seeing relationships, noticing change, identifying cause and effect, and seeing how form is related to function.

Attitudes and dispositions

Finally, a rich kindergarten science program supports the development of certain attitudes and dispositions that are important in all areas of learning. These include:

• Curiosity

• Seeing oneself as a learner of science

• Respect for life

• Willingness to take risks

• Perseverance

Key Concepts and Topics for the Kindergarten Year

Life science

Physical characteristics of living things

The basic needs of living things

Simple behaviors of living things

Relationship between living things and their environments—*What living things are there outside the classroom? What do they look like? How do they compare? What do they need to survive?*

The life cycle—*What happens to a seed as it grows and develops? What things make a difference in how it grows? What changes do animals go through as they grow?*

Variation and diversity—*What are all the living things we can find in a small plot? Are they the same? Are they different?*

People—*How are we all alike? How are we different? What do our senses tell us?*

Physical science

Properties of objects and materials

- Properties of solids—*What are the properties of our rocks? What are the properties of the soils? What are the properties of the leaves we collected? What are the properties of the different blocks we are building with?*

- Properties of liquids—*How does water move? How can water go up? What are drops like? How do they move? What happens to water when it is left in an open container? Frozen?*

Position and motion of objects—*How far will the ball go when it rolls down different ramps? What difference does it make if a ball is large or small? Heavy or light?*

Properties and characteristics of sound—*What kinds of sounds do different things make? How can sound be made louder? Softer? How can the pitch of a sound be changed?*

Properties and characteristics of light—*What happens to a shadow when a light moves? How many different shadows can be made with a light and an object?*

Earth science

Properties of Earth materials—*What is the ground like outside our classroom? What is in the soil?*

Weather—*What are the features of weather, and how can they be measured? What are the patterns of weather over a week? A month? A year?*

Space science

Patterns of movement and change of the Moon and Sun—*How does the Sun move across the sky? Is it the same every day? How does the shape of the Moon seem to change? Is there a pattern?*

- Respect for evidence
- Willingness to collaborate

How should science curriculum be structured?

Let us look back at the two vignettes and see how these four components of a rich science program—inquiry, subject matter, big ideas, and attitudes—come together in curriculum.

Putting it all together

In the first vignette, Derek has gone to his state standards and selected light and shadow as his subject matter. He has identified these concepts: light travels from a source; light can be blocked by objects; when light is blocked by something, there is a shadow; and the size and shape of shadows change if the light source or object is moved. Katie has chosen plants as her subject matter. She has identified that plants have a life cycle, plants have basic needs that must be met if they are to survive, plants develop and grow in predictable ways, and there is variation in the way seeds grow.

Derek and Katie have provided the children with many materials that allow them to inquire. In Derek's class, the children explore and notice what shadows and lights do, both indoors and outdoors. They describe what is happening and talk about their ideas. They use shadow boxes and the theater for simple investigations that follow up on their own questions and respond to Derek's challenge. Representation (drawing, writing, making models) is a constant part of the children's work, as are the science talks that help them draw out their ideas and conclusions. Katie's classroom is also engaged in a study that is taking place indoors and outdoors with many different kinds of plants. They are using simple tools—the magnifier and measuring tools—as part of their investigation of the growth of seedlings. As they collect and record their observations using graphs, drawings, and words over a couple of weeks, they continuously analyze the data looking for patterns and relationships, and they talk about their thinking.

Derek keeps the big ideas in mind as he interacts with children during their investigations and guides the science talks. He asks the children about relationships—in this case, the relationship be-

tween the light and the objects they are using and the shadows. Together he and the children wonder about cause and effect—what causes a shadow's size and shape and how they can control the effect. Katie considers the patterns of growth the children are watching. Rather than just naming parts of the plant, she talks about change—how the plants are changing and what functions new parts might serve and the relationship between form and function.

Finally, the materials and the events invite the children to question, to develop important attitudes and dispositions such as curiosity, a sense of themselves as science learners, perseverance, and collaboration. As Derek and Katie pose questions and challenge children to develop and share their own ideas, they are creating an environment in which learning science is an active and rigorous process that everyone can do, and a process that is based in the data they collect. This environment and culture also support children as they try out new actions and ideas. Children discover that sometimes things fall down or a light goes out, and they have to start again. They learn that they must work together—to investigate different shadows, one person has to hold the flashlight while another moves the object.

A simple framework

Each science study or investigation takes on a life of its own based on the content and the topic that is selected. But a science study has a simple structure that is useful to consider: engagement, focused exploration, extending the investigation through books and other media, and connecting to home and community.

Most studies begin with time for children to *become familiar* with the materials and events they will explore more deeply and pose some initial questions. A science study then moves on to *more focused exploration,* where the teacher challenges children to go deeper, to build understanding, and to document their work. Guided by the goals she has set, the teacher creates a focus using a child's question or one of her own.

A third part of this framework lies in the use of books and other media to *extend and enrich the firsthand experience.* Once they have grown seeds and studied the plants outside their classroom, children may be transported to a different plant world with a book on the giant redwoods. Once they have explored what the plants in their neighborhood need, they can read about desert plants and how they survive to learn more about basic needs and habitats. Reading a story about a scientist helps them to understand how scientists inquire.

Finally, the structure of a science study includes the *interplay between classroom, community, and home*. If science consists of activities only in the classroom, children will be less likely to see themselves as learners of science outside the classroom. Children and teachers can take trips to a plant nursery or science museum. Parents and community members with experience and expertise can be invited into the classroom. Teachers can send children home with letters that offer simple ways to support continued investigation at home.

How should science be taught?

Teaching inquiry-based science carries particular responsibilities for the teacher. Derek and Katie both demonstrate a variety of roles that promote science learning. They are both clear about the goals they have for learning and how their actions relate to those goals. They also have embedded the skills and the attitudes of inquiry into the daily routine of their classrooms. The children actively investigate. They record and discuss their experiences and observations. Teachers who engage a class in science inquiry play the following four roles:

Designing a science-rich environment

Direct hands-on exploration lies at the heart of inquiry, and effective teachers design the learning environment to stimulate and support children's exploration. To create this learning environment, teachers begin by making decisions about the central concepts. For example, a teacher may decide to focus on properties of liquids and, more specifically, on water flow and water drops. Then they select materials, carefully create spaces for exploration, and design the schedule.

Selecting materials. The materials for children's exploration must connect directly to the core science learning goals. This means that teachers may have to remove materials as well as add them. Children may not be able to focus on the science of water flow when there are dolls and dishes in the water table. Materials must be plentiful, too. For

example, each pair of students needs a flashlight to work with light and shadows. Basic science tools such as magnifiers, measuring instruments, and containers should be part of all classrooms.

Teachers also need to consider what materials to provide for documentation and representation. Books and other resources, such as pictures or posters, strategically placed around the room stimulate children's inquiry and provide them with needed information.

Teachers may worry, "I can't get all the materials needed for science."

With time and money limited, it can be difficult to get the varied materials needed for science inquiry. However, many of the materials of science are free or inexpensive. Nearby recycle centers are very useful. Printing stores, lumber yards, brick and gravel companies, and other businesses often will give away remainders and scraps. Members of the community might donate materials or money. Laboratories, science centers, colleges, and even high schools might give or loan materials. Libraries and the Internet offer free media resources.

Creating space for exploration. There are several ways to think about space. Teachers might have to temporarily rearrange a room in order to provide adequate space. For example, Derek uses his block area for the shadow theater. Katie dedicates several parts of her room to science so more children can participate. She puts the seedlings on one table and potted plants on the windowsill. Children keep track of the sprouting carrot tops and the potato on another table. It is also important to think about the way that display space can serve to stimulate and inform children's work. Posters, pictures, charts, documentation panels, and representations displayed at children's eye level help them revisit and build on their previous work and lead to new investigations. Finally, it is important to think about space beyond the classroom. Teachers extend children's learning by making connections between classroom investigations and the immediate environment of the school or community.

Teachers may express the concern, "I don't have any space to do this."

Many classrooms are small. Some have limited wall space. There may be only blacktopped playgrounds outside the school. However, any room can temporarily be rearranged, borrowing from one

© Ellen B. Senisi

area to add to another. Displays can be set up on the back of a cabinet or on an extra easel. Checking beyond the school yard can turn up places to expand investigations.

Designing the schedule. In-depth investigations take time. It can take weeks, even a month or two, for children to engage deeply with a topic and build new understandings. Some studies—such as weather patterns or how the world outside changes from season to season—can last all year. Regular choice times— at least 45 minutes of uninterrupted time—allow children to get engaged, see through an exploration, and spend some time representing their experience. Children also need regular opportunities to share their experiences and explore the patterns that emerge as they put a series of experiences together. This can happen at morning meetings, at circle time, and in small groups during choice time.

Teachers may worry, "I have to cover so many things. I have no time for science."

Classroom time pressures are very real. The emphasis on standards and basic skills in literacy and mathematics encourages teachers to view the daily schedule as a series of subject-specific activities. But time might be best spent by integrating competing demands. Katie's teaching is a good example. She makes science central to her kindergarten day. She emphasizes the role of documentation. The children chart, make observational drawings, and label. They learn the concepts of print, the connection between sound and print, and how to use print to label and explain their experiences and ideas. The children also have a variety of books available—from instructional books on how to grow plants to fiction such as *The Carrot Seed* (by Ruth Krauss). Katie also incorporates appropriate mathematics learning into the data-collection process. The children measure and discuss the seedlings. In the process, they build a vocabulary for discussing relative size and shape. They develop an understanding of numbers, number patterns, relationships, and the use of measurement to provide comparative data.

Guiding children's hands-on explorations

The teacher's guidance of children's hands-on explorations is essential to the success of any science investigation. While the environment does a lot of the work, the teacher's encouragement, guidance, probing, and challenges are vital to children's learning.

Setting the stage. A teacher's introduction to the day's science activities helps children focus on important science concepts. Ways to do that include these:

• Use documents from the previous day. Katie's children's growth charts provide opportunities to stimulate new investigations or extensions of previous experiences.

• Show children new materials and ask what they might do with them. "I have these new blocks. Feel them. What do you think you might build with these?"

• Offer a challenge. Derek introduces the shadow theater and challenges the children to make different shadows. A new investigation is launched.

Closely observe children's engagement. Once children begin to work, teachers need to watch their interactions with the materials and each other. These observations form the basis for selecting interventions that are relevant to what the children are doing and thinking and that improve their understanding. For example, Derek observed his children looking at the shadow of the flag pole in the playground and suggested they might look at it at different times of the day to see if it stayed the same.

Maximize engagement. Early in a topic, teachers need to notice who is engaged and who is not. Teachers should provide encouragement to any children who remain unengaged after several days. With knowledge of the children's interests, learning styles, background knowledge, and experiences, teachers can attempt to connect them with the exploration. Children who are reticent to interact with the materials might feel more comfortable taking on a documentation role at first. Others may need help learning to use the materials. Or, the teacher may need to add materials so that more children can be engaged.

Focus attention on the science. Teachers can use strategic comments or questions to help children focus on the science they are experiencing. "I notice that the roots of your seedlings are different lengths." Or, "I wonder how you made the shadow of the crayon look shorter." These kinds of comments heighten the children's attention to their science experience.

Extend children's learning. When the teacher's goal is to extend the exploration, these interactions will go further. For example, Katie might ask a child to measure the roots of the seedlings every other day to see what happens. Derek might select several objects and then ask a child to make three differently shaped shadows with each.

Deepening children's understanding

Experiences are the basis of science learning, but reflection on those experiences is what leads children to modify any previous naïve beliefs to form more sophisticated theories. Representation and discussion are two primary ways to encourage children's reflection.

Representation. The use of various media to reflect on and communicate experiences, observations and ideas is termed *representation*. Children learn to communicate in a variety of ways when they have regular opportunities to represent their experiences and ideas. Representation gives children a chance to reflect on a recent experience. They can think about the elements that were important to them, and ultimately gain new understandings of the science they are exploring (Wells 1986). Teachers encourage representation by:

• Making representation a regular part of the classroom routine

• Selecting materials that allow for an accurate representation of the object or experience and that provide opportunities for movement and story telling

• Providing easy access to materials where the science exploration takes place

• Building special times for representation into the schedule

• Valuing all children's work

• Talking with individuals about what they have done

Teachers may say, "But my children can't write."

Even at the beginning of the year, all kindergarten children can put something down on a piece of paper or in a science notebook. They can draw, they can begin to label drawings, and they can start to put letters down for words. The desire to represent the science work they have done may motivate some children to develop and use initial writing skills.

Discussions. A group discussion stimulates and makes explicit the thinking processes that underlie inquiry. They help build a shared vocabulary and encourage collaboration. Teachers can engage small groups in retelling the steps in their investigation, analyzing the data they have collected, or solving a problem. In large groups, children can share experiences, compare and contrast what they have found out, try out a new explanation, and ask a new question. Teachers guide meaningful conversations by:

• Keeping the dialogue open ended, accepting all contributions

• Maintaining a focus on the important science concepts that are being explored

• Probing for additional observations, more specifics, and alternate points of view

• Asking children: "Why do you think?" "How do you know?"

• Giving children time to think before expecting them to speak

• Using children's work and teacher documentation to encourage children to think back on what they have done and ideas they may have

• Asking children to comment on and question each other's experiences and ideas

• Avoiding explaining the science or looking for a right answer

Teachers may protest, "My kids won't sit still and don't listen to one another."

Children need to learn discussion skills and norms. They need to be taught explicitly how to listen and how to ask a question of another child. Sitting in a circle facing one another sets the stage. Discussions should be kept short at the beginning of the year. When children have discussions regularly, their participation will increase over time.

Using ongoing assessment to inform teaching

Children's engagement and learning is contingent on the relevance of what is being taught, and whether the learning opportunities match the level of their skills and understanding. Teachers can build a relevant curriculum through ongoing assessment. Important considerations include these:

What do you expect the children to do and learn? An essential step in assessing teaching and learning is to identify the learning goals related to each topic. These include both the conceptual learning goals and the inquiry goals.

How will the children display new understandings and skills? Children's understandings are best revealed as they explore, represent, and talk. Their ideas are often evident in their interactions with materials. For example, what process does a particular child go through to make a shadow smaller? Does he go through a lot of trial and error before he finds a successful strategy? Is he able to use past experiences to come to a solution quickly? Children's understandings are also revealed in their representational work. Have they included all of the parts of their seedling in their drawings? Can they talk about the seedlings' parts using accurate terms for the roots, stem, and leaves?

What questions are revealed in their work? Ongoing assessment is sometimes called "formative" assessment because the knowledge the teacher gains from the assessment helps him to determine what to do next. Often the assessment will uncover questions children are asking, in action or in words, which can then be used as the focus for another investigation. For example, while the children are investigating ways to change the size of shadows, Derek might observe that they show their interest in the varying shadows by using different materials. They may be curious about the materials that do or do not let some light through. This might serve as an excellent investigation for the future. Or, the teacher may realize that children are still struggling with a concept and need more time before moving on.

❖   ❖   ❖

Science is very important for kindergarten children for many reasons. Young children are naturally curious about their environment and are struggling to make sense of the world around them. A good science program engages all children in a way that builds on this natural curiosity, supports their attitudes and dispositions toward learning, and fosters inquiry skills. In addition to setting the foundation for later science learning, science investigations support other curriculum areas by providing many opportunities for developing literacy skills, applying mathematical ideas, and working together.

In this chapter, we have looked at appropriate goals for kindergarten children in science knowledge and abilities. We have emphasized the need for in-depth, long-term science studies that provide all children with the opportunities they need to develop an understanding of ideas and the nature of inquiry. We have looked at the teacher's role, highlighting the importance of the learning environment; the strategies that guide and challenge children's hands-on work; and perhaps most important, the strategies that teachers use to help children reflect on their experiences and develop science reasoning through discussion, representation, and documentation.

References

AAAS (American Association for the Advancement of Science). 1993. *Benchmarks for science literacy*. New York: Oxford University Press.

National Research Council. 1996. *National science education standards*. Washington, DC: National Academies Press.

Wells, G. 1986. *The meaning makers*. Portsmouth, NH: Heinemann.

Worth, K., & S. Grollman. 2003. *Worms, shadows, and whirlpools: Science in the early childhood classroom*. Portsmouth, NH: Heinemann; Newton, MA: EDC; Washington, DC: NAEYC.

Effective teaching leads to successful children's learning and healthy development. NAEYC's reading list provides innovative, research-based strategies for teaching and instructional practices.

Informing Our Practice: Useful Research on Young Children's Development

Eva L. Essa & Melissa M. Burnham, eds.

This volume contains 20 overviews of research on aspects of young children's social, emotional, cognitive, or physical development, as well as how the findings can be applied in the classroom.

Item #: 255   List: $29   Member: $23.20

Our Inquiry, Our Practice: Undertaking, Supporting, and Learning from Early Childhood Teachers Research(ers)

Gail Perry, Barbara Henderson, & Daniel Meier, eds.

This book explores what teacher research looks like, why it is important to the field of early childhood education, and how teacher educators can support it.

Item #: 357   List: $25   Member: $20

Powerful Interactions: How to Connect with Children to Extend Their Learning

Amy Laura Dombro, Judy Jablon, & Charlotte Stetson

A teacher interacts with the children all day long. But interactions in which teachers intentionally promote learning can be few. A "Powerful Interaction" may last only a few minutes, but in that time the teacher tunes out any distractions, tunes into the child, and then presents a learning experience tailored to that child at that moment. Written by the authors of *The Power of Observation*, this book will guide you through these three steps of a Powerful Interaction in a series of self-guided lessons enlivened with tips, hints, invitations to reflect, and vignettes.

Item #: 245   List: $30   Member: $24

The Intentional Teacher: Choosing the Best Strategies for Young Children's Learning

Ann S. Epstein

Planful, intentional teachers keep in mind the key goals for children's learning and development in all domains by creating supportive environments and selecting from a variety of teaching strategies that best promote each child's thinking and skills. *The Intentional Teacher* considers how and when each type of learning (child-guided, adult-guided, or a combination) is most effective, and what teachers can do to support them.

Item #: 165   List: $25   Member: $20

Scaffolding Children's Learning: Vygotsky and Early Childhood Education

Laura E. Berk & Adam Winsler

Why is this resource considered indispensable by teacher educators across the U.S.? It does a masterful job of introducing key Vygotskian concepts clearly and concisely and guiding teachers in applying these powerful ideas in the classroom. Includes discussion of key concepts such as play, language, assessment, development, special needs, and more.

Item #: 146   List: $14   Member: $11.20

Enthusiastic and Engaged Learners: Approaches to Learning in the Early Childhood Classroom

Marilou Hyson

Children's "approaches to learning"—*interest, joy, persistence, flexibility, self-regulation, engagement*, and *motivation to learn*—make up a key dimension of school readiness. Research shows that positive approaches to learning improve social-emotional and academic outcomes. With images of practice in diverse settings, Hyson illustrates the possibility of building greater enthusiasm and engagement through relationships, curriculum, teaching, assessment strategies, and family communication. Copublished with Teachers College Press.

Item #: 733   List: $24   Member: $19.20

For a complete listing of resources on teaching & instructional practices, please visit www.naeyc.org/store or call 800-424-2460.

Prices are subject to change.